PACKING THE COURT

PACKING THE COURT

*The Rise of Judicial Power and
the Coming Crisis of the Supreme Court*

JAMES MACGREGOR BURNS

THE PENGUIN PRESS | *New York* | 2009

THE PENGUIN PRESS
Published by the Penguin Group
Penguin Group (USA) Inc., 375 Hudson Street, New York, New York 10014, U.S.A. • Penguin
Group (Canada), 90 Eglinton Avenue East, Suite 700, Toronto, Ontario, Canada M4P 2Y3 (a division
of Pearson Penguin Canada Inc.) • Penguin Books Ltd, 80 Strand, London WC2R 0RL, England •
Penguin Ireland, 25 St. Stephen's Green, Dublin 2, Ireland (a division of Penguin Books Ltd) •
Penguin Books Australia Ltd, 250 Camberwell Road, Camberwell, Victoria 3124, Australia
(a division of Pearson Australia Group Pty Ltd) • Penguin Books India Pvt Ltd, 11 Community
Centre, Panchsheel Park, New Delhi–110 017, India • Penguin Group (NZ), 67 Apollo Drive,
Rosedale, North Shore 0632, New Zealand (a division of Pearson New Zealand Ltd) • Penguin
Books (South Africa) (Pty) Ltd, 24 Sturdee Avenue, Rosebank, Johannesburg 2196, South Africa

Penguin Books Ltd, Registered Offices:
80 Strand, London WC2R 0RL, England

First published in 2009 by The Penguin Press,
a member of Penguin Group (USA) Inc.

LIBRARY OF CONGRESS CATALOGING-IN-PUBLICATION DATA
Burns, James MacGregor.
Packing the court : the rise of judicial power and the coming crisis of the Supreme Court /
James MacGregor Burns.
p.   cm.
Includes bibliographical references and index.
ISBN 978-1-59420-219-3
1. United States. Supreme court—History.   2. Political questions and judicial power—United States.
3. Judges—Selection and appointment—United States.   I. Title.
KF8742.B79   2009
347.73'26—dc22   2009003987

Printed in the United States of America
1   3   5   7   9   10   8   6   4   2

Designed by Marysarah Quinn

For David, Stewart, Deborah, Antonia

Contents

PROLOGUE

ONE DAY in February 1937, a fellow student at Williams College burst into my room holding a copy of the local newspaper. At first, I thought the banner headline trumpeted another crisis in Europe, but instead it was sensational news from Washington. President Franklin Roosevelt had just handed Congress a controversial proposal to pack the Supreme Court by enabling him to name up to six new justices, expanding the court's size to fifteen. As more classmates flocked into my room, arguments erupted over the bill. Most of us with scholarships vehemently backed FDR, just as we had cheered his landslide reelection a few months before. We derided the Roosevelt haters in the more affluent "Gold Coast" dorm next door.

We watched the ensuing political fight as closely as we would the World Series. We were sorry, most of us, when the "court-packing" bill went down to defeat in Congress. We were also puzzled. FDR made his proposal to change the Supreme Court because the conservative justices had killed one New Deal law after another, blocking the president's efforts to lift the country out of the Great Depression. How could these justices, most of whom had been appointed to the Supreme Court decades earlier, paralyze a government twice elected by a huge majority of Americans and halt what seemed to us the march of progress? Where did the court's power to veto laws passed by Congress and signed by the president come from? A look at the Constitution's Article III, where the judicial power is set out, revealed no mention of a Supreme Court veto over the elected branches.

How could this be? We are all taught in school about the separation of powers, the checks and balances that give some veto power to the president and the houses of Congress. Could the great political and philosophical leaders who wrote the Constitution have wanted a judicial veto—a "judicial review" of legislation—without stating it? The authors of the Constitution were meticulous men, many of them lawyers. They knew exactly what they were doing—and not doing.

There is no mystery. The Framers did not include a judicial veto in the Constitution *because they did not want it*. They would not grant that supremacy over the elected branches to a nonelected judiciary.

The Supreme Court instead acquired its power through a brilliant political coup at the hands of Chief Justice John Marshall in 1803. It was Marshall who declared that it was the exclusive duty of the Supreme Court—not Congress and not the president—to say what the law is. The Constitution, Marshall insisted, was nothing more and nothing less than what a majority of the justices said it was. Building on Marshall's dictum, the Supreme Court has, over the last two centuries, made itself the center of constitutional action. In doing so, it has distorted the intricate checks and balances the Framers believed were essential to the success of the American experiment.

As the ultimate and unappealable arbiters of the Constitution, the

justices of the Supreme Court have become far more than the refer-
ees in constitutional disputes that the Framers intended. They have
gone beyond interpreting the rules—they have come to create them.
From John Marshall to John Roberts, as the court has evolved from
its makeshift quarters in New York City, the nation's first capital, to
its imperial courthouse in Washington, D.C., the justices have so
successfully enlarged and consolidated the power of judicial review
that they have become, in effect and often explicitly, *lawgivers*. And
unlike the president and members of Congress, the policy-makers on
the court don't face the judgment of the voters for their actions. They
are never held politically accountable to the American people.

But neither has the Supreme Court been *above* politics. Most justices have been political activists—*party* politicos—before joining
the court. Many have owed their elevation to party ties, as a reward
for loyalty, with every expectation that they will not turn coat on
the court. Justices might shed party labels when they take their seats
on the bench—newspapers don't print (R) or (D) after their names
when reporting decisions—but, with some notable exceptions, they
do not abandon their party doctrines. Instead, they become politicians in robes.

No sooner did Americans begin to fashion the first political parties in the 1790s than the Supreme Court became a magnet for partisan conflict. From George Washington to George W. Bush, the
opportunity for presidents to pack the bench with loyalists and so
gain political and ideological control of this potent third branch has
been irresistible. In this book I use the term "packing" in this general sense, to refer to the deliberate effort by the party in power—
sometimes across several administrations and over decades—to use
the presidential prerogative of appointing justices to ensure domination of the Supreme Court by its own partisans.

Court-packing has been abetted by the life tenure the Constitution gives justices. The *average* tenure of Supreme Court jus-

tices since the nation's founding has been more than fifteen years; since 1970, it has increased to more than twenty-six years. Justices throughout the court's history have clung to their seats long after their political patrons have retired and long after their parties have yielded to their opponents or even disappeared. They have often perpetuated ideologies and attitudes that are outdated or that Americans have repudiated at the ballot box. Inevitably, life tenure has produced a critical time lag, with the Supreme Court institutionally almost always behind the times. As a result, too often the Supreme Court has seemed to be fighting the progress of history.

The terms of elected officials are predictable, fixed by the Constitution. As of today, we know that, barring catastrophe, in 2020 or 2056, say, candidates for the presidency and Congress will be facing the judgment of voters. But the Supreme Court selection process is by nature unpredictable and erratic—America's biggest wheel of fortune, with high stakes but uncertain payoffs. Everything depends on which justice may die or retire, when, and with what party controlling the presidency and the Senate. A one-term president like William Howard Taft may pack the Supreme Court with as many as six appointments and retain an influence there for decades, even though he loses reelection by a landslide. Another one-termer like Jimmy Carter may leave no justices behind him. Over the years, this judicial roulette has produced a jagged line of personal and political selections and made what might have been the most stable of branches the most unstable—as well as the most unrepresentative of all the people.

THE AMERICAN constitutional system has no lack of obstacles to transforming leadership—the kind of leadership that sees the Constitution as the people's charter, not, as Thomas Jefferson put it, "a mere thing of wax" in the hands of judges. Transforming leadership is mobilized by people's real needs and shaped by the enduring American values of life, liberty, and the pursuit of happiness. It aspires to harness a majority of citizens behind deep and lasting change. For two centuries, such leadership has confronted—and rarely overcome—the *un*constitutional obstacle of the judicial veto that can reduce Congress to helplessness and make bystanders of presidents. All too often, the Supreme Court has resisted even modest efforts to improve the lives of the great majority of Americans, to give them hope and opportunity. And at critical times, minority rule by a handful of jurists has threatened the nation's welfare, as it did during the Great Depression, and even, in the crisis of the Civil War, its survival.

Increasingly in this century, the Constitution will be fought over as a creative or destructive force in American democracy. Within a generation or two—perhaps much sooner—justices wielding the power of judicial supremacy will again confront a majority of the American people, in a political crisis of the same magnitude as the Civil War or the Great Depression. Transforming leadership will again face the conservative, obstructive authority of the high bench. Beyond the issue of the Supreme Court's role in the American constitutional system, the crisis may pose the most fundamental question of all—who rules? Will it be "We, the People," as the Founders of our nation intended, or will it be the nine justices of the Supreme Court? Americans must, as Theodore Roosevelt once said, reclaim their place as makers of their own Constitution.

CHAPTER ONE

The First Courtpackers

GEORGE WASHINGTON was the first courtpacker. He *had* to fill the whole bench after Congress passed the Judiciary Act of 1789, which provided for a Supreme Court with a chief justice and five associates. By the end of his second term, the president had nearly packed the court twice over, with eleven appointments, nine in his first term alone. Justices were appointed for life, but judicial lives in the court's early years were often short.

The job back then was not all that appealing. There wasn't much to do as cases slowly worked their way up from the lower courts, and the justices spent most of their time traveling. Every spring and fall, they served as trial and appellate judges in the three federal circuits. Almost from the beginning, they begged Congress for relief from an onerous duty that, as they wrote in a 1792 "memorial," required "toilsome Journies through different climates and seasons," passing "the greater part of their days on the road, and at Inns, and at a distance from their families." The circuits ranged from New Hampshire to Georgia. Justices assigned to the southern circuit would travel nearly two thousand miles twice yearly. One of them, Thomas Johnson of Maryland, quit the court after little more than a year to escape the excessive fatigue of circuit riding. It shattered the health and sanity of Justice John Blair. By the time he retired to Virginia in 1796, he was afflicted with chronic headaches and complained of a "strange disorder" that deprived him of "nearly all the powers of mind."

Others grew restless and left for better jobs. John Jay, the Supreme Court's first chief justice, ran for governor of New York in 1792 while sitting on the bench. He lost, but—never mind the separation of powers—President Washington sent him as special envoy to England to negotiate a settlement of disputes lingering from the Revolutionary War. The chief justice never attended a session of the court after 1793. While he was abroad, New York elected him governor, and in 1795, he resigned from the court to take the job.

Seeking recruits for the new Supreme Court, Washington had touted the judicial department as "the Key-stone of our political fabric," but the early court showed little evidence that it would assume that role. In its first four years, it heard only a dozen cases, few of any significance. Its jurisdiction as the ultimate appeals court was ill defined even though Congress had tried in its Judiciary Act to fill in the blanks created by the Constitution's broad phrases. The early court was mainly a bystander to the furious political controversies that had begun to wrack the new nation. Far from threatening what some had feared as "a superiority of the judicial to the legislative power," the court in its first years was so deferential to—and dependent upon—Congress and the president that it appeared to be, as Alexander Hamilton had warned, "in continual jeopardy of being overwhelmed, awed or influenced by its coordinate branches." At the heart of the Constitution was its system of checks and balances.

Would the Supreme Court be able to hold its own against the constitutional and political resources of Congress and the presidency?

THE DAUNTING CHALLENGE of the Framers who invented the republic in 1787 had been to establish "government by the people" that would protect both the people from the government and government from the people. They wanted to overcome the infirmities of the Articles of Confederation, which had preserved extensive authority for the thirteen states by denying the central government powers to promote and defend the nation as a whole. But the Framers also wanted to guarantee that the new national government— or any one part of it—would not become too strong. They feared that it might be dominated by an "aristocratic" oligarchy or take on a "monarchical" cast. They also feared that it would be overrun by rampant popular majorities—"mob" rule that would crush minority rights.

The Framer who had led in solving the complex dilemma of a strong and efficient but limited national government was James Madison, whose ideas were grounded in a deep and realistic grasp of human nature. An obstacle to oppressive majority rule, he foresaw, was the fragmentation of people into factions, formed around geographical, religious, and myriad other differences—above all, those of class, rising from "the various and unequal distribution of property." Such divisions were, Madison wrote in the Federalist papers, "sown in the very nature of man." In the concentrated polities of the states, they could be decisive, producing either anarchy, as powerful factions clashed inconclusively, or, where a single faction predominated, oligarchies or untamed majorities that would "sacrifice the weaker party." But under the wider sphere of the nation, with "a greater variety of parties and interests," the ills of faction would be tempered, while providing essential insurance that the central government would not be dominated either by a narrow elite or by a popular mass.

Still, it was not enough that the people were fragmented. As Madison explained in another Federalist essay, "In framing a government which is to be administered by men over men, the great difficulty lies in this: You must first enable the government to controul the governed; and in the next place, oblige it to controul itself." To achieve this self-control in government, it must be divided as well, its powers separated among executive, legislative, and judicial branches that would constitute a permanent check on one another. President, senators in the elite upper house of Congress, and representatives in the popular lower house would be elected with such different and opposing constituencies as to guarantee conflict among and within the branches. The president was given a partial veto over Congress; Congress could override a presidential veto; and the House and Senate could veto each other.

That much was clear. What was not at all clear was the place of the judicial branch in the system of checks and balances. The Constitution authorized Congress to establish "one supreme Court," without fixing the number of judges to sit on it. That was left to the discretion of Congress—and until 1869, when the court's membership was set enduringly at nine, seats on the bench came and went as the party in control of Congress rewarded friends and punished enemies. But as to the court's role in the new government, the bare words of the Constitution's Article III gave limited clues: "The judicial Power shall extend to all Cases, in Law and Equity, arising under this Constitution, the Laws of the United States, and Treaties made, or which shall be made, under their Authority . . . to Controversies to which the United States shall be a Party; to Controversies between two or more States; between a State and Citizens of another State," and so on. Indeed, the very design of the new Constitution opened a host of such issues and controversies that seemed to cry out for adjudication, most notably the exact boundaries of power in the intricate scheme of checks and balances—among the three federal branches and between them and the states. Some constitutional provisions were spelled out in precise detail; others were left vague to evade controversy on divisive issues or to allow flexibility when the document's dry words came into living practice. But when that happened, when the inevitable controversies arose, who was to determine, authoritatively, finally, what was constitutional—within the charter's bounds—and what was not?

To FOLLOW the debates at the constitutional convention in Philadelphia's State House in the summer of 1787 through the diaries of Madison and other participants is to witness an extraordinary act of collective leadership. The fifty-five delegates were serious, strong-minded men, experienced both in waging a revolution and in building polities. They were meeting daily under almost intolerable conditions, alternating between heated debates in the lifeless air of the convention hall, its windows shut for privacy, and nights in stifling boardinghouses.

With George Washington augustly presiding, the debates revealed the delegates' obsession not only with empowering a new government, but with controlling it. One example was the clash between two future justices of the Supreme Court over how judges of the "National Judiciary" were to be chosen. To a proposal that Congress should fill judicial positions, James Wilson, a delegate from Pennsylvania, spoke for the common wariness of overweening legislative power—that "intrigue, partiality, and concealment were the necessary consequences." Instead, he argued, the appointment power should go to a "single, responsible person"—the president. South Carolina's John Rutledge objected that "the people will think we are leaning too much towards Monarchy." Then the irrepressible Benjamin Franklin lightened the mood by suggesting that they adopt the "Scotch mode" of picking judges—by lawyers, "who always selected the ablest of the profession in order to get rid of him, and share his practice among themselves." In the end, as so often, the Framers compromised for the sake of balance and caution: federal judges would be nominated by the president, subject to Senate confirmation.

Because it touched on the vital division of powers, the appointment of judges received extensive debate. This was not the case with another constitutional provision that would have huge implications for judicial power—that judges should "hold their Offices during good Behavior," removable only by the cumbersome process of impeachment. Experience in the states with what James Wilson called "the servile dependence of the judges" who bent to the will of the elected branches made it obvious to the Framers that federal judges must be insulated from political pressures and manipulations that would endanger, said Wilson, "the liberty and property of the citizen." But life tenure, as a leading critic of the Constitution who wrote under the pen-name "Brutus" would be quick to note, made judges "independent of the people, of the legislature, and of every power under heaven." Life tenure was an English practice, but in England, Brutus pointed out, it was designed to protect judges from a hereditary monarch who also had life tenure and therefore "much stronger inducements to increase the prerogatives of his office than those who hold their offices for stated periods." Moreover, the British House of Lords served as an ultimate, extrajudicial appeals court, while the judgments of the American Supreme Court would be "final and irreversible, for there is no court above them to which appeals can lie." But with scarcely a word of debate among the delegates, their Constitution granted unelected federal judges life tenure. That served as a check on the other branches, which might otherwise control them, but it also shielded them from the accountability to citizens that was central to republican theory and to which the other branches of the government were subject.

The powers that those judges would wield—over the states and the political branches of the federal government—remained to be clarified. Though James Madison considered it "absolutely necessary to a perfect system" of national power, a congressional veto over state laws roused widespread opposition in the convention. Rather than a legislative veto, the Framers adopted the "supremacy clause" that established the federal Constitution as "the supreme Law of the Land," binding on the states. This seemed to imply some form of judicial review of state laws by federal courts. After the convention, Virginia delegate George Mason would charge that "the Judiciary of the United States is so constructed and extended, as to absorb and destroy the Judiciaries of the several States." James Iredell of North Carolina, a future justice of the Supreme Court, replied that federal courts would have no jurisdiction "but where the Union is in some measure concerned." Still, Iredell acknowledged that the "construction of this authority" was undefined. At the convention itself, the role of the Supreme Court in relation to the states was not debated or spelled out.

Even more glaring was the absence of debate—and decision—on the powers of the judiciary over the laws of the federal government. Would the Supreme Court have a final, unchallengeable authority to veto acts of Congress it disapproved of? Few delegates even expressed an opinion on the subject, and when they did, it was mainly in connection with one of the convention's great preoccupations: preventing the legislative power from "swallowing up all the other powers." How would "unwise and unjust measures" be blocked from becoming law? Again and again, James Madison and others proposed that the president and the justices of the Supreme Court be united in a "Council of revision" with "authority to examine every act" of Congress and veto laws they deemed unsound. Opponents of the Council worried that it would grant the judiciary an "improper mixture of powers." "In some States," Elbridge Gerry of Massachusetts noted, "the Judges had actually set aside laws as being against the Constitution," but "it was quite foreign from the nature of the office to make them judges of the policy of public measures" as well.

While the Council of Revision was repeatedly rejected, few delegates explicitly endorsed or opposed a *judicial* veto over legislation. Maryland's John Mercer "disapproved of the Doctrine that the Judges as expositors of the Constitution should have authority to declare a law void. He thought laws ought to be well and cautiously made, and then to be uncontroulable." John Dickinson of Delaware echoed Mercer, rejecting "the power of the Judges to set aside the law," and warning, presciently, that the judiciary might become "by degrees, the lawgiver." But these comments provoked no debate over judicial power; no delegate leapt to defend the principle of judicial supremacy, no one moved to have it inscribed in the Constitution. Debate at once resumed on the doomed Council of Revision, until John Rutledge finally interrupted to complain of "the tediousness of the proceedings."

DID THE DELEGATES simply *assume* that the nation's highest court would exercise judicial supremacy? In years to come, as political leaders, scholars, and judges themselves struggled to reconcile what the Supreme Court had become with the Founders' intentions, some claimed to find in the convention's scattered references to judicial power over the laws of Congress proof that the delegates simply took for granted that the Supreme Court would exercise absolute authority over the Constitution—that by judicial review, the Founders meant more than a check on manifestly unconstitutional measures or on encroachments into the judiciary's own sphere, that they expected the Supreme Court to hold a monopoly on constitutional interpretation with the unlimited power to nullify the acts of the people—that, in short, they intended to make the court *supreme* in all matters constitutional. An early legal scholar, James Kent, argued in 1794 that the "interpretation or construction of the Constitution" was not a political but a "JUDICIAL act." Kent's own political views—most notably, a fear of popular rule—led him to conclude that the Framers had organized the courts "with peculiar advantages to exempt them from the baneful influence of Faction," making the judiciary the government's ultimate bulwark against an unruly majority of the people.

Over a century later, economic historian Charles Beard similarly saw the Framers as determined to frustrate popular rule in order to safeguard "the rights of private property against any levelling tendencies on the part of the propertyless masses." They empowered a judiciary "removed from direct contact with popular electorates," Beard claimed, to "control" legislation and guard the wealth and power of the propertied elite. In 1892, even as the Supreme Court was consistently knocking down laws that would regulate huge corporations or empower workers, a president of the American Bar Association would insist that, with the establishment of judicial review at the Founding, "the people by an unprecedented act of wisdom" had "effectually protected themselves against themselves."

But there is no proof of intentions such as these in the Constitution or in the convention's records. In the absence of proof, defenders of judicial supremacy have pointed to the colonial calls for American courts to defy acts of the British Parliament as evidence of what was in the minds of the Framers—never mind that this was a weapon forged in the struggle for independence. They have pointed to the emergence of judicial review in some states after the revolution, though the precedents were ambiguous and received scarcely a mention at the convention. They have pointed to the arguments of opponents like Brutus that the Supreme Court "would be exalted above all other power in the government, and subject to no controul." Never mind that Brutus was writing prophetically of what he feared the court might become, not of what the Framers intended it to be.

They have pointed to Alexander Hamilton's answer to Brutus, his vigorous defense of judicial review as essential to keeping Congress "within the limits assigned to their authority." But Hamilton dismissed fears of judicial *supremacy* over the legislature as a phantom. The judiciary was the "weakest" branch, Hamilton wrote, that could "never attack with success either of the other two."

The delegates were not in Philadelphia to practice constitution-making by omission. They were all practical men—lawyers, politicians, businessmen, state leaders. If they had favored something as radical as judicial supremacy, they would have argued for it at the convention and inserted it in the great charter.

Indeed, a plan for judicial supremacy would have run counter to the Framers' basic constitutional strategy. Under their checks and balances doctrine, *no* department was to be supreme. Each was to check and balance the others, using the tools provided by the Constitution. If that failed, if one branch overpowered the others, the system would lose its mooring in republican principles. One eminent authority on the Framers' intent, James Madison, doubted whether the Supreme Court could hold its own in the separated system—too weak to resist the "dangerous encroachments" of the states and, as his persistence in advocating the Council of Revision indicated, too weak to check Congress. But neither was Madison willing to grant the court supremacy over the Constitution, which had, he pointed out, no provision "for the case of a disagreement in expounding" it. As he noted in 1788, after Congress passed a law and the president signed it, the court was last in giving its interpretation; it could, therefore, stamp the law "with its final character." But this was an accident of the lawmaking process; it did not mean that the Supreme Court was "paramount" to the legislature, "which was never intended, and can never be proper."

In the debate over the Framers' intentions regarding judicial supremacy, the answer is clear. The Framers made no general grant of a judicial power to invalidate laws passed by Congress and signed by the president. They made no grant to the Supreme Court of supremacy over the Constitution or the other branches of the federal government.

LOYALTY TO the new Constitution and to his great idea that the United States must be more than a loose confederacy of states were George Washington's foremost criteria for appointments to what he called "the chief Pillar" of the exquisite balance of powers in the federal system. He sought men who had been fellow revolutionary soldiers, public servants, and statesmen. John Rutledge, an associate justice who served briefly as John Jay's successor as chief justice in 1795, had organized South Carolina's defenses against British invasion during the war for independence, and at the convention he had been instrumental in securing the "supremacy clause" that made the Constitution binding on the states. Pennsylvanian James Wilson, a brilliant Scottish-born legal scholar, had been an outspoken nationalist in the years after independence and a leading Framer of the Constitution. Chief Justice Jay, an author of the Federalist papers, had been among the Constitution's foremost advocates. Other justices had led their states in ratification of the new charter. On the court, they saw their task as supporting the fledgling government. With the president and Congress, they made a three-horse team. They were all, in a word, Federalists.

To Washington, this was not partisanship. The commitment to a single, unified nation under the Constitution was the *American* position. But even before the new nation had been launched, the roots of opposition to Federalism took form, and Washington's success in establishing federal power prompted that early Anti-Federalism, with its suspicion that the national government would crush the autonomy of the states and the liberties of the people, to metamorphose by the mid-1790s into a new, "Republican" opposition led by James Madison and Thomas Jefferson. Both men had backed the Constitution—Madison of course was its lead author, while Jefferson had offered qualified but positive support from his perch as minister to France. Both had been insiders during Washington's first term—Madison as the president's legislative leader in the House and Jefferson as secretary of state. But Washington's closest collaborator turned out to be Treasury Secretary Alexander Hamilton, whose plans for a centralization of national power and for rapid economic development, with government giving industry and finance a push, appalled both Madison and Jefferson. During Washington's second term, they built the framework for America's first political party.

Partisan conflict quickly became virulent and vindictive, as Republicans sneered at Washington's monarchical, "monocratic" pretensions. In his Farewell Address, the president warned that parties or "factions" were a threat to the survival of the republic. If elections were conducted on party lines, he feared that "the alternate domination of one faction over another" and the resulting "disorders and miseries" would "gradually incline the minds of men to seek security and repose in the absolute power of an Individual" who would stand on "the ruins of Public Liberty."

In 1796, at least, there was to be no alternation. In the first contested presidential election, John Adams, Washington's loyal vice president and heir, eked out a three-vote victory over Jefferson in the electoral college. As Washington's successor, Adams had the right credentials. He had been a leader in Massachusetts' revolt against British rule and in the Continental Congress and then a strong supporter of the Constitution, whose form his writings on balanced government had influenced. But unlike Washington, this vain, ambitious, cantankerous man made no pretense of nonpartisanship. He was quick to discover sedition and treason in his opponents. Like

Washington, Adams viewed the judicial department as a coordinate branch of government, working with the president and Congress to achieve common goals. But Adams also saw it as a vehicle to crush opposition. He was much more conscious of the party implications of judicial appointments than Washington had been, and he was determined to pack the judiciary with party loyalists, making it a Federalist stronghold—and a scourge to Republicans.

Adams did most of his packing at the lower levels of the federal judiciary, but after one of the most spectacular flame-outs in Supreme Court history, he had an opportunity to secure Federalist domination of the high bench. James Wilson, whose hunger for fame as a lawgiver was frustrated by the early court's relative inconsequence and by his equally powerful thirst for riches, had plunged headlong into ruinous debt, pyramiding one disastrous investment on top of another. Describing himself as "hunted like a wild beast" by creditors even while riding circuit, he was arrested and flung into debtors' prison, where his health broke down. In 1798, he died a justice of the United States Supreme Court and a pauper. To replace him, Adams offered the job to a proven Federalist loyalist, John Marshall, who turned it down to run for a seat in Congress but recommended his close friend Bushrod Washington. Only thirty-six years old, Washington had studied law with James Wilson after service in the Continental Army and established impeccable Federalist credentials as a delegate in Virginia's legislature. He also happened to be the beloved nephew of the Father of His Country. Bushrod Washington would promote Federalism from the high bench for more than three decades.

If the courts were to be used to bludgeon Republicans, they would need laws for the job. In 1798, Congress passed and President Adams signed the Sedition Act, which outlawed not only "insurrection, riot, unlawful assembly, or combination" but writing, printing, or uttering words that would bring the president or Congress "into contempt or disrepute." The law, designed to suppress the Republican opposition, made a mockery of First Amendment free speech guarantees. But Chief Justice Oliver Ellsworth, who had been named by Washington to replace Rutledge, assured the administration privately that he saw no "constitutional difficulty" in the act.

The escalating partisanship drew in other justices. On circuit, they pitched in to apply the new law. Justice William Paterson was an enthusiastic Hamiltonian from New Jersey appointed in 1793 to replace Thomas Johnson. Presiding over the 1795 treason trials of two tax protesters in the Whiskey Rebellion, Paterson had directed the jury to find the men guilty. In 1798, he similarly secured the Sedition Act conviction of a Vermont congressman, Matthew Lyon, who had mocked Adams's "unbounded thirst for ridiculous pomp, foolish adulation or selfish avarice." Paterson was ready to tell the jury to find Lyon guilty before it could hear his defense. The press was not spared. In another case, Paterson obtained the indictment of the leading Republican publisher in New England, Thomas Adams, for his criticism of the Sedition Act as a Federalist attempt to "screen from scrutiny the conduct of your own Government and to silence by an argument of force the remonstrances of reason." But Thomas Adams died before he could be brought to trial.

Even more ardent in persecuting Republicans was Justice Samuel Chase, appointed to the Supreme Court by Washington in 1796. Chase was a onetime Anti-Federalist from Maryland who had turned hyperpartisan Federalist, even stumping for John Adams while serving on the Supreme Court. He brought Sedition Act indictments against Republican journalists and printers, during one trial telling the jury, "I cannot suppress my feelings at this gross attack upon the President." He indignantly accused a handbill author of attempting to influence voters in the next election. He even obtained the conviction of one David Brown, a semiliterate itinerant orator, for "sowing sedition in the interior country" of Massachusetts. Though Brown apologized for "uttering his *political* sentiments," Chase gave him the heaviest sentence under the law—eighteen months in jail and a $480 fine.

But the nadir of Sedition Act prosecutions was reached when an old fellow named Luther Baldwin was clapped into federal jail. On his way to a tavern in Newark, New Jersey, Baldwin had been sourly observing the president and Mrs. Adams drive down the city's Broad Street to the accompaniment of a sixteen-gun salute. Someone nearby him commented, "There goes the President and they are firing at his a——." The drunken Baldwin replied that he "did not care if they fired *thro* his a——." *That* was sedition.

EXTREMES BEGET extremes. Even as some Republicans talked of secession, the Sedition Act prompted Jefferson and Madison to frame resolutions asserting the rights of states to reject federal laws that violated the Constitution. Because the Sedition Act was "expressly and positively forbidden" by the First Amendment, Madison wrote in 1798, states "have the right, and are in duty bound, to interpose" and declare it unconstitutional. Only the Kentucky and Virginia legislatures approved such resolutions. Ten states rejected what they considered the dangerous and subversive doctrine of the resolutions, with Vermont replying that it was not for the states to decide the constitutionality of laws, "this power being exclusively vested in the judiciary courts of the Union." But what if those courts were eagerly abetting repression and voiding the First Amendment?

The brutal partisanship reached a climax with the 1800 elections, a resounding repudiation of the Federalists and a triumph for the Republicans. Politically, the Federalist era was over, but Adams and his congressional allies would not leave the scene without an attempt to ensure that the judiciary would remain packed with their partisans far into the next century. The Judiciary Act of 1801 became law on February 13, 1801, a mere three weeks before Thomas Jefferson was to be inaugurated as president. The act put sixteen new circuit court judgeships at the disposal of President Adams. Republicans denounced it as the "law of the midnight judges" as Adams set feverishly to work to distribute judicial plums to worthy Federalists, and Congress made haste to confirm them.

Then, just four days before Adams's time ran out, Congress created a new court for the nation's new capital, the District of Columbia, with three judgeships—one went immediately to a nephew of Adams and a second to the brother of his secretary of state, John Marshall—as well as a mass of new marshals, clerks, registers, and justices of the peace. To fill all these offices, the president and Marshall worked late into the night on the eve of Jefferson's inauguration, signing and sealing commissions. There wasn't time enough to deliver them all before Jefferson became president. One who never received his was a prosperous Georgetown Federalist, William Marbury.

There was one last poison pill for Jefferson in the 1801 Judiciary Act, meant to frustrate him not by addition but by subtraction. Anticipating that a justice might retire early in Jefferson's term— the rigors of circuit riding continued to make invalids of judges— congressional Federalists cut the court's membership from six to five in order to deny Jefferson the opportunity to replace a departing justice. While Republicans would make short shrift of this ploy when they repealed the act after coming into power, Jefferson had to wait three years for a chance to unpack the Supreme Court as the Federalists clung tenaciously to their seats.

LITTLE MORE THAN a decade after the founding of the new federal government, the Supreme Court had shifted from its docile partnership in George Washington's three-horse governing team to

become a vortex of partisan controversy. Though the court's authority remained uncertain, the potential dangers of judicial power were
amply revealed in the abusive Sedition Act prosecutions, when
unelected judges aggressively served the political purposes of the
ruling party.

James Madison recognized those dangers and also saw what must
be the remedy. Defending his Virginia resolution in 1800, Madison
again denied that "the judicial authority is to be regarded as the sole
expositor of the constitution." If the legislative process meant that
the Supreme Court would have the last word on constitutional issues
within the government, the court did *not* have the ultimate last word.
That belonged to the people: "The authority of constitutions over
governments, and of the sovereignty of the people over constitutions,
are truths which are at all times necessary to be kept in mind; and at
no time perhaps more necessary than the present."

Despite the fears he had shared with other delegates to the constitutional convention about runaway legislative power, Madison had
always understood that "in our Governments the real power lies in
the majority of the Community." it was this conviction—that republican government, however checked and balanced, must be *popular*
government—that drove him away from Washington and the Federalists in the 1790s. Government must be responsible to the people.
Under the Constitution, members of the House were directly elected
by the voters, the president and senators indirectly, through electors
and state legislatures. All of these officeholders could be unelected
at the next polling. If the people were indeed to be the final arbiters
of the Constitution, lawmaking justices accountable to no one presented a special danger.

Many years after the Founding, greatly vexed by the Supreme
Court's aggrandizement of power, and especially its claim to supremacy because "there must be an ultimate arbiter somewhere," Thomas
Jefferson replied, "True, there must"—"The ultimate arbiter is the
people of the Union."

CHAPTER TWO

John Marshall's Constitution

ON MARCH 4, 1801, John Marshall and Thomas Jefferson stood stiffly face-to-face in the Senate chamber as the new chief justice of the Supreme Court administered the oath of office to the new president of the United States. Then Marshall stepped aside as Jefferson gave an address marked by its conciliatory tone after the bitterness of the 1800 election. Declaring that "we are all republicans: we are all federalists," Jefferson said that those were merely different names for the same principle—"our attachment to union and representative government." The new president and new chief justice were old political enemies, but Jefferson had invited Marshall to swear him in—a notable gesture, given Marshall's role in the creation of the "midnight judges" and the fact that he himself had been the most prominent of John Adams's late appointments.

Marshall's promotion to the court was a spectacular example of the right man standing in the right place at the right time. Chief

Justice Oliver Ellsworth, like John Jay before him, had been sent on a peace mission to Europe in November 1799. Taken ill in France, he had sent a letter of resignation that Adams received in December 1800. Had Ellsworth waited to resign until his return to the United States in March 1801, the naming of his replacement would have been Jefferson's. Instead the plum was in Adams's hands and he asked Jay to take it again. Adams also considered a promotion from within the court—William Cushing, a Massachusetts Federalist and Washington appointee who had filled in as acting justice while Jay had been abroad, or William Paterson, who had made his mark persecuting Republicans. But Cushing, at age sixty-nine, was the court's oldest member, his health already beginning to fail, while Paterson was the favorite of a Federalist faction that had turned bitterly against Adams after the election debacle.

Adams had to act quickly. If he waited until passage of the Judiciary Act, which would reduce the court's numbers from six to five at the next vacancy, he would have been forced to elevate a sitting justice. As John Marshall told the story, he came to the president on the evening of January 19, 1801, with Jay's letter declining the appointment. "Who shall I nominate now?" Adams asked thoughtfully. Not Paterson, he decided. "After a moments hesitation he said 'I believe I must nominate you.'" Marshall recalled that he was "pleased as well as surprized, and bowed in silence. Next day I was nominated. . . ."

Though Adams had two years earlier asked Marshall to fill the vacancy left by James Wilson's death, there is no evidence that the president considered his secretary of state for the chief justiceship before that moment. Yet the choice—an act Adams later would call "the pride of my life"—was understandable. Marshall had proven his loyalty to the president first by tirelessly defending the administration's policies in the House of Representatives and then by joining his cabinet in May 1800 when Adams's political fortunes were sinking and his leadership was under siege even within his own party. But Marshall was a moderate Federalist—absolutely sound on the core principles of nationalism and federal power, while averse to extremes of partisanship. His opposition to the Sedition Act as unnecessarily divisive had earned him the grudging respect of some Republicans. Moreover, Marshall believed that the Constitution, as the supreme law of the land, was "the rock of our political salvation," preserving Americans from "misery, division and civil wars," and he assigned the Supreme Court a lofty role in defending the new constitutional order. It was to be the ultimate guardian of what in 1798 he termed "the genuine principles of the constitution, as sanctioned by the will of the people, for their general liberty, prosperity and happiness."

Marshall was, above all, of the school of George Washington, "the greatest Man on earth," as he called him. Their backgrounds could hardly have differed more—Washington born and bred to Virginia's gentry, given to the pose of Cincinnatus, his people's reluctant savior who readily surrendered power once he had fulfilled his duty; Marshall with roots in Virginia's wild northwest frontier and a thrusting ambition that led to almost feverish land speculation and a scramble for every political office that opened up. But Marshall's service in the revolutionary army was a transformative experience, when he stopped thinking of himself as a Virginian first and was "confirmed in the habit of considering America as my country."

George Washington embodied that almost mystical sense of nationhood, and like him, Marshall would be dismayed by the ebbing of revolutionary unity in the 1780s as the states squabbled and competed in pursuing their self-interests. All that Marshall most valued—legal stability, social order, economic progress—was threatened by weak and incompetent government. He had firsthand experience of the fecklessness of state legislatures when he served in Virginia's House of Delegates, convincing him that "no safe and permanent remedy could be found but in a more efficient and better organized general government." Marshall defended the Constitution at the Virginia ratification convention in 1788, not fearing to challenge that hero of independence, Patrick Henry, head on. The new design, Marshall argued, offered "a well regulated Democracy," with life, liberty, and property secured by a "strict observance of justice and public faith." To Anti-Federalists like Henry who feared Congress would overpower the states, Marshall pointed to judicial review as a check. If Congress exceeded its authority in passing a law, "it would be considered by the Judges as an infringement of the Constitution which they are to guard." They would, he promised, "declare it void."

It was Marshall, this "Federalist of the good old school," who, after Adams departed the capital in the predawn darkness of inauguration day to avoid the sight of his successor's swearing-in, remained as the most powerful Federalist in the national government, left to protect the party's principles against the onslaught sure to come. After the peaceful handover of power, comity vanished, as Jefferson's conciliation proved an illusion. Republicans were fiercely determined to demolish the Federalist legacy, especially what Jefferson termed its "stronghold," the judiciary, where "the remains of federalism are to be preserved and fed from the treasury." Among the new president's first acts were pardons of the Sedition Act victims and a halt to further prosecutions. When Congress convened in December 1801, Republicans made repeal of the Judiciary Act—the law that had enabled Adams to pack the courts after his election defeat—a very early order of business.

Some Republicans wanted to go much further in reducing and caging judicial power. In a letter to Jefferson, Virginia congressman William Branch Giles suggested a purge: "the only check upon the Judiciary system" was "the removal of all its executive officers indiscriminately." The president's close friend Senator John Breckinridge of Kentucky, defending the repeal measure, borrowed passages from a paragraph Jefferson had omitted from his first annual message to Congress to define the limits of judicial power. He adopted the president's "departmentalist" view of constitutional interpretation—that each branch of the government had "an equal right" to determine for itself the constitutionality of measures and actions affecting its own sphere. Thus, the Supreme Court was supreme only in matters judicial. "To make the Constitution a practical system," Breckinridge said, "this pretended power of the courts to annul the laws of Congress cannot possibly exist."

But that power, never yet exercised, hung over the repeal debate. Republicans feared—and Federalists hoped—that the court would declare Congress's repeal of the Judiciary Act unconstitutional at the earliest opportunity—its June 1802 session. In the partisan atmosphere of the moment, this was a logical expectation: a vindictive Republican measure—passed strictly on party lines—would be rejected by a solidly packed Federalist court. Moreover, since repeal directly affected the judiciary, the court was entitled to strike it down even under Jefferson's narrow departmentalism. To forestall this, Republicans passed a law that simply abolished the court's June sitting, ordering it to reconvene in February 1803, after repeal had been implemented.

The threatened showdown never happened. When a case challenging the constitutionality of the repeal act, *Stuart* v. *Laird*, arrived at the court in February 1803, Marshall skillfully lobbied and maneuvered to secure unanimity—or at least silence—behind the court's minimalist opinion. The decision stated tersely that "there are no words in the constitution to prohibit or restrain the exercise of legislative power." Adams's attorney general, Charles Lee, lamented that "the judiciary is certainly gone." Lee was premature. Marshall's prudence had saved the court from a worse confrontation with aroused Republicans. He had shown that it was not purely a mouthpiece for

Federalist politicians. Still, it was as clearly a retreat by a court under siege.

How was the Supreme Court—holed up in dingy quarters in the new Capitol, shared with the District of Columbia courts, and widely despised by the public as the tool of a discredited political party—to become what John Marshall fervently believed it should be: the final authority in all matters constitutional?

SUDDENLY AN opportunity opened up, one that perhaps only a politician of Marshall's vision and determination might have seized. It first appeared in a most humdrum fashion. In early March 1801, Marshall, already chief justice but still serving as Adams's secretary of state, had been so overwhelmed by last-minute business that he failed to see to it that William Marbury's commission—for the modest post of justice of the peace in D.C.—was delivered to him. When the commission fell into Jefferson's hands, the new president ordered his acting secretary of state to withhold it. Seeing a chance to embarrass the Republican administration, Marshall's good friend Charles Lee brought the issue to the Supreme Court in December 1801, asking for an order that would compel the commission's delivery to Marbury. With the court on its congressionally mandated recess, the case did not come to trial until February 1803. The administration treated it as a political stunt, and the defendant—new secretary of state James Madison—was not even represented in court. But Lee argued that under the Judiciary Act of 1789, the Supreme Court had the authority to compel Madison to perform his legal duty to deliver commissions duly signed and sealed.

The Marbury case threw Marshall into a personal, political, and judicial thicket. Apart from his own role in the matter, his brother James was a key witness for Marbury. The chief justice might have—perhaps, should have—recused himself, but he chose not to and instead confronted the options. If he agreed with Marbury and ordered the commission delivered, Jefferson and Madison might happily defy him, setting a precedent that could hobble the court for years to come. But if he found in favor of the administration, that would expose the court's weakness in the face of executive authority, again setting a dismal precedent.

Marshall's opinion in *Marbury* v. *Madison* was a brilliant solution to the dilemma. First the chief justice found that Marbury had a right to receive his commission and that Jefferson was not entitled to withhold it. Further, Marbury had the right to turn to the courts to compel its delivery. To this point, Marshall seemed to be paving the way for confrontation with the president. But then he performed a dramatic sidestep that would transform American constitutional history. He ruled that the grant of jurisdiction to the Supreme Court in such cases as Marbury's by the 1789 Judiciary Act "appears not to be warranted by the constitution," in conflict with Article III, which defined the court's jurisdiction. In such instances of conflict, Marshall wrote, "the constitution, and not such ordinary act, must govern the case." Thus, that portion of the Judiciary Act was unconstitutional and void. The Supreme Court was powerless to remedy the obvious wrong done to Marbury.

But by striking down a measure that gave him a tiny authority, Marshall secured a far greater one—the power to declare acts of Congress unconstitutional. "It is, emphatically, the province and duty of the judicial department to say what the law is," Marshall asserted. This judicial power "extended to all cases arising under the constitution." With these words, Marshall laid the basis for a power of judicial review of acts of Congress—indeed over the acts of all branches of the national and state governments—so absolute and sweeping that it would eventually create a *supremacy* of the Supreme Court over American government.

How did Jefferson and his fellow Republican leaders respond to

Marshall's coup? With outrage, denunciation, threats? The reaction was in fact quite muted. Some in Congress used the decision as further proof of the Federalist plan to dominate the government from the judiciary. Defendant Madison, father of the Constitution, left no written trace that he gave, then or ever, a moment's thought to *Marbury* and its implications. In the most obvious sense, the decision was a win for Republicans—Marbury never would receive that commission. What galled Jefferson—and he returned to it for the rest of his life—was Marshall's lecture to the president that he *should* have delivered the commission. For one thing, it was, as Jefferson would point out, a "gratuitous interference," since Marshall had gone on to hold that the court lacked jurisdiction. More important, it was an invasion into the executive's department, where the president must have the final word on such issues. As Jefferson saw it, it was this that "would make the judiciary a despotic branch." Marshall, "travelling out of his case," asserted power the court did not possess. On these same grounds, Jefferson never disputed the court's authority to strike down a portion of the Judiciary Act of 1789, since the issue was its own jurisdiction.

In the end, the president's insistence on viewing the decision through narrow, departmentalist eyes blinded him to the wider implications of Marshall's muscular claim that it was the "duty" of the court to "declare what the law is." The chief justice's huge, historic victory, with its twining of politics and principle that would become characteristic of landmark Supreme Court rulings, was all the more effective because his foes seemed hardly aware of it.

THE REPUBLICANS' small win in *Marbury* did not stall their push to overturn the Federalist bench, though by evading open conflict, Marshall had made the task more difficult. Even more frustrating to the Republicans was the Constitution itself. Justices, with their life tenure, were immune from a "general purgation of office." "By a fraudulent use of the Constitution, which has made judges irremovable," Jefferson wrote sourly, Federalists "have multiplied useless judges merely to strengthen their phalanx."

The Constitution provided but one remedy—impeachment. Before tackling the Supreme Court, Republicans made a trial run with lower court judge John Pickering, who had long suffered from nervous disorders that deteriorated into alcoholism and insanity. Even Federalists acknowledged his incapacitation—but they wanted to keep him on the bench so that their enemies could not name a replacement. After a year of preparation, Republicans had little trouble convicting Pickering in the Senate, on a straight party vote in March 1804, but to do so they had to find a deranged alcoholic guilty of "high crimes and misdemeanors." It was an ugly affair. Even before the trial began, Jefferson conceded that "this business of removing Judges by impeachment is a *bungling way.*" Would it not be better, he had suggested, if "the President, on application of Congress should have authority to remove any Judge from office"? But that would require a constitutional amendment, an even slower and more uncertain process.

Since, as Jefferson insisted, "the good work of *reform* cannot be delayed," congressional Republicans next set their sights on a member of the high court, the rabidly partisan Samuel Chase, whose recent outrages included a jury charge while on circuit in Baltimore that featured condemnations of the Judiciary Act's repeal, a harangue against universal suffrage as leading to *"Mobocracy,"* and a warning that Jefferson's *"modern* Doctrines" of *"equal Liberty* and *equal rights"* would be the destruction of "peace & order, freedom and property." The effort to impeach Chase had started in 1803, but the justice did not come to Senate trial until 1805, when the Republican managers bungled away their case, unable to show, even to the satisfaction of Republican colleagues, where Chase's gross misconduct amounted to an impeachable offense. In the end, Chase was not convicted of any of the eight charges against him.

Impeachment as a political weapon proved, as Jefferson later wrote, "a mere scare-crow." But it had so frightened John Marshall that he proposed a remarkable compromise of the judicial independence he otherwise defended so ferociously. Rather than impeach justices who delivered objectionable opinions, Marshall suggested, Congress should be given an "appellate jurisdiction" over the court—the power to reverse opinions it "deemd unsound." The chief justice mooted this idea in a private letter to Chase; after the impeachment scare passed, it was never heard of again.

IF REPUBLICANS could not abolish the Federalist Supreme Court, nor pick off its members one by one through impeachment, they would have to rely on the president's power of appointment to pack it with their own partisans. But here they suffered a double frustration. The rapid coming and going of justices in the court's first decade, which gave Washington and Adams fourteen appointments, all but ceased after the Republicans took power. Justices now clung to their seats, even as health or finances failed. Over the course of twenty-four years, three Republican presidents—Jefferson, Madison, Monroe—had a total of only seven appointments, just enough for a full bench after Republicans in Congress made a gift to Jefferson by enlarging the court with a seventh seat in 1807. And Marshall and Bushrod Washingon continued to occupy two of those seats well past the end of the Republican era in the mid-1820s.

A second, graver disappointment was that Republican packing could not make the Supreme Court a vehicle for the party's principles. Its appointees failed to shake John Marshall's Federalist grip. It was not that Republicans lacked talent in their huge pool of lawyers and politicians. The first of Jefferson's three appointments, in

1804, was his most distinguished—William Johnson, a brilliant young attorney and state judge from South Carolina with impeccable Republican credentials, termed a "zealous democrat" by a Federalist senator. Johnson was also described as bold and independent, but, once on the court, his Federalist brethren brought him to heel. After he dissented in an early case, he would recall years later, "during the rest of the session I heard nothing but lectures on the indecency of justices cutting at each other" and decided that he "must either submit to circumstances or become such a cypher in our consultations as to effect no good at all. I therefore bent to the current." It would take many years—and Jefferson's dismayed promptings—before Johnson would speak in an independent voice.

Jefferson's two other justices also quickly joined the chorus of silence behind John Marshall—Brockholst Livingston, to all appearances a Republican stalwart in New York who on the court regressed to the Federalism of his youth; and Thomas Todd, who at forty-two had been chief justice of Kentucky's highest court for six years when Jefferson nominated him to the Supreme Court. Though Todd came from a region where Marshall's nationalizing jurisprudence was especially resented, he never disagreed with the chief justice in a constitutional case. He was on the court for nineteen years and wrote one dissent, five lines in 1810.

But Jefferson could continue to hope. After his retirement, he greeted the death in 1810 of the last survivor of Washington's original bench, Justice Cushing, with the cheering thought that at last "we have a chance of getting a republican majority in the supreme judiciary." In fact, Madison's two appointments—the second when Samuel Chase died in 1811—made five nominal Republicans on the bench. But those two epitomized the unpredictability of Supreme Court appointments, since they actually strengthened Marshall's grip. Gabriel Duvall was an early Republican with long experience as a Maryland legislator and judge. For nearly a decade he had served

Jefferson and Madison as comptroller of the United States. But after he fell into the black hole of Marshall's court, he was scarcely heard from again, the author of fifteen opinions in twenty-three years, all in minor cases.

Madison's other appointment was the most consequential of the Republican era. Joseph Story was a man of inexhaustible interests and ambitions, a lawyer, politician, poet, banker, constitutional scholar, and Republican leader in Massachusetts. But Federalist domination of the state made compromise necessary for advancement, and Story's willingness to cross national Republicans led Jefferson to label him a "pseudo-republican." When he saw that Madison might consider him for the court, Jefferson warned his friend that Story was "unquestionably a tory." But after three failed attempts to fill Chase's seat, Madison named Story, who, sure enough, soon became Marshall's most powerful intellectual collaborator in a partnership that lasted until the chief justice's death a quarter century later. Sharing Marshall's determination to expand judicial power in the service of aggressive nationalism, Story was anything but a silent justice, second only to Marshall in authoring opinions, many in landmark cases, but with only a handful of dissents.

With Story's appointment, the Marshall Court took enduring form. Between 1811 and 1823, there were no vacancies, the longest such period until the end of the twentieth century. Though packed with Republicans, it was, emphatically, John Marshall's court. Its voice—the "opinion of the Court"—was, in major cases, Marshall's, and though he would consult with Story and Bushrod Washington, he did not circulate drafts, which meant that his opinions, "although subscribed to by the Associate Justices," as historian G. Edward White put it, "had not even been read by the subscribers."

But Marshall's real strength was in the forcefulness and consistency of his ideas. His determination to secure and extend the power of the court as the supreme interpreter and final arbiter of the Constitution—as the center of constitutional action—dovetailed with his unwavering nationalism, just as Republican hostility to Marshall's power was of a piece with the party's defense of states' rights. At a time when the proper relation between the nation and the states remained unsettled, with wide implications for the founding values of life, liberty, and the pursuit of happiness, John Marshall put the Supreme Court firmly and effectively behind the drive for national power.

LIBERTY, PROPERTY, and the nation's economic growth were closely interwoven in Marshall's mind. All three depended on the security of private rights of property, their protection against interference by government. An aggressive land speculator himself, Marshall believed that if entrepreneurs did not think that their investments were safe from "invasion" by law or regulation, they would not put their capital at risk. In a long series of cases involving the Constitution's contract clause, Marshall enshrined property rights as a core constitutional value.

The foundation was laid in 1810, with *Fletcher* v. *Peck*, a case with origins in 1795, when corrupted Georgia legislators had authorized the sell-off of 35 million western acres the state claimed to own. The acreage was scooped up by the four large companies that had bought off the lawmakers, and they in turn marketed it to other speculators. But in the 1796 elections, outraged Georgians gave the corrupt legislators the boot and the new legislature rescinded the land grant. But what about those who had bought the land? Did the repeal also rescind their title? Congress for years tried and failed to settle the disputed claims.

Then John Marshall stepped in. His decision in *Fletcher* came down squarely for the speculators and against Georgia's reform legislature. He held that the 1795 act was a contract to sell the land, and when "a law is in its nature a contract, when absolute rights have vested under that contract, a repeal of the law cannot divest those rights." The state legislature, Marshall wrote, could not be "absolved from those rules of property which are common to all the citizens of the United States." By transforming a political or public-policy issue into one of the common law of property and contract, and then embedding it in the contract clause, Marshall gave constitutional status to the "absolute right" of property.

But the chief justice was, as usual, up to something more. While cloaking his decision in judicial restraint—by deferring to the 1795 Georgia legislature—he also asserted the court's power of judicial review by rejecting the reformers' 1796 reversal of the land grant.

Fletcher was the Supreme Court's first major decision to strike down a state law. As Marshall went on to assert federal power, he dropped the cloak of restraint. In another complex real estate case, decided in 1816, *Martin* v. *Hunter's Lessee*, the court forcefully overrode a defiant decision by Virginia's highest court. Because he had an interest in the case, Marshall recused himself, but his memorandum was the basis for Story's opinion. To the assertion of the Virginia Court of Appeals that, under "a sound construction of the constitution," the Supreme Court lacked jurisdiction to review state court judgments—and that states could defy federal mandates with impunity—Story answered that the Supreme Court's reach did indeed "extend to cases pending in the state courts." He reminded Virginians that because of the "jarring and discordant judgments" emitted by state courts, the Supreme Court's "revising authority" was essential, lest the laws and the Constitution itself be different in different states. "The public mischiefs that would attend such a state of things," Story concluded, "would be truly deplorable."

Story's insult to Virginia's sovereignty provoked little outcry, but a decision three years later ignited a firestorm across the South. At issue was the constitutionality of the Bank of the United States, which had long been a hate object for Republicans as an intrusion by the federal government into the economy. Jefferson's break with the Washington administration in 1793 had been hastened when he lost the constitutional argument over the Bank to Alexander Hamilton. Washington's treasury secretary had insisted that the Bank was authorized by the "liberal latitude" of the Constitution's "necessary and proper" clause, which recognized a wide range of "implied powers" beyond those enumerated.

The Bank had been chartered in 1791 and when the charter expired twenty years later, Republicans had blocked its renewal. But the financial demands of the War of 1812 and an outburst of nationalism provoked by the war led to the chartering of the Second Bank in 1816. For two years, the Bank supplied easy credit, fueling a land boom in the West and South. But when the bubble burst, the Bank foreclosed on thousands of farm mortgages and called in loans to state banks, forcing many to close their doors. States retaliated by passing laws to curb the Bank's power. Maryland imposed a tax on all notes the Bank issued, which a cashier at the Bank's Baltimore branch, William McCulloch, refused to pay. After Maryland courts upheld the tax, the Bank appealed to the Supreme Court.

In *McCulloch* v. *Maryland*, decided as the Panic of 1819 was roiling the country, Marshall delivered his most sweeping declaration of national power. The federal government, he wrote, "is, emphatically and truly, a government of the people," not of "sovereign and independent states." It was "the government of all; its powers are delegated by all; it represents all, and acts for all." Its powers were defined by the Constitution but not limited to those enumerated. There were also "implied powers" that were "necessary and proper." The chief justice defined them in memorable words: "Let the end be legitimate, let it be within the scope of the constitution, and all means which are appropriate, which are plainly adapted to that end, which are not prohibited, but consistent with the letter and spirit of the constitution, are constitutional." And who was to give a "fair construction" to the "great outlines" of the Constitution? "On the supreme court of the United States has the constitution of our country devolved this important duty." Should Congress exceed its powers, it would become the court's "painful duty" to say that an act of Congress "was not the law of the land."

Marshall spoke as an absolutist. If Maryland were allowed "to retard, impede, burden, or in any manner control" constitutional acts of Congress like the Bank, the federal government would be prostrate at the foot of the states. The "supremacy" Americans had vested in the nation would be transferred to the states. But Americans "did not design to make their government dependent on the states."

Some states believed otherwise, notably Virginia, Jefferson's home, which was the last stronghold of the old Republicanism and the birthplace of the new, more aggressive states' rights doctrine. Marshall too was of course a Virginian, but he was no "Virginia judge." His *McCulloch* decision set off a heated debate over state sovereignty that would persist to the Civil War—and beyond. At a time when Congress was barreling toward a showdown over the extension of slavery into the territories, the subtext of Southern rage over *McCulloch* was the fear that Congress might seize the boundless "implied powers" Marshall afforded it to limit and gradually undermine and destroy slavery—and receive the Supreme Court's stamp of approval for it.

Critics zeroed in on the decision's assertion of judicial power. It seemed to them a dangerous complement to unbounded legislative license; between Congress and the Supreme Court, the states would be annihilated. Virginia judge Spencer Roane, the man Jefferson would have made chief justice of the Supreme Court in 1801 had Adams not beaten him to it with Marshall's appointment, attacked the court's "judicial *coup de main*" in *McCulloch*. The power of the Supreme Court, Roane insisted, "does not extend to every thing; it is not great enough to *change* the constitution"—to destroy what had been a compact of the "several states, in their highest sovereign character" and erect on its ruins a consolidated and unlimited federal government. The power of federal judicial supremacy was nowhere to be found in the Constitution, Roane pointed out, yet Marshall had asserted the court's authority to rule in all cases whatsoever.

While avoiding public comment, Jefferson cheered Roane on. "I subscribe to every tittle," he wrote the judge. Decades earlier Jefferson had objected to Hamilton's "liberal" interpretation of the Constitution's "necessary and proper" clause. The doctrine of "implied powers," he had argued, would erase the entire careful system of checks and balances and "reduce the whole instrument to a single phrase," giving legislators "a distinct and independent power to do any act they please, which might be for the good of the Union." Now the former president struggled to imagine how a court with five Republicans on it could render a decision like *McCulloch*: "An opinion is huddled up in conclave, perhaps by a majority of one, delivered as if unanimous, and with the silent acquiescence of lazy or timid associates, by a crafty chief judge." And so the Constitution became, he lamented to Roane, "a mere thing of wax in the hands of the judiciary, which they may twist and shape into any form they please."

Marshall's answer to critics of his court's power came in *Cohens*, an 1821 case that again involved Virginia and again questioned the court's jurisdiction over state courts. Dismissing the Supreme Court's judgment in *Martin*, Virginia's attorneys argued that the Constitution mandated a total separation between federal and state courts—"Let each operate within their respective spheres; and let each be confined to their assigned limits"—and warned that Marshall's claims to "unacknowledged power" were undermining "the confidence of the people" and "exciting the hostility of the state governments. With them it is, to determine how long this government will endure."

The chief justice met the challenge—and veiled threat—unflinchingly. Restating his doctrine of national supremacy, Marshall reasoned that as the federal government was supreme, so were "all its departments supreme" with respect "to objects of vital interest to the nation." And if constitutional law was supreme, so must the Constitution's highest court be supreme. The constitution and laws of a state were another matter. "So far as they are repugnant to the constitution and laws of the United States," they must be "absolutely void."

Marshall could not have made it plainer.

THE FRAMERS had given judges life tenure to insulate them from the whirligig of politics, but as John Marshall's decades as chief justice lengthened, his independence from partisanship waned in step with his fading domination of the court. The political terrain was shifting dramatically against him. A so-called era of good feelings had followed the final collapse of the Federalist party in 1815. Almost everyone was a Republican now, but party labels meant little and partisanship was seen, much as it had been in the early days of the republic, as an expression of faction and bigotry. President James Monroe, reelected against token opposition in 1820, was Jefferson's heir in name only, blurring Republican and Federalist principles in the cause of moderate and efficient public service.

But in the early 1820s, as the economy rebounded after the Panic of 1819, new cleavage lines of class and sectional interests sharpened, fueling a political awakening and the reemergence of partisan conflict in the battle for control of the national government. North and South clashed over slavery and states' rights. The East, with its financial centers and industrializing cities, faced off against the West, where commercial agriculture was erasing wilderness. The 1824 presidential election proved a watershed, when four candidates—each calling himself a Republican—battled it out. None won a majority in the electoral college, so the decision fell to the House of Representatives. After bitter disputes and tough bargaining, John Quincy Adams emerged the winner. It was a Pyrrhic victory with, as Adams himself sadly noted, "perhaps two-thirds of the whole people adverse to the actual result."

Most of those people had preferred Andrew Jackson, the fierce and volatile hero of the War of 1812, giving him 151,271 votes to Adams's 113,122. The seeds of a revived party system were planted by Jackson's thirst for revenge. Mobilizing rapidly after 1824, especially in the South and West, the new Democratic party assumed the Jeffersonian mantle of economic populism and states' rights and tarred its foes—entrenched Eastern banking and manufacturing interests and their pawns in the federal government—with the "revival of Federalist heresies."

Jackson's Democrats framed his second run for the presidency in 1828 as, among other things, a referendum on that original and unrepentant Federalist, John Marshall. The chief justice himself let it be known that he would vote for the first time in decades and reportedly said, "I should consider the election of Jackson as a virtual dissolution of the government." But Jackson, riding a surge of anti-court feeling in the South, was elected, beating President Adams by a landslide, and arrived at the White House spoiling for a fight. Like Jefferson, he was determined to challenge the court's self-appointed role as the Constitution's supreme interpreter, which, like Jefferson, he saw as a vehicle for federal aggrandizement at the expense of the states.

To Marshall, Jackson was an even more formidable foe. Jefferson's revolution had been essentially conservative, an effort to restore the republic to what he saw as its first principles of limited government and majority rule. Now it was Marshall, determined to protect his nationalist legacy, who was the conservative in an age of change. And where Marshall had beaten back Jefferson's challenge with a unified court, the leadership of the seventy-four-year-old chief justice was now not so steady. With President Monroe's nomination of an independent-minded New Yorker, Smith Thompson, in 1823, and the emergence, under Jefferson's prodding, of his first appointee, William Johnson, as the court's first "great dissenter" after nearly two decades as a justice, Marshall was finding it more difficult to mass the brethren behind his sweeping nationalist decisions.

And Andrew Jackson was willing to hit at the very roots of Marshall's authority. In 1832, the Supreme Court struck down a Georgia statute that conflicted with U.S. treaty obligations to the Cherokee nation. *All* Georgia laws dealing with the Cherokees, Marshall held, were unconstitutional; federal jurisdiction was absolute. Jackson refused to indicate that he would enforce the court's order with the armed force that might be needed to suppress Georgian resistance. He denied that the court could place in the president's hands "a power to make war upon the rights of the States and the liberties of the country." In a remark that was perhaps apocryphal but that accurately and memorably captured his stance, Jackson was reported to have said, "John Marshall has made his decision; now let him enforce it." In fact, the president's defiance encouraged Georgia's. As a result, he boasted, "the decision of the supreme court fell still born."

That same year, Jackson vetoed as unconstitutional the rechartering of the Bank of the United States—the bank John Marshall had emphatically declared constitutional in the landmark *McCulloch* decision. Drafted with the help of his attorney general, Roger Taney, Jackson's veto message was a ringing declaration of presidential independence that echoed Jefferson's departmentalist theory of constitutional interpretation. The Supreme Court could not "be permitted to control the Congress or the Executive when acting in their legislative capacities," Jackson held; rather, each branch must "for itself be guided by its own opinion of the Constitution." The court should be permitted "only such influence as the force of their reasoning may deserve."

Marshall coped with the Jacksonian onslaught by sacrificing doctrinal purity, making compromises and adjustments to accommodate states' rights challenges without yielding core principles. But his heart wasn't in it. By 1831, ill and discouraged, unwilling to "hazard the disgrace of continuing in office, a mere inefficient pageant," he was ready to retire. Still, it would depend on the 1832 presidential election. With Jackson's reelection, Marshall became determined to hang on, to deny the president the chance to replace him with a man who might repudiate his life's work.

Jackson was well aware that by naming the right men to the Supreme Court he could extend his influence long after his administration ended. Personal loyalty was paramount, but Jackson also wanted nominees whose "principles on the Constitution are sound, and well fixed"—that is, Jacksonian. His first appointment, in 1829, exposed other considerations. John McLean, as postmaster general, had obstructed the Jacksonian campaign to flush out Republican officeholders and replace them with Democratic loyalists. Jackson bumped him up to the Supreme Court to get him out of the way. McLean proved a moderate nationalist who mainly backed Marshall, but he also hoped to use his court seat as a base for a presidential run and brought an unwelcome "modern" air of partisan politicking into the court's sanctum.

Marshall suffered a greater blow the same year when his closest friend and ally, Bushrod Washington, died after three decades on the bench. To replace him, Jackson named the man who had managed his Pennsylvania campaign in 1828, ex-congressman Henry Baldwin. Mentally unstable, Baldwin constantly quarreled with other justices and became a chronic dissenter, defending extremist states' rights positions against Marshall's nationalism.

With such colleagues, Marshall was unable to sustain the court's façade of unanimity. Decision-making became less collective and more individualistic. The chief justice was even obliged in 1834 to acknowledge publicly that the seven-member court now operated on the radical Jeffersonian principle of majority rule, with four votes needed for a decision. This "revolutionary spirit," as Marshall called it, was the cause of much "inconvenience and mischief." Even more embarrassing, in a number of constitutional cases, no four justices could agree on a single position and decisions were deferred for years. And in one decision that upheld the power of state governments to revoke or modify private contracts in bankruptcy proceedings, John Marshall found himself, for the first and only time in his thirty-five years on the bench, in the minority in a constitutional case, a *dissenter.*

These were indeed strange and troubling times for a chief justice who, over the decades, had so closely identified his own authority with the power of the federal government, his nationalism with the Union. Politicians of Marshall's era had wavered, compromised, and contradicted themselves in the struggle to define the dividing line between federal and state power. President Jefferson had ventured grand, even radical assertions of national power in the purchase of France's vast Louisiana territories in 1803 and with the 1807–08 Embargo Acts that barred all American exports to insulate the United States from Europe's wars. It was only after his retirement back in Virginia that he indulged in the states' rights extremism of Spencer Roane and company.

But Marshall, secure in his seat on the bench, accountable not to voters or to political rivals but only to his own constitutional faith, never wavered. He built the Supreme Court into a driving force for his nationalism, and more than any man since the Founding, he had shaped the Constitution into an image of his own beliefs. So it was small wonder that as his powers ebbed, he should see that not only his judicial legacy was at stake, but the United States itself. "I yield slowly and reluctantly to the conviction that our constitution cannot last," he wrote in 1832 to his ally Justice Story. The case in the South was "desperate" and even the North now seemed doubtful. "The union has been prolonged thus far by miracles," but he was afraid "they cannot continue."

CHAPTER THREE

The Dred Decision

WHEN CHARLES DICKENS visited Washington in 1842, he found a place of "slavery, spittoons, and senators—all three are evils in all countries." His indignation rose as he stood with a congressman looking out a window of the Capitol—the Temple of Equality, as the congressman ironically called it. In the open street below, they saw "a gang of male and female slaves for sale, warranted to breed like cattle, linked to each other by iron fetters." Where now, Dickens asked, was Equality and Liberty?

Slavery had long been established in North America, with the English beginning the importation of Africans early in the seventeenth century. By the end of the 1780s, after the Declaration of Independence and the adoption of the Constitution, African Americans in the Middle Atlantic and Southern states numbered over 700,000, nearly all of them slaves, and 17,000 in New England, about a quarter of whom were slaves. Many Northern writers attacked this bondage as cruel and unchristian, but only Quaker Pennsylvania, which Dickens also visited, had passed an act of gradual abolition.

Since the revolution, slavery had been a flash point between North and South, the single issue that threatened to make the union of the states impossible. It fueled the South's resistance to Marshall's nationalism, the fear that the federal government would one day "interfere" with—even abolish—slavery. The South sought, if not to turn the United States into a "slaveocracy," as Northern abolitionists warned, then at least to secure slavery's constitutional status and the right to extend it into the great expanses of the western territories. The North sought, if not to abolish slavery, then to confine it to the Southern states where it already existed and where, isolated, it might wither and die.

For decades, American political leaders struggled to find a balance between these positions, beginning with the Framers themselves, whose Constitution made union possible by avoiding any explicit mention of slavery, thus leaving its status—and that of the slaves themselves—undefined. The Framers, though, allowed the South, for purposes of apportionment in the House of Representatives, to add three fifths of what the Constitution termed "all other Persons" to their total of free persons.

That provision augmented the South's representation in the House by 30 percent, crucial because it was Congress that bore the burden of striking that balance between the sections. Congressmen fought repeated battles over slavery's extension into the territories and whether new states should be "free" or "slave." The first grand settlement was the Missouri Compromise of 1820, which admitted Missouri as a slave state and Maine as a free state, while seeking to head off future conflict by banning slavery from the huge territory acquired in 1803 by Jefferson's Louisiana Purchase north of an agreed-upon line. This set the pattern for three decades. Periods of calm were shattered by desperate slave rebellions in the South and by outrage in the North over the capture of fugitive slaves who were dragged from freedom back into bondage. There was violence and talk of war—but not yet war.

By the late 1840s, though, the chasm between North and South had become so wide that further compromise seemed nearly impossible. The balancing act over slavery, maintained by evasion and ambiguity, between the Northern and Southern branches of the two major parties—the dominant Democrats and the Whig party that had emerged in the 1830s to represent the old Federalist strain—had begun to collapse. Northern abolitionists from both parties fused into the first antislavery party, Free Soil, and opposed further extension of slavery as unconstitutional. Southern Democrats, ever more insistent on the South's "rights," argued that it was congressional interference with slavery that was unconstitutional. That left little middle ground. In 1846, Pennsylvania congressman David Wilmot proposed that slavery be excluded from all territories acquired in the war with Mexico that began that year after the American annexation of Texas. The Wilmot Proviso and the vast Mexican cession—500,000 square miles, including California—reignited the issue of national power over slavery, driving a sharp wedge between Northern and Southern Democrats, and making a new grand bargain imperative if the Union was to survive.

In an epic act of transactional brokerage, managed by Senators Henry Clay of Kentucky, a Whig, and Democrat Stephen Douglas of Illinois, Congress hammered together a new bundle of agreements in 1850 that included admission of California as a free state. In return, the South received a tougher Fugitive Slave Law and the ambiguous prospect of "territorial sovereignty" that would allow territories to decide for themselves whether to exclude slavery, so long as their actions were "consistent with the Constitution." Firebrands North and South, with their radically different views of what the Constitution required, condemned the Compromise of 1850 as an evasion, and so it was, undermining the Missouri Compromise without settling the central question of federal power over the territories. The issue of slavery in the United States could not be faced squarely. The Compromise was politics both at its best and at its worst as the art of the possible. At stake, the great Massachusetts senator Daniel Webster insisted, was "the preservation of the Union."

EVEN AS POLITICIANS bickered and bargained, the Supreme Court was largely a bystander. For decades after the nation's founding, no questions of slavery's constitutional status came before the court, nor did justices seek them out. John Marshall's nationalizing crusade raised Southern fears that federal power would strike at slavery, but the chief justice, a slave owner himself and well aware of the dilemma slavery posed for the Union's survival, shunned confrontation. The man who spread federal power over the widest ranges of politics, law, economics, and society decided that slavery was the business of the states.

As polarization over slavery had intensified in the decades between the two great compromises, the Supreme Court was packed by aggressively pro-slavery Southerners and Northerners sympathetic to the South's concerns. Control of the presidency and Congress by the Democratic party with its dominant Southern base ensured this distorted representation. Nominees had to be sound on states' rights—no more Marshalls!—and attuned to the South's peculiar sensitivities. Four of Andrew Jackson's six appointments in his two terms were Southerners and slave owners. One, Philip Barbour, had played a prominent role in his native Virginia's resistance to Marshall. Though Barbour died after only four years on the court, in 1841, President Martin Van Buren, a New Yorker who was the heir to Jackson's Democracy, quickly named an even more extreme antinationalist Virginian, Peter Daniel.

But Jackson had already left a time bomb on the Supreme Court—Marshall's successor as chief justice, Roger B. Taney. Born in Maryland to a family of planters, Taney joined the Federalists in the 1790s, becoming a party leader in his home state and a supporter of the Bank of the United States in the controversy that led to Marshall's *McCulloch* decision. But in the early 1820s, when he was in his forties, Taney underwent a conversion. With the Federalist party in tatters, Taney fell back on the states' rights doctrine. By 1824, he was the most loyal of Jacksonian Democrats. Later, as Jackson's attorney general and, on a recess appointment, secretary of the treasury, his enthusiastic support of the president's war on the Bank earned him Jackson's lasting gratitude—and the enduring enmity of the opposition Whigs. After pro-Bank Whigs in the Senate blocked Taney's confirmation as treasury secretary in 1834, an angry Jackson vowed to discharge the "debt of gratitude and regard" he owed Taney as a "martyr" to the "corrupting domination of a great moneyed power."

The retirement of Justice Gabriel Duvall in January 1835 gave the president his chance. He named Taney to the court as an associate justice. But Whigs stalled the nomination. When Marshall died a few months later, Jackson sent Taney's name back to the Senate, now for the chief justiceship. This time Democrats pushed the nomination through.

Taney's late conversion to anti-Marshallian doctrines was apparent in his first major decision, the 1837 Charles River Bridge case. The corporation that owned a half-century old bridge between Boston and Charlestown had sued to stop the construction of a competitor chartered by Massachusetts in 1828, arguing that the new bridge violated its own 1785 charter with the state. Its appeal rested on the Constitution's prohibition of state laws that impaired "the obligation of contracts." The case had first come before Marshall's Supreme Court in 1831, but divisions among the justices prevented a decision. By the time it was reheard in 1837, the competing bridge had been in operation for nearly a decade—and Taney was chief justice. In his opinion for the court's majority, Taney put into the balance a corporation's property and contract rights and the responsibilities of government. Marshall would have favored the "sacred" rights of property and contract over a state law, but Taney wrote that "while the rights of private property are sacredly guarded, we must not forget, that the community also have rights, and that the happiness and well-being of every citizen depends on their faithful preservation." Over the objections of Marshall's old collaborator Justice Story, who dismissed Taney's invocation of social benefits as "speculative niceties or novelties," the court upheld the Massachusetts charter of the competing bridge. Some Democrats who had feared that Taney might revert to Federalism once on the bench breathed a sigh of relief.

But Taney did not aim to overthrow his predecessor. In cases involving implied powers, while not rejecting Marshall's *McCulloch* holding, Taney construed the sphere of federal authority more narrowly, all the while cautiously extending the powers of state governments in areas where Congress had not legislated, especially in matters of commercial regulation and public health. And in 1849, in *Luther* v. *Borden*, Taney announced an appealing new doctrine of judicial restraint, writing that certain inherently political issues were the exclusive province of the political branches, whose decisions "could not be questioned in a judicial tribunal." Even many Whigs were impressed by the modesty and pragmatism of the chief justice's jurisprudence.

There was, though, one exception to Taney's moderation and restraint, where those qualities might best have served the court and the country. As Jackson's attorney general, he had held a racist conception of the constitutional status of African Americans, writing in an unpublished opinion that "the African race in the United States even when free, are every where a degraded class." Even when free, blacks "permitted to be citizens by the sufferance of the white population . . . hold whatever rights they enjoy at their mercy."

As chief justice, Taney would brook no tampering with the status quo of slavery, no matter the source, and especially not from Congress, whose power he saw as limited to the *protection* of slavery and slave owners. The chief justice lost no opportunity to make that clear. In one of the first slavery cases to come before Taney's court, in 1841, the chief justice wrote a concurrence—one of only fourteen separate opinions he wrote in thirty years—to underline his view that the federal government had no power whatever to regulate the interstate slave trade, an issue that did not happen to be before the court in that case.

A decade later, a case arrived at the Supreme Court that involved a group of slave musicians from Kentucky who had been taken to perform in the free state of Ohio. They returned to Kentucky but later, with the aid of sympathetic whites, escaped to Canada. Their owner sued the white sympathizers for damages, his loss of property in the slaves. The defendants argued that they were not liable because the musicians had not been the owner's property at the time of their escape—their sojourn on free Ohio soil had made them free men.

Deciding *Strader* v. *Graham* in 1851, Taney first denied that the Supreme Court had jurisdiction—thus allowing a Kentucky court's ruling against the white defendants to stand—and then went on gratuitously to opine that the slave state, Kentucky, had exclusive control of the legal status of its black residents. It was not the business of the federal government or for that matter of Ohio. For Taney, states' rights reached their limit when a state's laws protected the rights of blacks. In an earlier decision, *Prigg* v. *Pennsylvania*, the Taney Court had upheld the constitutionality of the 1793 Fugitive Slave Act even though, as abolitionists pointed out, the law interfered with the rights of Northern states to offer procedural safeguards, such as jury trials and habeas corpus, to fugitive slaves pursued by "slave catchers."

It was no wonder that Taney's court, packed as it was with slave owners, consistently returned decisions supporting slavery. The real wonder was that, in the mid-1850s, desperate politicians, including Northerners, were looking to this Supreme Court for the ultimate compromise—the final settlement—that would save the Union from political collapse and war.

As the case of Dred Scott worked its long way through state and federal courts, the Compromise of 1850, whose authors had promised it would bring "finality" to the slavery conflict, was inciting new rounds of violent talk and action. Fire-breathing secessionists mobilized in the South, while abolitionists vowed defiance of the new Fugitive Slave Law. In 1854, a last, futile compromise was forced through Congress to get the lawmakers out of the hopeless business of deciding slavery in the territories. The Kansas-Nebraska Act enshrined the principle "that all questions pertaining to slavery in the Territories, and in the new States to be formed therefrom," should be left to the people who lived there. By explicitly repealing the Missouri Compromise's exclusion of slavery from northern territories, Congress opened the Great Plains to colonization by slaveholders. It ignited a proxy war in Kansas as free-state and pro-slavery emigrants flooded in to battle for control of the territory. The act was also a political catastrophe: the Whig party collapsed and Democrats split between North and South. A new Republican party emerged from the ashes, pledged to resist the slave power.

Dred Scott was born a slave, probably in Virginia, and taken by his first owner to Missouri in 1830, when he was about thirty years old. After that owner died two years later, Scott was sold to an army doctor, John Emerson, and taken to posts in the free state of Illinois and the Wisconsin Territory, which was free soil under the Missouri Compromise. After six years, Scott returned to Missouri, and in

1846 he filed the first suit for his freedom in a Missouri court. Scott claimed that he had been emancipated by his long residence in free jurisdictions and could not be reenslaved on his return to Missouri. A lower court, relying on state precedents that went back to the 1820s, granted Scott his freedom, but in 1852, the Missouri Supreme Court overturned the decision. It threw out the precedents because "times are not now as they were." Now "a dark and fell spirit in relation to slavery"—abolition—was threatening "the overthrow and destruction of our government."

Scott and his supporters—including children of his first owner—turned to the federal judiciary, bringing a new freedom suit in circuit court in 1854. By now Emerson was dead, and Scott had become the property of his brother-in-law John Sanford. Filing as a Missouri citizen, Scott again claimed that his stay on free soil had made him a free man and he could not be held by Sanford against his will. But Sanford's attorney argued that as a black man, Scott could not be a citizen of Missouri and so could not file a federal suit. Without settling the issue of Scott's citizenship, the federal judge accepted the suit. But when the case came to trial, the judge, citing Taney's opinion in *Strader*, instructed the jury to find against Scott.

Then the case moved to the Supreme Court, where it was first argued in February 1856. To their brief against Scott's citizenship, Sanford's attorneys added a new—and potentially explosive—contention. Part of Scott's claim to freedom rested on his residency in the free Wisconsin Territory. But, Sanford's lawyers maintained, the legislation that had established Wisconsin as a free territory was unconstitutional because Congress lacked the power to regulate slavery in the territories. In other words, the Missouri Compromise was unconstitutional. Though Congress had repealed it in 1854, the principles the Compromise embodied—above all, Congress's authority over slavery—were still dividing the nation in 1856. A few newspapers noticed the daring argument, but the press was distracted by the

Kansas violence, volatile debates in Congress, and the start of the presidential campaign.

Early signs suggested that the justices would prudently avoid ruling on the Compromise, but they could come to no decision on Scott's citizenship and ordered a rehearing on that issue in December 1856. By that time, a Pennsylvania Democrat, James Buchanan, had won the presidency in a bitterly fought election that settled nothing. Congress was racked by debates over an inflammatory statement by the outgoing president, Franklin Pierce, that Congress had no power over slavery in the territories. The Missouri Compromise, Pierce declared, was unconstitutional, a "dead letter in law." Eyes now turned to the Supreme Court, where a case involving that very issue was being heard.

At the December rehearing, the lawyers only briefly addressed Scott's citizenship. Instead, in an echo of the political debates in Congress and across the country, they clashed over congressional power. Sanford's attorney acknowledged that the Missouri Compromise may have been a "compromise of principle necessary to the existence of the Union," but that did not justify Congress's unconstitutional action in legislating limits on slavery.

The justices again seemed reluctant to involve themselves in the furor. The initial opinion, drafted by Samuel Nelson, a New York Democrat expert in admiralty and patent law who had been appointed to the high court by the lapsed Whig John Tyler in 1845, was a model of judicial restraint, little more than an affirmation of the circuit court's ruling against Scott. Political questions would have been left to the political branches to resolve—or fail to resolve. On any issue other than slavery, the chief justice might have drafted such an opinion himself, as Nelson subtly suggested by quoting Taney to prove there was no reason to rule on the Missouri Compromise.

But in mid-February, on a motion by Justice James Wayne, a slaveholding Jackson appointee from Georgia, the court abruptly shifted course. The Southern justices abandoned Nelson to form a new majority behind a strong pro-Southern opinion. Taney, who until then had been sitting neutrally in conferences on the case, agreed to write it himself.

Why the sudden switch? The Southerners blamed the two Northern dissenters from Nelson's opinion, Justice McLean, Jackson's first appointment, and Benjamin Curtis, the court's sole Whig, a Massachusetts conservative named by Millard Fillmore in 1851. The Southerners claimed that they had been willing to go along with Nelson, but when McLean and Curtis insisted on defending the Missouri Compromise in their dissents, they could not leave them unanswered. James Buchanan also came in for blame. The president-elect was in touch with John Catron, the Tennessee slave owner who was Jackson's last justice, nominated on Jackson's last day in office to fill one of the two new seats Congress had created in 1837 to cement the Democratic hold on the Supreme Court. Buchanan indicated that he was eager for the court to settle the territorial question before he took office. A pro-Southern Pennsylvanian, he feared that the issue would otherwise swallow his presidency. He successfully pressured his fellow Pennsylvanian, Justice Robert Grier, to join Taney's Southern bloc so that it should not appear, in Grier's words, that "the line of latitude should mark the line of division in the court."

The true reason for the Southern switch may have been the simplest. The Southern justices, while ostensibly backing Nelson, had waited for the excuse to issue the pro-slavery opinion they had wanted in the first place. And Taney's passivity in conference? As historian Don Fehrenbacher concluded in his exhaustive study of the case, "The Chief Justice wrote the opinion that he had wanted to write all along."

That opinion was not long in coming, only two weeks after the Southern coup in conference. Perhaps Taney had been writing it all along. The verdict could scarcely have been more sweeping and decisive. On the jurisdictional issue, Taney constructed an intricate and confused distinction between state and federal citizenship, but his conclusion was stark: Dred Scott was not—could never be—a citizen of the United States. No black man or woman descended from an American slave could claim national citizenship under the Constitution, which relegated blacks to a "subordinate and inferior class of beings who had been subjugated by the dominant race" and who had "no rights which the white man was bound to respect," including the right to seek redress in a federal court. In Taney's reading, Scott could not be a citizen of Missouri either—or of any state for that matter, since, the chief justice mistakenly asserted, no state had accorded blacks that status—but Scott was subject to Missouri law, and by the ruling of the state's highest court, he remained a slave.

Having vehemently denied his court's jurisdiction, Taney had no need to go further. But further he did go, on to the Missouri Compromise. For the first time since *Marbury*, the Supreme Court exercised the power of judicial review of acts of Congress that Marshall had so emphatically claimed a half-century earlier. What Taney now declared "void," though, was not an obscure provision in an "ordinary act," but the keystone to a carefully wrought structure that for three decades had kept the Union from exploding. Also void, by implication, was the Compromise of 1850 and any *future* attempt by Congress to "interfere" with slave owners' rights. "The powers over person and property of which we speak are not only not granted to Congress, but are in express terms denied, and they are forbidden to exercise them. And this prohibition is not confined to the States, but the words are general, and extend to the whole territory over which the Constitution gives it power to legislate." The only power over slavery that the federal government could "constitutionally exercise"—indeed, it was its "duty"—was "that of protecting the rights of the owner."

The chief justice's opinion, with its distorted reading of the Constitution as a charter for slave owners, its illogic, bigotry, and partisanship, was not the Supreme Court's only word in the case. Each of the other six justices in the majority issued separate concurrences, including Nelson, who published his original draft opinion, while Justices McLean and Curtis wrote separate dissents. Curtis's opinion was an overwhelming rebuttal of Taney's evidence and reasoning, and he warned that the chief justice had abandoned the law for politics and assumed an authority that rightfully belonged to the political branches.

Yet Taney's was the voice that counted, and its effect on the political branches was devastating. The chief justice, who had aspired to break the country's political deadlock over slavery with his exercise of John Marshall's power of judicial review, succeeded in smashing it to pieces. Two days before the opinion was read in court, on Inauguration Day, March 4, 1857, James Buchanan, tipped off by his friends among the justices, expressed to the crowd outside the Capitol his confidence that the Supreme Court would "speedily and finally" settle the territorial controversy. To its decision, he said, "I shall cheerfully submit." It was an inauspicious start to a presidency that never would recover from Buchanan's submission to *Dred Scott.*

The decision also inspired cheerful submission in the South, where John Marshall's Supreme Court had once inspired threats of secession. Finally, Southern rights had been given their just recognition. Now, as the Augusta (Georgia) *Constitutionalist* crowed, the South's opinion of slavery was "the supreme law of the land."

Outside the South, the reaction was outrage and horror. Many Northerners interpreted it as an initial step in the nationalization of slavery, even as a dark plot involving Taney, Buchanan, and Southern extremists to impose slavery on the free states. As a Republican senator from Wisconsin paraphrased Taney's "momentous and revolutionary" logic, if the Constitution "is the paramount law of every State; and if that recognizes slaves as property, as horses are property," then "no State constitution or State law can abolish [slavery], or prohibit its introduction."

Taney's opinion finally dragged into the open issues that political moderates in the North and the South—starting with the Framers themselves—had tried to keep obscure, lest compromise for "the preservation of the Union" become impossible. By ignoring extremist claims—and slavery's terrible realities—transactional leaders had been able to forge a middle ground. Much of that ground had eroded by 1857. There was none left after Taney put the authority of the Supreme Court on the side of the South's pro-slavery extremists. The Democratic party irreparably broke in half, with Southern Democrats rallying behind Taney's dogmas as the "final settlement," while those Northerners who didn't bolt to the Republican party clung to the tattered ideal of "popular sovereignty" in the territories.

As Taney's main political target, Republican leaders perhaps understood the implications of *Dred Scott* better than others. There could be no more papering over the differences between what New York senator William Seward called "opposing and enduring forces." It meant, he said, "that the United States must and will, sooner or later, become either entirely a slave-holding nation or entirely a free-labor nation." It was now "an irrepressible conflict."

CHAPTER FOUR

War Powers: Lincoln vs. Taney

"I DO NOT FORGET the position assumed by some," the new president declared to an expectant, anxious throng assembled in front of the Capitol in Washington for his Inauguration, "that constitutional questions are to be decided by the Supreme Court." It was March 4, 1861, just four years after the Dred Scott decision. *But*, Abraham Lincoln went on, "if the policy of the government, upon vital questions, affecting the whole people, is to be irrevocably fixed by decisions of the Supreme Court, the instant they are made . . . the people will have ceased, to be their own rulers, having, to that extent, practically resigned their government, into the hands of that eminent tribunal." It was the people, Lincoln insisted, who were the "rightful masters"—of president, court, and Constitution.

After Lincoln concluded with a plea for reconciliation between North and South, the aged chief justice of that eminent tribunal came forward to administer the oath of office. To an observer, Roger

B. Taney appeared "very much agitated, and his hand shook very perceptibly with emotion."

The Union was dissolving, with war imminent—in five weeks Confederate cannon would fire on Fort Sumter. The Republican party that had made resistance to *Dred Scott* its battle cry, determined to overturn "that bench-full of Southern lawyers," had won control of the popular branches in the 1860 elections. Lincoln himself had said three years earlier, "Somebody has to reverse that decision, since it is made, and we mean to reverse it, and we mean to do it peaceably." His inaugural remarks indicated the new president's intent to challenge the Supreme Court's supremacy. Meanwhile, the Democratic party, built into an electoral powerhouse by Taney's mentor Andrew Jackson, had been shattered by the chief justice's effort to rescue it. Northern, Southern, and border-state Democrats each nominated a presidential candidate in 1860, effectively handing the presidency to Lincoln. After the election, a rumor spread that Taney had resigned. It was not true, the chief justice wrote late in December 1860. "I am sensible that it would at this moment be highly injurious to the public." He had expected slave rebellions to flame across the South on news of Lincoln's victory. Instead it was the slaves' owners who rebelled.

IN THE DECADES since Andrew Jackson's dynamic administration, American presidents had been enfeebled by sectional conflict. Suddenly, with the country breaking apart, desperate need was met by a shock of action. President Lincoln delayed the reconvening of Congress to July 4 and proceeded to wage war as if the legislature—and judiciary—did not exist. On his own authority, he called out the militia and expanded the regular army by ten regiments; proclaimed a blockade of Southern ports and ordered the navy to buy and arm steamboats; and gave public funds and weapons to private antisecessionists.

Lincoln's energetic response to the Southern revolt was greeted enthusiastically in the North, but the Union government's situation was dire. Confederate troops were massing in Virginia, across the Potomac from Washington. Maryland's legislature teetered on the precipice of secession. Lincoln resisted advice to, as he put it, "arrest, or disperse" that body. But to prevent secessionist mobs from blocking the passage of reinforcements through Maryland to the capital, the president in late April quietly authorized the military to arrest disloyal civilians and, in order to forestall judicial interference, suspend the writ of habeas corpus.

One night a month later, Union troops arrested a wealthy Maryland secessionist, John Merryman, in his home. Alleged to have burned railroad bridges, among other treasonable acts, Merryman was imprisoned at Fort McHenry in Baltimore harbor. His attorney quickly submitted a habeas corpus petition to the judge presiding over the local federal circuit—who happened to be Roger Taney. The chief justice issued an order to Fort McHenry's commanding general to produce Merryman. The commander refused, citing the president's instructions, and rebuked Taney for seeking confrontation at such a time: "Errors, if any, should be on the side of the safety of the country." Taney issued a second writ, ordering the general to a hearing, and prepared a public spectacle for the next day. When the general failed to appear, Taney declared to a Baltimore courtroom packed with reporters that Lincoln had acted unconstitutionally in suspending habeas corpus. The chief justice said his marshal might well have ordered a posse to Fort McHenry to haul the commander into court, except that such action would have been repelled by the army. With only the Constitution in his arsenal, Taney would submit a formal opinion to Lincoln calling on him "to perform his constitutional duty, to enforce the laws."

Hastily produced and widely publicized, Taney's opinion in *Ex parte Merryman* ranged far from Lincoln's suspension of the writ to a dissertation on presidential power that was startlingly at odds with the broad and independent authority Taney had claimed for Andrew Jackson during the Bank war. Taney's doctrine in *Merryman* would leave Lincoln almost powerless to respond to the rebellion. Praised by pro-Southern newspapers as "a vindication of the principles of the republic" and damned by Unionists for giving "aid and comfort to public enemies," the opinion was met with silence by its presidential target. Lincoln continued to impose martial law selectively in areas under Union control. His response to Taney came only weeks later, in his July 4 address to Congress. Must a "government of the people, by the same people," Lincoln asked, be "too *weak* to maintain its own existence" against a discontented minority determined to break it up? Were "all the laws, *but one*"—habeas corpus—"to go unexecuted, and the government itself go to pieces, lest that one be violated?" In what Lincoln called a "People's contest," the president's duty to the people was to preserve the Union. It was a doctrine of necessity.

But Roger Tancy did not believe in that necessity because he did not believe the Union was worth saving. It was a voluntary compact of the states and, with irreconcilable differences acknowledged, the South should have been allowed to secede peacefully. The war was, in Taney's mind, unnecessary, and a constitutional disaster. But, aside from making futile gestures, what could he do about it? He led a court that many in the North regarded as a nest of traitors.

BY THE BEGINNING of the Civil War, that nest had been much depleted. Virginian Peter Daniel, the most aggressive of the pro-slavery justices, had died in May 1860. For almost a year, Buchanan had dithered, finally nominating a successor only a few weeks before his term ended. He chose his attorney general, who had advised him that the president had no constitutional power to resist secession. After the Senate swiftly rejected the nomination, the seat remained vacant. In early April 1861, Justice McLean died. That same month, John Campbell left the court. Appointed by Franklin Pierce in 1853, the Alabaman had opposed secession but, appalled by Lincoln's violent response and convinced that, as a Southern sympathizer, he would bring the court into discredit, he resigned, eventually to become a Confederate assistant secretary of war. No other Southerner followed him. John Catron, the slave owner from Tennessee, was a devoted Unionist who saw support for the rebellion as treason. James Wayne, the pro-slavery extremist from Georgia, nevertheless backed Lincoln's expansive war powers.

With three of nine chairs empty, Taney's Supreme Court was nearly a rump, barely a quorum. Lincoln did not make his first appointment until January 1862, over a year and a half after Daniel's death. The delay was excused by the effort to reorganize the federal circuits. Five of nine in the old system were based in the South, and Republicans were determined to shift that balance northward. But neither were they in a hurry to restore the Supreme Court to full manpower, with the author of *Dred Scott* and now *Merryman* still in control. The empty seats were a mark of Republican disdain.

Lincoln's reorganization plan in fact included a subtle way to reshape the court. Among his proposals was the suggestion that Supreme Court justices be relieved from circuit duty. That would loosen the bonds between geography and Supreme Court seats that for so long had guaranteed the South a majority on the court. Outlined in his first State of the Union message to Congress, Lincoln's proposals triggered a round of court-bashing that echoed 1857—except that, now, enraged Republicans had the legislative power.

Leading the radical charge was New Hampshire senator John P. Hale, with a shocking proposal to abolish Taney's Supreme Court altogether and create a new one. The Constitution provided for "one Supreme Court," but, Hale argued, that did not mean it had to be *this* one, which was nothing more than "part of the machinery of the old Democratic party," its justices mere politicians in robes. Now that Republicans were in power, they were entitled to a Supreme Court of their own. While that was a widespread sentiment among Republicans, Hale's path to a Republican court was dismissed as anarchic. Was every change in political control of Congress to bring a new Supreme Court? But neither did Republicans frontally attack what *Dred Scott* had so disastrously shown was the real source of the court's power: judicial review. Even Lincoln, while deriding the reverence for the court's rulings demanded by Taney's defenders, acknowledged that Supreme Court decisions, when "fully settled" and accepted by the people, might control "the general policy of the country."

Republicans did not want to destroy judicial power; they wanted that weapon in their own hands. A more moderate proposal than Hale's was to pack the court under cover of circuit reorganization, by expanding its membership from nine to as many as thirteen, which, with three pending vacancies, would give Lincoln seven appointments and an instant majority. But more patient Republicans pointed out that the remnant of the Taney Court had an average age of above seventy; the chief justice himself was in his eighties. Republican control would simply be the short work of time. Meanwhile, there were those three open seats.

Early in his presidency, Lincoln had been besieged by office seekers. Hundreds of would-be clerks, postmasters, and custom officers jammed the halls of the White House. As his secretary, John Hay, described it, the president had "literally to run the gantlet through the crowds" wanting a word with him. It was only a little less disorderly with aspirant Supreme Court justices. The long delay before Lincoln made his first appointment enabled rumors to gather steam,

ambitions to swell, and campaigns to be mounted. The reorganization of circuit courts was not completed until July 1862, but Lincoln
was obliged to act before that. With illness often keeping Taney and
Catron off the bench, the court frequently lacked the quorum of five
it needed legally to convene.

Ohio lawyer Noah Swayne was ready for the moment. He had
launched a campaign for McLean's seat shortly after the justice died
in April 1861, mobilizing Ohio's entire Republican establishment to
help Swayne beat off rivals. There was much to recommend him in
Lincoln's eyes. A native Virginian and Quaker, he had left the state
out of disgust with slavery and set up successfully as a corporate lawyer in Ohio. After playing a prominent role in several fugitive slave
cases, he embraced the Republican party on its founding and campaigned for Lincoln in 1860. He was a stalwart of the Republican
ascendancy—impeccably loyal to the party and its president, who
named him to McLean's seat in January 1862.

Lincoln's second appointment, which he made the day after he
signed the circuit reorganization bill, followed a similar pattern.
A country doctor who became an ardent emancipationist, Samuel
Miller had left his native state of Kentucky when it retained slavery in its 1849 constitution and moved to the free state of Iowa,
where he became an early Republican and practiced law. He had
less claim to being a "Lincoln man" than Swayne—Lincoln in fact
confused him with Daniel Miller, a former Iowa congressman, as
did the first news reports of his nomination—but Samuel Miller's
obscurity was more than offset by recommendations from everyone
who mattered in Iowa, as well as a raft of petitions from "Iowa state
citizens."

That left one open seat. The three leading contenders were all
true Lincoln men—all Illinoisans, all friends and associates of the
president for decades. But none had been closer or more important to
Lincoln than Judge David Davis of the Illinois Circuit Court. He had

managed Lincoln's nomination at the 1860 convention and then the winning presidential campaign. Other Lincoln friends were miffed that the president had passed over Davis with his first two nominations and wondered if the president was an ingrate. They pushed him even harder now. Yet Lincoln seemed unwilling to nominate Davis, perhaps because he was *too* close to him. Months passed after the Miller nomination, and it was only in October 1862 that Lincoln appointed Davis to the court.

THERE WAS NOT YET a Lincoln Court—it was still Roger Taney's—but even as Davis took his seat, a case was reaching the Supreme Court that would prove the difference that even a partial packing could make. The "Prize Cases" were an amalgam of a dozen suits brought by shipowners who claimed that the Union's seizure of their property under Lincoln's blockade proclamations of April 1861 was unconstitutional. By early 1862, the cases had worked their way through the federal courts to the Supreme Court, and the shipowners, anticipating that the court's three open seats would soon be filled with Lincoln supporters, pressed for an early hearing. For the same reason, the administration sought, and won, a delay.

Taney's attitude toward Lincoln was only too well known. Of the five other sitting justices, four had backed Taney in *Dred Scott*. Two were Northern Democrats—Robert Grier, who, though a loyal Unionist, had criticized Lincoln's war policies, and Samuel Nelson, who had agreed with Taney that the Union was beyond saving and that the war was "without any useful purpose." The fifth justice, Nathan Clifford, had not been on the court when *Dred Scott* was decided. A New Hampshire native, he had made his legal career in Maine, where he also became a leading figure in the state's Democratic party. Buchanan appointed him in 1858 to replace Benjamin Curtis, who resigned from the court after his great dissent in the case led to a bitter clash with Taney. But Clifford was no Curtis—he was pleased to say that Taney's *Dred Scott* opinion "fully expressed" his own pro-Southern views. To win the "Prize Cases," the administration, if it could count on the Lincoln three, would need to peel away at least two of the Taney six.

The stakes could scarcely have been higher. Had Lincoln acted constitutionally when he ordered a blockade of Southern ports before Congress declared war on the Confederacy? The shipowners argued that only Congress could declare a state of war and authorize the president to act. Of Lincoln's doctrine of "necessity" that justified his emergency action, their lawyer said, "The Constitution knows no such word."

After twelve days of argument, the justices retired for deliberations, as tension mounted throughout the country. Would Taney deliver a great victory to the South—greater perhaps than any it had won on the battlefield—by exposing Lincoln as a usurper and throwing into question the legitimacy of the war? Three weeks later, the justices returned to the bench to deliver the court's opinion—all except Taney, who was said to be indisposed. That itself was a strong signal; surely the chief justice would not have denied himself the satisfaction of reading out an anti-administration decision. And in fact, the court went against Taney, but by the narrowest margin, 5–4, with Grier and James Wayne joining the Lincoln three.

The opinion was read by Grier, who in vigorous terms dismissed the shipowners' claims. "A civil war is never solemnly declared," he said. When the South commenced its rebellion, "the president was bound to meet it in the shape it presented itself, without waiting for Congress to baptize it with a name." It was a matter of fact, not of law. "To affect a technical ignorance" of "the greatest civil war known in the history of the human race" would "cripple the arm of the Government and paralyze its power by subtle definitions and ingenious sophisms." The president had acted within the Constitution by treating the rebels as belligerents, "and this Court must be governed by the decisions and acts of the political department"—a deference to politics that the court, Grier included, had failed to show to the Missouri Compromise.

To demonstrate how far astray the court might have gone had Taney been able to swing a single vote, Nelson's dissenting opinion held that Lincoln had acted unconstitutionally by waging war on the South before Congress declared it. The existence of a state of war was a matter of law, not of fact, and Lincoln's war was illegal, a "personal" war against the South. It was a startling construction—that a president of the United States might mobilize all its resources to wage a "personal" war on half of the nation.

The *Prize Cases* decision was dramatic evidence that a new majority on the court was unwilling to challenge the political branches in the midst of the war. To finance the military, Congress in February 1862 passed the Legal Tender Act, which for the first time allowed the Treasury to print paper money—"greenbacks," or as Taney called them, the "paper trash of the government"—backed not by specie, but by the government's good faith. When a case challenging the measure's constitutionality reached the Supreme Court, fears spread that a decision that struck down the act would destroy the North's ability to pay for the war. But in June 1863, the court, with the chief justice again indisposed and not taking part, sidestepped the issue. It denied jurisdiction, allowing a lower court's ruling in the law's favor to stand.

WAGING A FEROCIOUS civil war for the survival of the Union, the Lincoln administration feared the subversive influence of Southern sympathizers and spies in the North and on battle fronts. It responded with limitations of civil rights and liberties, most controversially the president's suspension of habeas corpus. Disregarding *Merryman*, the administration broadened its use of martial law throughout the

war, extending it in September 1862 to "all persons discouraging vol-
unteer enlistments, resisting militia drafts, or guilty of any disloyal
practice, affording aid and comfort to Rebels." Military commissions
were set up to try detainees, even where civil courts were functioning. In the course of the war, the military arrested some eighteen
thousand civilians, though most were quickly released on a promise
not to resume "disloyal" activities.

For two years, the writ of habeas corpus was suspended solely on
Lincoln's authority, a use of presidential power that disturbed not only
Taney and other anti-administration Democrats, but many Republicans as well. Even an old Whig, retired Justice Curtis, Taney's scourge
in *Dred Scott* and a warm supporter of the Union cause, saw Lincoln's
September 1862 extension of martial law as a watershed. By Lincoln's
doctrine of necessity, Curtis warned, the president might "disregard each and every provision of the Constitution, and . . . exercise
all power, *needful, in his opinion*, to enable him 'best to subdue the
enemy.'" The answer, Curtis believed, was to restore the balance of
powers among the three federal branches, beginning with congressional action on Lincoln's suspension of the writ.

But for two years Congress failed to act. When it had reconvened in July 1861, Congress confirmed most of Lincoln's unilateral
war measures but not his suspension of habeas corpus. For eighteen
months, Congress debated the issue repeatedly but could not decide
what to do. Some opposed the suspension but were unwilling to
rebuke the administration in time of war. Others backed it, but were
stuck on a constitutional question: did the president derive his power
to suspend the writ directly from the Constitution or must Congress
delegate it to him? Lincoln's September 1862 proclamation spurred
action, but not without more months of bitter debate. Finally, in
March 1863, Congress passed a bill stating that the president "is
authorized to suspend" habeas corpus. Uncertain to the last, the legislators left unclear whether that authorization came from Congress
or the Constitution.

Such a fine-grained constitutional issue seemed ready-made for the Supreme Court to decide, but in fact the wartime court never ruled on the writ's suspension, while lower courts almost invariably deferred to executive power. Even Justice Clifford, sitting in circuit in Boston, declined to challenge Lincoln. Much as Taney had earlier, Clifford issued a writ for a Southern sympathizer held by the military. But when the writ was rejected, Clifford released no indignant blast. He simply dropped the matter, saying the courts had no power to enforce the writ.

But neither was the administration eager for a test in the courts, especially not in Roger Taney's. In December 1862, the Wisconsin Supreme Court had ruled unanimously that the president lacked the power to suspend habeas corpus. To avoid a confrontation with the military, though, the court had issued no enforcement order and invited the federal Supreme Court to make the final decision. It was up to the administration to appeal the adverse finding, which Edwin Stanton, Lincoln's secretary of war, was ready to do, until Attorney General Edward Bates intervened. Bates had little doubt that, even with three Lincoln appointees, the court's majority was of Taney's "political school" and would deal the administration a devastating defeat. Bates managed to delay the appeal for months until Congress passed its Habeas Corpus Act. The Wisconsin court, deferring to Congress, withdrew its ruling.

The mutual prudence and wariness of the Supreme Court and the Lincoln administration was evident in the case of Clement Vallandigham. The former Ohio congressman had become one of the most vivid and vituperative Northern foes of the war, damning it as "wicked, cruel, and unnecessary" and urging Northerners to knock "King Lincoln" from his throne. For his "disloyal sentiments and opinions," Vallandigham was arrested in May 1863—like Merryman, in his home in the middle of the night by a squadron of soldiers— and tried and convicted by a military commission, then sentenced to "close confinement in some fortress" for the war's duration. Vallandigham immediately filed a petition in federal court for habeas corpus, disputing the military commission's constitutionality. The judge dismissed the plea, writing that "when the national life is in peril," it would be "an unwarrantable exercise of the judicial power" to question the acts of the president. This was no time, he said, to "embarrass" Lincoln.

It was already too late for that. Even Republican politicians and newspapers attacked the government's suppression of free speech. Lincoln, who had had nothing to do with Vallandigham's arrest, sought to rid himself of the problem by commuting Vallandigham's sentence to banishment behind enemy lines.

But the "wily agitator," as Lincoln called him, was determined to get his case before the Supreme Court, where, he figured, the mixed bench of Taneyites and Lincoln men would become embroiled in conflict over his arrest and the president's war powers. While Vallandigham made his base in Ontario, his lawyer appeared before the justices in January 1864 to argue that, since the military commission acted as a court, the Supreme Court could and should review its proceedings, particularly whether it had jurisdiction over civilians like Vallandigham, and if so, whether Vallandigham had been properly charged. The government simply contended that the commission was not a court; it was a military body created on the president's authority to deal with military issues. That put it beyond the reach of judicial review.

In a unanimous opinion, the court closed all doors to Vallandigham. It declined to look into the charges against him or the military commission's jurisdiction. But neither was the decision a vindication of the military's treatment of Vallandigham. To have attempted either would probably have split the court, as Vallandigham had intended. Instead, the opinion was narrowly confined to the Supreme Court's jurisdiction over military commissions, deciding that nothing empowered the court "to review or pronounce any opinion upon the proceedings of a military commission." The Supreme Court had spoken as one—but in silence over the arrests of civilians, the denials of habeas corpus, the military trials, and the powers of the president in whose name these things occurred.

That unanimity—and silence—very possibly would not have been achieved had Taney participated in the decision, but once again he was indisposed, ill at home, one of the many forced absences from his seat at the head of the Supreme Court. Shunned by the capital's new Republican and Unionist political establishment, trapped in what he described as the "foul and corrupt atmosphere of Washington," the chief justice spent many long hours brooding, frustrated by his powerlessness to check Lincoln, making notes for cases that had not yet come before the court and for some that never would. Legal tender?—unconstitutional. Conscription?—unconstitutional. Taxes on judicial salaries?—unconstitutional. Had it come before the Supreme Court, would Taney have found the Emancipation Proclamation—which Lincoln offered not as an act of liberation but as a "necessary war measure"—unconstitutional? The administration feared that the chief justice and his brethren would. Abolitionists were certain of it: "the hot-new purpose of today" would be "filtered through the secession heart" of Roger B. Taney, Wendell Phillips thundered, and "tested and measured by the fossil prejudice and iron precedents of a century back." But, Phillips warned, "Don't try to bind earthquakes with parchment bands!"

To this, Taney might have replied, as he wrote in 1863, that civil war could not "absolve the judicial department from the duty of maintaining with an even and firm hand the rights and powers of the Federal Government, and of the States, and of the citizens, as they are written in the Constitution which every judge is sworn to support." Taney still longed to do his duty, to restore the court to its place at the center of action as the supreme arbiter of rights and powers, to do battle in defense of the Constitution, but now the fighting was on different fronts, on other terms, a long way from Taney's roots in Jacksonian America. He was not the first justice, nor would he be the last, to outlive the political era that raised him to the Supreme Court. But now it was Lincoln's time.

CHAPTER FIVE

Deconstruction: Republican Reversal

DURING THE three decades after the Civil War, Americans endured some of the most wrenching economic and social changes in the nation's history. Confederate soldiers returned to a transformed world of devastated farms, where newly freed blacks struggled to find their own footing. Northerners shifted from war privation to a growing industrial economy of boom and bust. In those three decades, the nation's population would double, from around 35 million to 70 million. Huge numbers of immigrants would encounter the delights and disillusionments of a strange culture. Railroads would spearhead changes in old cities and new frontiers.

Who would preside over the daunting problems posed by the nation's reconstruction after the Civil War and its social and economic transformation? As it turned out, some of the most inadequate or unfit presidents in the nation's history: Andrew Johnson, who succeeded Lincoln after his assassination in April 1865 and was immobilized by a hostile Congress; Ulysses S. Grant, a war hero baffled by postwar problems; then a series of Republican single-termers, Rutherford B. Hayes, James A. Garfield, succeeded after his assassination by Chester A. Arthur, and Benjamin Harrison, who was bracketed by the separate single terms of Democrat Grover Cleveland.

And what sort of men, appointed to the Supreme Court by these presidents, would deal directly with the aftermath of the Civil War and the endless conflict arising from an ever-changing polity and economy? Decades of Republican dominance meant that most of the justices would come out of the party of Lincoln, the party empowered by his vision of an indissoluble Union dedicated to the Founding principles of equal and inalienable rights to life, liberty, and the pursuit of happiness. "This terrible war," Lincoln had declared in his second Inaugural Address, was a judgment on American slavery, necessary to remove "the offence." The war's dual purposes—Union and liberation—had become intertwined. And, as Lincoln told a Union general in July 1863, seven months after he issued the Emancipation Proclamation, there could be no turning back. "Those who shall have tasted actual freedom I believe can never be slaves, or quasi slaves again."

But the justices of the Supreme Court—the Lincoln men and those appointed by his successors—would betray the "new birth of freedom" for all Americans that Lincoln had promised at Gettysburg. In the postwar decades, liberty would be broadened for some—mainly entrepreneurs and speculators, those who possessed or scrambled after riches. Even corporations would come to be endowed with the full dignity of citizenship. But for many millions of others—the poor and working classes and, above all, the freed slaves—the space of freedom would shrink as the nation's wealth and power burgeoned. The Union would be reknit, but with the sacrifice of black equality and liberty in the betrayals of Reconstruction.

. . .

THE TRAGEDIES of postwar America began with triumphs. The proposed Thirteenth Amendment, abolishing slavery, passed the House of Representatives in January 1865 after Republicans picked up just enough seats in the 1864 elections for the needed two-thirds majority. The climactic House vote set off wild cheering, with some members in tears of joy. After the Confederacy's surrender a few months later, Reconstruction appeared to be on the way. When a wave of terrorism against blacks—lynchings, pillages, and massacres—swept through the South, outraged Republicans passed the Civil Rights Act of 1866, granting full citizenship to all native-born Americans and guaranteeing them "full and equal benefit" of the laws and "security of person and property." The act empowered the federal government to enforce these guarantees.

President Johnson, already suspect in Republican eyes for Reconstruction policies too weak to protect beleaguered freedmen, vetoed the measure, only to be overridden by Congress. The struggle persuaded Republican leaders that guarantees of citizenship and equal rights must be written into the Constitution. They passed a Fourteenth Amendment that, after recognizing the national citizenship of "all persons born or naturalized in the United States," went on: "No State shall make or enforce any law which shall abridge the privileges or immunities of citizens of the United States; nor shall any State deprive any person of life, liberty, or property, without due process of law; nor deny to any person within its jurisdiction the equal protection of the laws." These unadorned promises of "due process" and "equal protection" would become more enduring sources of conflict over their meaning than any other clauses of the Constitution. The amendment's last section empowered Congress "to enforce, by appropriate legislation, the provisions of this article."

But the Fourteenth Amendment faced a daunting prospect.

It would have to be ratified by two thirds of the states, including those of the South. After every state but one of the old Confederacy rejected the amendment, Congress passed the Reconstruction Act of 1867, which imposed military rule in place of the state governments that Andrew Johnson had created. Congress ordered Southern states to organize new governments with full black participation and, as a condition for representation in Congress, to ratify the Fourteenth Amendment. That was how this reversal of Taney's *Dred Scott* disaster was thrust into the Constitution.

It was followed two years later by the climactic Fifteenth Amendment, which wasted no words: "The right of citizens of the United States to vote shall not be denied by the United States or by any State on account of race, color, or previous condition of servitude." Under the 1867 Reconstruction Act, black voting rights in the South were protected by federal troops, who organized elections and presided over the drafting of state constitutions. Turnout by black voters topped 70 percent in some areas. Blacks sat in state constitutional conventions and won seats in Congress. All this aroused unreconstructed Southerners to intense fear and fury, and the Ku Klux Klan and other vigilante groups mobilized across the South. In an atmosphere of anger and mistrust, congressional Republicans responded with a series of harsh laws to enforce the Reconstruction Amendments—especially the 1871 Ku Klux Klan Act providing that persons conspiring to "injure, oppress, threaten, or intimidate any citizen" or threaten the exercise of his constitutional rights could be prosecuted in federal court.

Nationally Democrats and Republicans were returning to the traditional two-party contests and compromises of American politics, and as they did the radical thrust of Reconstruction was inevitably blunted. The Republicans were split between radicals and moderates, though united against Andrew Johnson, impeaching him for what they saw as his alliance with white Southerners to restore the prewar political order and reduce freedmen to peons. Johnson escaped conviction in the Senate by one vote. Luckily for the Republicans, they had in hand a new hero to unite them—Ulysses S. Grant, who had led the Union armies to victory. At the 1868 convention in Chicago, General Grant carried the party's nomination on the first ballot. For their part, Democrats were reuniting the wings of their party. Northerners secured the nomination of Horatio Seymour, former governor of New York, but he ran on a Southern platform of opposition to Reconstruction. In November 1868, Grant won twenty-six of thirty-four states and 214 of 294 electoral votes, but his winning margin in the popular vote of merely 300,000 out of 5.7 million ballots cast suggested that the two parties were establishing a competitive balance, while the widespread intimidation of black voters in the South signaled a dimming hope for full freedom and equality for black citizens.

THOUGH CLOSELY IDENTIFIED with Abraham Lincoln and Republican Reconstruction, Grant had run on a platform of peace and reconciliation, and when it came time to replace the remnants of the Taney Supreme Court with Republican loyalists, the views of his nominees on the new constitutional amendments had little weight with him. It was not that the president ignored the duty and pleasure of court nominations—in fact, he spent countless hours discussing possibilities with Republican politicos. His first nomination, of his own attorney general, Ebenezer R. Hoar, seemed respectable, but Republican radicals deemed Hoar too moderate for having opposed Johnson's impeachment, and he was voted down in the Senate. The radicals pressured Grant to name Lincoln's secretary of war, Edwin Stanton, who was confirmed by a lopsided Senate vote just before Christmas 1869—and died four days later. By then Justice Grier, in poor physical and mental health, had finally been persuaded by his colleagues to retire, and Grant had two seats to fill. His choice, a pair of railroad lawyers, William Strong and Joseph P. Bradley, was expedient. He knew that they would take the right position on the issue of legal tender that was roiling the country—and so they did—but he evidently didn't inquire into their views on race and Reconstruction. Of Grant's first three appointees, only Ward Hunt, another railroad lawyer, would provide an occasional dissenting voice on behalf of black rights.

Grant would have one more opportunity when Salmon P. Chase, the chief justice who had been named by Lincoln as Taney's successor in 1864, died in May 1873, two months after Grant began his second term. The president could now offer the most glittering prize in American politics. Alas, the opportunity turned into a nightmare for the former general. He first offered the post to Republican New York senator Roscoe Conkling, telling his old friend that the appointment would be "entirely fitting." In fact, it was entirely unfitting to liberals and reformers who looked on Conkling as a party boss and master spoilsman. The senator wisely declined the prize. Grant offered the job to his secretary of state, Hamilton Fish, who preferred his current eminence. The president then considered another close friend, Caleb Cushing, a distinguished Masssachusetts attorney, but Cushing, at seventy-three, seemed too old for a job that Marshall had taken in his midforties and Taney in his midfifties. Moreover, Cushing had been a prominent pro-Southern Democrat before a late conversion to the Republican party. Grant turned next to his attorney general since late 1871, George Williams, a man widely regarded as incompetent, an embarrassment to the bar. His nomination, in December 1873, was shot down when the press revealed his misuse of Justice Department funds, including the hiring by Mrs. Williams, at government expense, of a coach and footmen. In desperation, Grant turned back to Cushing, but when a letter surfaced from Cushing to the traitorous Jefferson Davis recommending an old friend for a job with the Confederacy, the nomination was hastily withdrawn. After Conkling rejected another overture, Grant finally, in January 1874, almost nine months after Chase's death, found his man, Morrison R. Waite.

And who was Morrison Waite? At least, wrote diarist Gideon Welles, we should be thankful that Grant hadn't chosen an old acquaintance of his, perhaps a stage driver or bartender. A more measured commentator estimated that Waite stood in the front ranks of the army of second-class lawyers in the country. Waite himself confessed that his new eminence filled him with "fear and trembling." Newspapers checked their archives—Connecticut-born, schooled at Yale, moved to Ohio, and practiced law in Toledo. Railroad law, naturally, though on a small-town scale. He had been a Whig until helping to organize the state's Republican party in 1856. He was always a strong party man.

But the kind of party man he was—a Lincoln Republican who would take judicial leadership for African-American liberation, or a Grant Republican, intent mainly on protecting railroad and other corporate interests—remained to be seen.

AT THE HEART of both the civil rights and economic issues that would face the Supreme Court in the postwar decades lay the historic conflict over national versus state power. Taney had helped bring on the Civil War with his rabid support of state—that is, Southern— control of slavery. Republican voters and Lincoln's army had established national authority to protect freedmen's rights, especially through the Reconstruction Amendments. But the interpretation of these amendments—the extent of the rights and liberties they guaranteed and the reach of federal power to enforce them—became the province of the Supreme Court.

Under Chief Justice Chase, a leading antebellum abolitionist, the court had, despite Republican fears, shown a strategic deference to congressional Reconstruction in the late 1860s, allowing the legislature wide latitude in its campaign to remake the South and secure black rights. But as the nation began a retreat from Reconstruction in the 1870s, the Supreme Court fell into step.

The pacesetter was an 1873 case that had nothing directly to do with black rights. A group of New Orleans butchers—all white men—had brought suit against a state-chartered monopoly of slaughterhouses. Louisiana had decided to centralize the city's chaotic system of private stockyards in a "grand slaughterhouse" to better regulate an unsanitary trade. Butchers objected that under the law they were forced to submit to the monopoly, paying the fees its investors demanded, or go out of business. Their appeal rested on the Fourteenth Amendment. Louisiana, they said, had infringed their "privileges and immunities" as United States citizens, and by favoring the monopoly, the state had deprived them of "property" in their livelihoods without "due process" and denied them "equal protection of the laws."

In its first great test, the sweeping promise of the Fourteenth Amendment for liberty and equality was reduced to little more than empty words. Justice Samuel Miller, the Lincoln man who wrote for the court's majority in the *Slaughterhouse Cases*, acknowledged that the Civil War had "given great force to the argument" for a more powerful national government that would protect the rights of all Americans—and then he pushed that argument aside. The Supreme Court, he wrote, must maintain "the balance between State and Federal power." Rejecting the Fourteenth Amendment's clear intent to nationalize citizenship, Miller reinstated the two classes of citizenship—state and national—that had become a key element in Taney's denial to Dred Scott of any "rights which the white man was bound to respect." The rights Miller attached to national citizenship were meager—the right of access to Washington, D.C., and to coastal ports and navigable rivers, as well as the rights to habeas corpus and to petition and assembly. Congress could impose no other constitutional "privileges and immunities" on the states; it could not bring within its power "the entire domain of civil rights heretofore belonging exclusively to the States." Those rights were not "embraced" by the Fourteenth Amendment. They must, Miller wrote, "rest for their security and protection where they have heretofore rested"—on the states.

For white New Orleans butchers, this meant that their status as United States citizens did not protect them from Louisiana's regulation of their trade. But what did it mean for Reconstruction, which was all about congressional interference in the states, not least the garrisoning of several thousand troops in the South to enforce its policies? Even more, what did it mean for the freed slaves of the South? Though Miller, who supported those Reconstruction policies, noted that the Fourteenth Amendment had been framed for "the protection of the newly-made freeman and citizen from the oppressions of those who had formerly exercised their unlimited dominion over him," his deconstruction of the amendment would seem to leave the rights of freed slaves to the mercies precisely of those who had formerly dominated them.

One day before the court issued its *Slaughterhouse* ruling, on an Easter Sunday in April 1873, came the makings of the case that would directly test the Supreme Court's interpretation of the constitutional status of black rights. On that Easter Sunday, the black community in a Louisiana county seat suffered what historian Eric Foner called "the bloodiest single act of carnage in all of Reconstruction," the Colfax massacre. In a bitter election dispute between black Republicans and white Democrats, blacks had been deputized to safeguard the courthouse in Colfax against a rumored white takeover. A mob of local whites used a cannon to blast open the courthouse and set it ablaze. Scores of fleeing blacks were mowed down.

Amid outrage across the nation—and predictable inaction by state and local authorities—ninety-six white men were indicted in federal court for violating the Ku Klux Klan Act, charged with conspiring to deny black men their constitutional rights. Of the ninety-six, only nine stood trial and only three were convicted. One of the three was William Cruikshank, and it was his name that would be attached to the epochal case presented to the Waite Court three years after the massacre.

The chief justice wrote for a unanimous court. As he searched the Klan Act and the indictments for legal defects, Waite's opinion turned into a case study of ignoring all the human aspects of the matter, seizing on dubious precedents, and, most significantly, denying the African-American victims the federal guarantees that the Reconstruction Amendments were supposed to have secured them.

After reaffirming the differential citizenship, state and national, the court had resurrected in *Slaughterhouse*, Waite went on, as historian Peter Irons wrote, to slam "every legal door in the face of federal officials who tried—and ultimately failed—to protect southern blacks against intimidation and violence." Conspiracy to murder, the chief justice held, could be no federal crime. It was "the very highest duty of the States," Waite wrote, to protect their citizens, neglecting the fact that Congress had passed the enforcement acts because states had been notoriously unwilling to prosecute whites for crimes against blacks, as the aftermath of the Colfax massacre itself had proved. But "sovereignty, for this purpose," Waite insisted, "rests alone with the States."

Then the chief justice discovered another way that the Fourteenth Amendment could not be applied. The amendment barred "any State" from depriving any person of life, liberty, or property, and inasmuch as Cruikshank et al. *were not states*, the federal government was powerless to enforce those rights. Finally, since the violence had occurred during an election dispute, prosecutors had brought charges under the Fifteenth Amendment, accusing the defendants of hindering the victims' exercise of their right to vote. But Waite pointed out that the amendment condemned only racial discrimination, and the chief justice could only *"suspect* that race was the cause of the hostility. . . ."

With rulings like *Cruikshank*, with Democrats surging at the polls, and their own party eagerly embracing the new hustling spirit of industrialism, radical Republicans were fighting a rearguard battle. Old abolitionists like William Lloyd Garrison and Wendell Phillips were "not exactly extinct from American politics," the *New York Times* wrote in 1876, "but they represent ideas in regard to the South which the majority of the Republican Party have outgrown." In a final thrust, before they gave up control of the House to Democrats in 1875, Republicans passed a civil rights act that reached for social equality. The measure barred racial discrimination from "inns, public conveyances on land or water, theaters, and other places of public amusement." During the debate over the bill, a black congressman from Mississippi, John Lynch, described how, traveling through the South to Washington, "I am treated, not as an American citizen, but as a brute." But the radicals were too weak to push through a ban on school segregation. Nor did the act provide for federal enforcement. Instead, individuals would have to sue for their rights in federal court.

Still, five determined souls fought through the judicial system to bring their cases of discrimination to the Supreme Court in 1883. That august tribunal—with one dissenter—responded with a brusque dismissal of their claims and a patronizing lecture. In the *Civil Rights Cases*, the court spoke in the voice of Joseph Bradley, who had confided to his journal his view that "depriving white people of the right of choosing their own company would be to introduce another kind of slavery." To save whites from that fate, Bradley confirmed the *Cruikshank* finding that only actions by states were forbidden by the

Fourteenth Amendment, not the acts of innkeepers, theater owners, or coach drivers. Nor was the Thirteenth Amendment relevant.
That pertained "not to distinctions of race, or class, or color, but to
slavery," and "it would be running the slavery argument into the
ground," he wrote, a note of exasperation in the words, "to make it
apply to every act of discrimination." Having cut the constitutional
ground out from under it, Bradley ruled that the 1875 Civil Rights
Act "must necessarily be declared void."

But before concluding, Bradley turned to address black citizens,
to tell them bluntly that it was about time for them to get over slavery.
"When a man has emerged from slavery," he opined, "and by the aid
of beneficent legislation has shaken off the inseparable concomitants
of that state, there must be some stage in the progress of his elevation
when he takes the rank of a mere citizen, and ceases to be a special
favorite of the laws, and when his rights as a citizen, or a man, are
to be protected in the ordinary modes by which other men's rights
are protected." Speaking for a court that, packed though it was with
Republicans, had repeatedly ignored the clear intent of Congress,
nullifying or distorting its "beneficent legislation," Bradley could
not have made it plainer that any hope black Americans might still
have harbored that the Supreme Court would put its awesome power
behind the principles and policies of Reconstruction was vain.

A FEW YEARS EARLIER, Justice Bradley had in fact played a central role in the political burial of Reconstruction. The 1876 election
had ended in a bitter stalemate. Neither the Democratic candidate,
New York governor Samuel Tilden, nor the Republican, Ohio governor Rutherford Hayes, had the 185 electoral votes needed to win,
as the outcome in three Southern states, where there had been widespread intimidation of black voters, was in dispute. Amid feverish
controversy, Congress invented an "electoral commission" to award

the disputed electors. It was made up of ten congressmen, divided equally between the parties, and five Supreme Court justices. The propriety of members of the Supreme Court involving themselves in a political—and furiously partisan—conflict was apparently not discussed.

The justices lent a noble air to an extraordinarily tawdry business rife with horse-trading and double-dealing, even as they were expected to vote along party lines. Congress named four of the justices—two Democrats, two Republicans—and those four were to choose the fifth. That swing voter was Justice David Davis, Lincoln's old Republican ally and campaign manager who had become an "independent" in politics, though he was thought to favor Democrat Tilden. But even before the commission could convene, the Democratic legislature in Illinois elected Davis to the Senate. Republicans charged that this was the payoff for his support of Tilden, but if so, it came prematurely. Davis resigned from the commission and Justice Bradley, Republican loyalist, took his place. Bradley cast the decisive vote for Hayes.

But the controversy didn't end there. Tilden supporters threatened to block a final count of electoral votes. After intense negotiations, a deal was struck, less than a week before the new president, still undetermined, was to be inaugurated. In return for the presidency, Hayes would withdraw all remaining federal troops from the South and stop enforcing the civil rights laws. "The negro," *The Nation* prophesied, "will disappear from the field of national politics. Henceforth, the nation, as a nation, will have nothing more to do with him." Reconstruction was over.

CHAPTER SIX

A Court for the Gilded Age

As African Americans were erased from national politics in the tragedy of Reconstruction, entrepreneurs and corporations took their place as the recipients of "beneficent legislation" from the political branches of the federal government. They received even more beneficent decisions from the United States Supreme Court. The long era of Republican domination of the presidency after the Civil War coincided with an unprecedented economic expansion that was closely abetted by Republican appointments to the Supreme Court. Indeed, this collaboration among capitalists, politicians, and justices was a defining feature of the Gilded Age, as captured by an episode that took place during the Grant administration.

In 1862, Congress had passed the Legal Tender Act, authorizing the government to print paper currency called greenbacks. This cheap money was especially loathed by bankers, who favored a stable currency backed with gold. But a depreciating currency was much favored by anyone with debts to pay, including a government that needed to finance total war.

The wartime court had managed to duck the question of the act's constitutionality, but in February 1870, in *Hepburn* v. *Griswold*, the Supreme Court struck down the Legal Tender Act by a 5–3 vote. Because the Constitution empowered Congress to provide for a national currency without limiting it to money backed with gold, the court's ruling against greenbacks applied only to debts incurred *before* the act's passage. Those who had borrowed hard money could not discharge their debts with paper. Retroactive operation of the law, the court held, would impair the contractual obligations of borrowers— though the words of the Constitution forbade only the states, not the federal government, from doing that—while it deprived creditors of property, under a novel reading of the Fifth Amendment. Astonishingly, Chief Justice Chase, who as Lincoln's treasury secretary had promoted the act as a wartime necessity, himself authored the tortured opinion that declared it unconstitutional.

That opinion struck one young legal scholar and editor, Oliver Wendell Holmes, Jr., as presenting "the curious spectacle of the Supreme Court reversing the determination of Congress on a point of political economy." If the ruling stood, all prewar debt would have to be paid off in gold. Borrowers, and especially railroad entrepreneurs who had taken on massive debt to finance expansion, faced disaster.

President Grant still needed those greenbacks. Luckily for him, there happened to be two openings on the Supreme Court. To block the hated Andrew Johnson from appointing a successor to Justice Catron after his death in 1865, congressional Republicans had reduced the court's membership to seven. No sooner was Grant in office than Congress restored the old complement of nine, giving the new president one free pick, for what had been Catron's seat. The other seat was Justice Grier's, who had decided to retire, though not before voting with Chase's majority in *Hepburn*. On the very day that decision was delivered, the president nominated William Strong and Joseph Bradley, the two railroad lawyers. They were speedily confirmed, and two days after Justice Bradley was seated in late March 1870, the government petitioned urgently for a rehearing of *Hepburn*'s constitutional issues. That almost unprecedented request was granted, though not without a furious battle in the court's conference room, according to Justice Miller, a *Hepburn* dissenter. As he reported to his brother-in-law, "The Chief Justice has resorted to all the stratagems of the lowest political trickster" to prevent the new cases from being heard. The "excitement" among the justices had been "fearful."

In its next term, on March 1, 1871, the Supreme Court overturned *Hepburn* by a 5–4 margin. The decisive votes to constitutionalize greenbacks in the *Legal Tender Cases* were cast by the two new justices, and Justice Strong spoke for the new majority. Never before had the court so quickly reversed itself so completely. A howl of indignation rose from Wall Street and other financial centers. There were charges that the new justices had promised support of paper money in exchange for their appointments. The New York *World* described the decision as "a base compliance with Executive instructions by creatures of the President placed upon the Bench to carry out his instructions." Democrats echoed the accusation in the 1872 campaign, portraying the justices as tools of Grant, who himself was the tool of corporate power. The president's defenders dismissed the notion. Surely the guileless, good-hearted, straight-shooting Grant would never have made such a foul bargain. The president himself had no public comment on the matter.

The question simmered for decades until it was revealed, in the diary of Secretary of State Hamilton Fish, that Grant a few years later had indeed admitted to Fish "that although he required no declaration from Judges Strong and Bradley on the constitutionality of the Legal Tender Act, he knew Judge Strong had on the bench in Pennsylvania given a decision sustaining its constitutionality, and he had reason to believe Judge Bradley's opinion tended in the same direction, that at the time he felt it important that the constitutionality of the law should be sustained, and while he would do nothing to exact anything like a pledge or expression of opinion from the parties he might appoint to the bench, he had desired that the constitutionality should be sustained by the Supreme Court."

So Grant, by his own admission, had packed the court with justices who would give him the decision he wanted in an immediate case, but he did not negotiate or extract a promise from them. None was needed. As the historian Charles Fairman wrote years later: the president regarded *Hepburn* as "profoundly wrong, and nominated judges whose opinions, according to the best information available, he approved. Would anyone in his place have done otherwise?"

LEGAL TENDER was an early and notorious example of the postwar Supreme Court's intervention in "political economy"—and of a president's use of his appointing power on behalf of powerful economic interests. This would prove to be not an exception in the Gilded Age but the rule. Indeed, observing the high bench in the decades after the war, Americans might have mused that corporation heads packed the court as much as presidents. Exerting their overpowering influence on the White House and Congress, an astonishing number of railroads and other industries put their people on the Supreme Court. All of Grant's appointees—including the *Legal Tender* duo and Chief Justice Waite—were railroad attorneys. Railroads were the most dynamic, visible, and controversial sector of the economy, and the railroad frenzy after the Civil War raised countless human and social as well as legal questions. In one year, 1889, twenty thousand railway workers were killed or injured. Simply in laying out new routes, the railroad corporations could bypass and isolate one city or town, create or enrich another. A torrent of disputes emerged from charges of unfair competition, profiteering, monopolistic control, tax issues—especially from the attempts of states to regulate the railways. But what part of the rail empire would the Supreme Court respond to—the executives and stockholders, or the railroad workers and passengers and the villages, towns, and cities that felt its impact?

Few personified the judicial politics of the time better than Stanley Matthews, an Ohio antislavery Democrat who had turned Republican on the advent of the Civil War. He was a railroad lawyer and stout defender of free enterprise. A fellow student of Rutherford B. Hayes at Kenyon College, Matthews was his friend's representative in the bargaining over Reconstruction that secured the presidency for Hayes. Matthews got his reward when Hayes, in the last days of his presidency early in 1881, chose him to fill retiring Justice Swayne's place on the court. The nomination blew up such a storm, especially from vengeful Tilden supporters and those who saw Matthews as a railroad mouthpiece, that the Senate Judiciary Committee refused to act as Hayes's term ended. But James Garfield, the new president, salvaged the nomination, as he had promised Hayes, and after a hard battle, Matthews was confirmed by a single vote. His eight years on the court were all anticlimax. Justice Matthews left no distinctive mark, but simply typified the postwar Republican devotion to laissez faire—and the ubiquity of railroad power.

THE POSTWAR Republican Congress had created the Fourteenth Amendment to guarantee the rights of newly liberated, still beleaguered and impoverished African Americans against state repression in the South, but within a few years, the amendment would instead become a potent weapon for the rich and powerful, and a brutal crushing of the rights and hopes of the black and the poor.

While the majority's decision in the 1873 *Slaughterhouse Cases* would severely restrict the national government's power to protect the civil rights and liberties of freed slaves and other citizens with its narrow construction of federal rights binding upon the states, it was the ideology of a dissenter, Justice Stephen J. Field, once it became accepted as the dogma of the Supreme Court, that would most threaten the ability of government to control the explosive forces of industrial capitalism.

Unlike the court's majority, Field saw no distinction between national and state citizenship. A citizen of a state was simply a citizen of the United States living in that state. But rather than vindicate its framers' vision of the Fourteenth Amendment as a broad federal guarantee of Americans' political and civil equality, Field interpreted it in his *Slaughterhouse* dissent as securing what he termed "the distinguishing privilege of citizens of the United States"—nearly boundless *economic* liberty. Invoking the Declaration of Independence and Adam Smith's *Wealth of Nations*, Field condemned Louisiana's licensing of the slaughterhouse monopoly as an invasion on the liberty of New Orleans butchers "to acquire property and pursue happiness"—"the fundamental idea upon which our institutions rest, and unless adhered to in the legislation of the country our government will be a republic only in name." This was Field's first great blow—and for the moment, a minority view—on behalf of private property and liberty of contract, one that eventually would severely restrict government in its power to regulate enterprise. Who was this justice so ideologically addicted to laissez faire?

Field was an oddment on the Supreme Court, the first justice nominated by a president of the opposing party, a Buchanan Democrat but loyal Unionist chosen by Lincoln in 1863 to represent a new circuit centered on the booming state of California. Years earlier, Field had journeyed the long way to the West Coast across the Panama Isthmus and by sail up to San Francisco. Unlike other

"Forty-niners," he planned to mine not gold but the men mining gold, and he became remarkably successful as a land speculator. Always preaching the values of liberty and individualism, he became chief justice of the state's highest court until Lincoln brought him to Washington. People wondered about the source of Field's fiery commitment to individual enterprise. Did it emerge from his family's stern religiosity, rooted in Puritanism, back in rural western Massachusetts, or from Mark Hopkins's libertarian teachings and moralizing admiration for men of property and wealth at Williams College, where Field graduated in 1837, or simply from the jousting ground of free enterprise in California? Whatever its source, Field's laissez-faire absolutism in his *Slaughterhouse* dissent would in the 1880s make all-encompassing property rights the supreme value of the Constitution, transforming the Fourteenth Amendment into a charter for capitalists, at the expense of millions of American workers and farmers.

Farmers faced growing burdens in the Gilded Age: rising production and falling prices, higher costs for land, seed, machinery and, above all, for credit. They paid local taxes to finance bonds issued to build rail lines and in return railroads charged them monopoly prices for grain transport and storage. Rebellious farmers began to mobilize, especially in the prairie and western states where in 1870 they launched the Grange movement to protect their common interests. In some towns Grangers allied with merchants against the railroads' price gouging. State governments began to respond to the pressure with a series of Granger laws to regulate rates. In 1873, the Illinois legislature approved a measure that fixed maximum rates for grain storage in Chicago, where produce carried in rail cars was stored in immense elevators. The owners of the storage company appealed to the Supreme Court, complaining that they had been deprived of their liberty to engage in business by an arbitrary state regulation and without due process of law.

In keeping with its narrow interpretation of the Fourteenth Amendment and its almost antebellum idea of states' rights, the Waite Court's majority had proved sympathetic to economic regulation by the states. In *Munn* v. *Illinois*, in 1876, the Supreme Court voted to uphold the Illinois statute as a "reasonable" regulation of a "virtual monopoly." The chief justice, a former railroad attorney, reached back two centuries to the great English jurist Lord Matthew Hale, and wrote simply that when "private property is devoted to a public use, it is subject to public regulation." Waite was not ready to accept the idea of "substantive" due process—the testing of a law's impact to judge whether it violated rights protected by the Fourteenth Amendment—for instance, as the railroads insisted, their property rights in the form of profits—in contrast to "procedural" due process, which tested laws on the much narrower ground of whether they had been enacted by proper procedures. The Illinois legislature had acted within its discretion and for the general welfare, the court found; whether those rates were fair was not a judical question. If the rail roads objected, the chief justice wrote, the remedy was at the polls, not in the courts.

In an impassioned dissent, Field charged that the "legislation in question is nothing less than a bold assertion of absolute power by the State to control at its discretion the property and business of the citizen, and fix the compensation he shall receive." For Field, the court had opened the ultimate chamber of horrors by holding that private property could be regulated by states. "If this be sound law," he thundered, "all property and all business in the State are held at the mercy of a majority of its legislature."

The issue was liberty—individual liberty. Field had his priorities— liberty of contract, free enterprise, protection from state interference, liberty for entrepreneurs and investors. To the Grangers and other populists, however, liberty—for farmers, consumers, railroad workers—might require protection *from* entrepreneurs and investors.

Munn struck a blow for them. But Field had taken a narrow line that would challenge both national and state reform efforts for years to come.

THE REPUBLICAN PARTY had its roots in the antebellum "free labor" movement, which not only campaigned against slave labor but championed equal opportunity and social mobility for all workers. Lincoln himself in 1859 had contended that "labor is prior to, and independent of capital." In fact, he said, "capital could never have existed without labor" and therefore "labor is the superior—greatly the superior—of capital." Several early Supreme Court verdicts suggested that, at least on economic issues, if not on those of civil rights, postwar Republicanism might take a moderately progressive and reformist course. The court's reversal on greenbacks was a blow to hard-money conservatives and a relief not only to entrepreneurs and speculators but to farmers and other small debtors. *Slaughterhouse*, while it distorted the Fourteenth Amendment, at least recognized government's power to regulate the economy in the public interest—in this case to protect public health by providing for the "grand slaughterhouse."

As for *Munn*, in a memorandum to guide Waite in drafting the opinion, Justice Bradley expressed, albeit in terms more forceful than Waite would use, the court majority's temper: "Unrestricted monopolies as to those things which the public must have and use, are a canker in any society, and have ever been the occasion of civil convulsions and revolutions. A people disposed for freedom will not tolerate this kind of oppression at the hands of private corporations or powerful citizens." Bradley knew exactly whereof he spoke—he had advised just such monopolies and powerful citizens as his clients in private practice. For all of his hostility to Reconstruction, Justice Bradley was a rare justice who sought to strike a balance between national power—objecting to the *Slaughterhouse* construction of dual citizenship with his view that "citizenship of the United States is the primary citizenship in this country," with state citizenship "secondary and derivative"—and the power of states to regulate railroads and other corporations.

Bradley did not always disappoint his former corporate clients but he stood out as the court's spate of liberalism faded. By the 1880s, it was giving way to a conservatism that grew more and more extreme in its hostility to the halting efforts by the popular branches of government to regulate the economy. That conservative ideology would dominate the court not only for a decade or two but well into the next century. Crucial in this long stalemate was the role of political parties. Not only did conservative Republicans win presidential election after election for almost half a century after the Civil War, but the two Democratic victories, by the conservative Grover Cleveland, did not offer voters a meaningful alternative approach to the fundamental economic and social problems plaguing millions of Americans.

This failure lay in political leadership embedded in ineluctable historical circumstances. Reconstruction had left the Democratic party more dependent than ever on the South, embittered by defeat and dominated by leaders almost as conservative or reactionary as in prewar days. Race, not economics, controlled Southern politics. Economic reform, especially if it had Northern origins, was seen as a threat to the racial order. No Democratic candidate—not even Cleveland with his political skills—could win a presidential election without the South, nor could he carry the South without deference to states' rights and the continued denial of civil rights to blacks. Inevitably, as the two major parties clung to the right—the Republicans on economic policy and the Democrats on the race issue—a huge gap opened on the left.

In the 1870s, as the Granger movement faltered, farm and labor leaders tried to fill the gap with a wide range of organizations. The Greenback party defended debt-ridden farmers against Wall Street demands for hard money and fought Supreme Court rulings that upheld vast grants of public lands to railroad, timber, and mining interests. The Farmers' Alliance campaigned for government control of the "oppressive and tyrannical transportation system" created by the railroads. "Taxpayers Associations" protested Supreme Court vetoes of laws that would have relieved cities and towns of railroad bond obligations obtained by fraud and corruption. After years with little to show for their efforts, reform leaders concluded that they must be more unified. They laid plans for a grand third-party effort, variously called the People's or Populist party. Its 1892 platform demanded "that the power of government—in other words, of the people—should be expanded . . . to the end that oppression, injustice and poverty, shall eventually cease in the land."

The Populists had an ambitious agenda of cheap currency, the abolition of national banks, government ownership of transport, a graduated income tax, and shorter workdays in industry, but they understood that the ultimate enemy of reform was "our Imperial Supreme Court," as it was called by Iowan James B. Weaver, a former congressman and the Greenback presidential candidate back in 1880. By usurping the "supreme power in the State," Weaver wrote in 1892, the court "dethrones the people who should be Sovereign and enthrones an oligarchy." The court, he insisted, must be held to its proper sphere and "brought back to a sense of its accountability to the people." But that would mean first overcoming the great Democratic-Republican duopoly of power.

With Weaver leading the charge at the top of the ticket, Populist hopes ran high in 1892. Running strongly in the West, the Populists became the first third party since the Civil War to win seats in the electoral college. But, overall, the outcome was devastating as the party took less than 10 percent of the national vote. Most disappointing were the results in the South, where Weaver's background as a Union officer and supporter of Reconstruction drew a furious attack. The Populists campaigned hard for African-American support but were foiled by Democratic leaders who saw to it that blacks were led to vote in gangs, by the cartload, "marched to the polls by beat of drum."

AS A RESULT of this one-sided political combat, the Supreme Court turned even further right in the 1880s and 1890s, while reformers—and one justice on the court—looked on helplessly.

By the mid-1880s, Samuel Miller was, with Stephen Field, the last of Lincoln's justices and the one who had remained truest to Republican ideals. Author of the *Slaughterhouse* opinion, he had scarcely imagined that it would become the defining construction of the Fourteenth Amendment, used to deny federal support to blacks. As he saw it, he had been addressing the case in front of him, involving a group of white butchers, not the amendment's intended beneficiaries. He had given state governments the power to regulate economic activity for the public good, which he considered "the best and most beneficial public act" of his life. And Miller remained an opponent of Field's campaign to use the Fourteenth Amendment to shield business from public controls.

This meant that his later years on the court were not happy ones. He was sorely disappointed by his brethren's increasing conservatism, by their obsessive protection of railroad bondholders, their casual use of free railroad passes. "It is vain," he would say, "to contend with judges who have been, at the bar, the advocates of railroad companies, and all the forms of associated capital, when they are called upon to decide cases where such interests are in contest." As politically minded as ever, Miller felt so unhappy about the decline of the party of Lincoln that he allowed supporters to push for his nomination for president on the Republican ticket in 1880 and 1884. He didn't have a chance. No wonder Miller's sympathetic biographer, Michael Ross, entitled his book *Justice of Shattered Dreams*.

Miller's final disappointment came in 1888, after the death of Morrison Waite, with the news that Melville Fuller had won the chief justiceship that Miller had long hoped for. President Cleveland did consider him but concluded that Miller was too old for the job— in fact, he would die two years later at the age of seventy-four. After rejecting others, Cleveland turned to Fuller, a fifty-five-year-old fellow Democrat from Illinois, a Harvard Law graduate, prominent railroad attorney—and, above all, unflinching conservative. Fuller believed that it was "the duty of the people to support the government and not of the government to support the people," and he could be trusted to rule properly on private property, free trade, government regulation, and other laissez-faire issues. Fuller too had been an active politico, maintaining his party contacts by attending four Democratic National Conventions.

More ideological than intellectual, Fuller was expected to be a skillful mediator who could unite a divided court. His fellow justices stretched from Miller and John Marshall Harlan on the left to Bradley in the center and Field on the right. Harlan had been an unusual Hayes pick, a liberal who was more idiosyncratic than ideological. Born into a slaveholding family in Kentucky, he too had been politically engaged, but rather erratically: before the Civil War, he was first a Whig, then a Know-Nothing, and then a founder of Kentucky's short-lived "Opposition Party." These shifts won him a reputation for opportunism, but what was he to do? His parties kept collapsing under him. In 1860, dismayed by the extremism of the major parties, he became a Constitutional Union activist, devoted to preserving the Union at all costs, including the perpetuation of slavery. Harlan stuck to what he saw as the middle ground throughout the war, opposing Lincoln's reelection in 1864 because he believed the president had "perverted" the Union cause by embracing emancipation. But the Unionist party's collapse and the South's violent response to Reconstruction made him an initially reluctant convert to the Republicans.

Later he helped rejuvenate the Kentucky Republican party and ran two failed campaigns for governor. He slowly came to adopt with fervor not only Lincoln's philosophy but even the conviction that the Fourteenth Amendment made the Bill of Rights enforceable on the states. This ensured that Harlan became a frequent and forceful dissenter from the court's conservative consensus on a wide range of issues involving civil rights, economic regulation, the rights of criminal defendants, and even a case of seamen kept in employment conditions that Harlan denounced as approaching slavery.

IN THE LATE 1880s, as Americans celebrated the framing and ratification of the Constitution a century earlier, the Supreme Court shouldered a series of cases arising out of the titanic economic forces transforming the nation—cases that would test the flexibility and adaptability of the great charter. The court was undergoing changes too, but only slowly, as justices resigned or died. Hayes's choice of Harlan turned out to be the only liberal appointment in the late 1870s and 1880s. His pick of William B. Woods, who served only six years on the bench, was notable for Woods's unusual background: an Ohio native who moved to Alabama after service in the Union army, a Republican who adopted extreme states' rights views and the Jim Crow "separate but equal" doctrine of racial segregation. Hayes also nominated Stanley Matthews, who was confirmed during Garfield's brief administration. Chester Arthur, who became president when Garfield was assassinated in 1881, appointed Horace Gray of Massachusetts, a "Federalist Republican" who would serve on the court for twenty years. Though the strongest nationalist on the bench, Gray, unlike Harlan, was a reluctant dissenter, believing that disagreement injured the court's reputation. Arthur also named Samuel Blatchford of New York, a specialist in admiralty and patent law with major industrialists among his clients, who served eleven years. The comings and goings of these justices illustrated again the vagaries and uncertainties of lifetime tenure on the court.

During the 1880s, a flock of major railroad cases arrived for decision by a high court packed with railroad attorneys. The 1886 case of *Santa Clara Co.* v. *Southern Pacific R.R.* was a landmark in the expansion of corporate power. The court ratified the argument former senator Roscoe Conkling had made while representing a railroad in another case: that the word "person" in the Fourteenth Amendment had been chosen twenty years before by its congressional framers, including Conkling himself, to extend the due process clause to "legal persons"—that is, to corporations. There was little evidence to back up Conkling's claim, but neither did anyone contradict him— most of his colleagues on the framing committee were dead. As a result, corporations now gained the "privileges and immunities" of American citizens.

That same year, in *Wabash, St. Louis & Pacific R.R.* v. *Illinois*, the court denied the states any jurisdiction in interstate commerce and created a no-man's-land where neither the states nor the federal government could regulate interstate railroad practices. In response, Congress the next year established the Interstate Commerce Commission, whose regulatory powers the court would dismantle piece by piece.

And with *Chicago, Milwaukee & St. Paul R.R.* v. *Minnesota*, in 1890, the Fuller Court's first major railroad decision, the justices completed their creeping abandonment of *Munn* by drastically curtailing the powers of state regulators. By failing to provide for judicial review of its rate decisions, the court now ruled, the Minnesota rate commission had interfered with the property rights of railroads. For the first time, a majority of the justices recognized "substantive" due process, holding that the reasonableness of rates was "eminently a question for judicial investigation, requiring due process of law for its determination." This was too much for Justice Bradley, who in a dissent defended *Munn*'s holding that the fairness of rates was a "legislative question, not a judicial one" and suggested that the court was on the path to granting corporations a constitutional right to a fair return on their investments.

Bradley was right. These conservative rulings were only the prelude to decisions in the 1890s, pioneered by Chief Justice Fuller and the "Fuller Team," that would play a huge role in shaping the nation's economy and human life.

Today the members of the Fuller Team are but footnotes in a general history of the court, but their collective impact was overwhelming. They were the four appointees of Benjamin Harrison during his one-term presidency and reflected his business-oriented conservatism. David J. Brewer of Kansas, a Yale-educated clergyman's son and nephew of Stephen Field, was the court's leading Social Darwinist. In his version of that doctrine, the struggle for survival centered on the "love of acquirement," the "real stimulus to human activity." This led Brewer to extreme laissez-faire views, fiercely protective toward "the acquisition, possession, and enjoyment of property" as sacred pursuits of happiness "which human government cannot forbid, and which it cannot destroy."

Brewer led the court's climactic assault on *Munn* and was author of the 1894 opinion in *Reagan* v. *Farmers' Loan and Trust* that fully realized Bradley's fears. Brewer drew out of the Fourteenth Amendment's equal protection clause a new, substantive constitutional right to a "fair return" for corporations. Because the regulation of rates prevented a corporation from charging as much as it could get away with and denied "some profit to those who have invested their money," an "unreasonable" regulation would amount to a now unconstitutional "taking of private property for public purposes without just compensation." It was the "judicial function" to prevent legislators from "wresting" property from its owners. In making the justices the ultimate arbiters of profit margins at the largest corporations in the United States, Brewer spoke for a unanimous court.

Bradley by then was dead, replaced in 1892 by Pennsylvanian George Shiras, another Yale man and another enormously successful corporate lawyer, nominated by Harrison on Andrew Carnegie's powerful recommendation. Shiras was one more laissez-faire conservative, but unique in that he became a justice without ever having held public office or taken an active role in politics. Henry B. Brown, still another Yaley and Social Darwinist, who took the place of Samuel Miller, was less dogmatically conservative but otherwise undistinguished. Harrison's last appointment, Howell Jackson of Tennessee, a former Confederate officer and a corporate lawyer, was ill for much of his two years on the bench but managed to return from his sickbed to distinguish himself from other members of the Fuller Team with a forceful dissent from one of three watershed decisions of 1895, *Pollock* v. *Farmers' Loan and Trust Co.*, calling it "the most disastrous blow ever struck at the constitutional powers of Congress."

In *Pollock*, the court overturned precedents dating back to the 1790s to strike down the first peacetime federal income tax, a 2 percent levy on annual income above $4,000 that would have affected less than 1 percent of Americans. A key demand of the Populists and taken up by Democrats from the South and the West, the tax was enacted after acrimonious debates in Congress, with Republicans denouncing the measure as class legislation and an assault on property. Chief Justice Fuller insisted in his opinion that the court was not "concerned with the question whether an income tax be or be not desirable," but the highly technical ruling could not cloak the fact that the majority saw the tax as an attempt to alter what Brewer called "the unvarying law" of civilization, "that the wealth of a community will be in the hands of a few." It would take a constitutional amendment, ratified two decades later, to overcome the Supreme Court's opposition to the income tax.

With *U.S.* v. *E. C. Knight Co.*, also decided in 1895, the court underscored its dedication to that "unvarying law" by drastically narrowing the scope of the 1890 Sherman Anti-Trust Act, which had

been hailed as the first federal effort to regulate the huge monopolistic corporate combinations that were rapidly forming. Only after
another decade of political agitation would "the third House of Congress," as a law review called the court, loosen its grip on the regulation of monopolies, while retaining its own power to decide the
"reasonableness" of regulations.

And most ominously in this same year of 1895, the court upheld
a contempt citation against the president of the American Railway
Union, Eugene Debs. Beginning in the 1880s, railroads had learned
to turn to friendly courts for injunctions to break up strikes. When
workers at Pullman, the Chicago sleeping car maker, walked out in
1894, Debs led his 160,000-member union in a sympathy strike that
paralyzed the nation's rail system. Grover Cleveland's Justice Department quickly won a federal injunction to stop the strike. When Debs
defied it, he was convicted of contempt. The Fuller Court, eager as it
was to uphold the Debs conviction in the name of public order—and
to teach other union leaders a lesson—faced a quandary. The court
had long held, most notably in its Reconstruction decisions, that
security—"the chief end of government," as Justice Brewer said—
was the function of *state* governments. In the Debs case, though,
Brewer found a "special exigency" that demanded an exception to
that rule—even if Debs broke no federal law, the strike was a danger
to the national economy, threatening widespread "interference" with
"property or rights of a pecuniary nature."

The attorney for Debs had pleaded with the court to remain
neutral in the battle between labor and capital. But in its three 1895
decisions, the Fuller Court had made it unmistakably clear where it
stood—with the powerful and the propertied. Such holdings were
the triumph, wrote the New York *World*, of "greed over need." They
destroyed the few tools fashioned by Congress and by workers to
contain corporate power and to temper the massive inequalities of
America's industrial revolution.

The decisions triggered an anti-court uproar unmatched since *Dred Scott*. Outrage carried into the 1896 presidential campaign. The Populists sacrificed their party in order to "fuse" with radical Democrats led by William Jennings Bryan, who, much to the dismay of conservative Clevelandites, became the Democratic nominee. The fusion campaign challenged as never before the Republican reign of "government by injunction," with its courts that served as "at once legislators, judges, and executioners." But not even the combined "Demopop" forces could defeat the Republicans, who proved that the electoral power Lincoln had bequeathed them remained largely intact. Warning in turn of "government by the mob," they elected William McKinley. It looked as though the Republicans—and their "judicial oligarchy"—might rule forever.

As MCKINLEY added Joseph McKenna, still another Republican politico, to the court's Fuller Team, it was evident that, more than three decades after the Civil War, Americans were witnessing the greatest, most enduring episode of court-packing in American history. The acid test was the ideology of the justices who so dominated the court decade after decade. They looked imposing in their dark gowns as they assembled for their group picture, differentiated mainly by their diverse combinations of beards, mustaches, and sideburns. Their faces seemed benign, perhaps a bit complacent. On their $5,000 annual salaries, which would have made them subject to the income tax they vetoed in *Pollock*, they were able to live in the DuPont Circle area of Washington, some taking the trolley to work on Capitol Hill. Still, one wonders, considering some of their earthshaking economic and social decisions during the postwar era, whether they paused for a moment to consider the impact of their decisions on the wretched lives of ill-paid and overworked laborers, mortgaged farmers, penniless immigrants, and slum dwellers.

The mystery deepens with the Supreme Court's 1896 decision in *Plessy* v. *Ferguson*, which sustained a Louisiana law that didn't simply permit but *required* segregated railway cars. Even though the court acknowledged that the Fourteenth Amendment's intent was "undoubtedly to enforce the absolute equality of the two races before the law," it ruled that if equal accommodations were offered to blacks, segregation did not constitute discrimination, since they were not denied equal protection of the laws. The court in *Plessy* reacted as though blacks were attempting to force social equality upon whites. While denying that "the enforced separation of the two races stamps the colored race with a badge of inferiority," the court contended that "legislation is powerless to eradicate racial instincts or to abolish distinctions based upon physical differences. . . . If one race be inferior to the other socially, the Constitution of the United States cannot put them upon the same plain." In reality, the Jim Crow laws, widespread in the South by 1896, *forbade* blacks, under penalty of law, from occupying the same public, work, living, recreational, and school places as whites. There was only one dissent to this decision, by Justice Harlan, who called the ruling as "pernicious" as *Dred Scott*. Harlan saw Jim Crow as an assault on liberty, a degradation of "the personal freedom of citizens." "Our Constitution is color-blind," he wrote, "and neither knows nor tolerates classes among citizens."

Not one of Harlan's colleagues agreed. Their abandonment of the Republican party's founding principles still haunts Americans more than a century later. *Plessy* delivered a final blow to the civil rights that they—or at least their fathers and uncles—had fought for in the "war between the states." That war had been framed by many Republicans as a great moral crusade, posing issues on which their party had prospered, securing the power that put most of these justices on the Supreme Court. But from the high bench they had left the momentous civil rights amendments in tatters, before going on to block initiatives to improve the lives of farmers, laborers, and the poor. Why? They were influenced by their straitlaced religious upbringings as Protestants in an era when that faith gave moral underpinning to laissez-faire capitalism and individualistic material striving. They lived in an age when rags-to-riches was the defining myth, when fortunes burgeoned and wealthy families rose to rival European aristocrats. Most of the justices of the Gilded Age Supreme Court had spent their earlier years in service to, and earning handsome incomes from, the new breed of rich and powerful capitalists. They were themselves among the privileged creatures of the Gilded Age, of laissez faire in all its unbounded glory. So why fight it?

Still, it is striking that these men, members of a ruling elite that possessed a near monopoly of power—political, legal, economic, social, military—so often felt themselves threatened, even besieged, by the dispossessed. In the unrest of powerless workers, David Brewer, for instance, could imagine "the black flag of anarchism, flaunting destruction to property" plus "the red flag of socialism, inviting a redistribution of property." Reflecting the urgency and determination of his fellow justices of the Gilded Age Supreme Court, Brewer concluded that, as revolution loomed, the law had "to do all that it can."

CHAPTER SEVEN

The Triumphant Mr. Taft

THE LONG DECADES of conservative domination of government were interrupted not by an electoral upset but by a sudden and shocking death—the assassination of William McKinley in September 1901—that propelled Theodore Roosevelt into the White House. With his bravado, bellicosity, and impatient, reformist energy, TR was a dramatic departure from the long line of Republican mediocrities in the presidency, an instinctive antagonist to the party's Old Guard, who would never have put such a man into the office. But of course they had nominated him only for the vice presidency. Running for reelection in 1900, McKinley had picked Roosevelt as a sop to the small but growing progressive wing of the GOP. Six months into his second term, McKinley was killed by an anarchist's bullet, and TR burst onto the stage determined to make the presidency the center of action "in a strong and efficient National Government" and to drag the Republican party into the modern age. He declared war on the monopolistic trusts that dominated the industrial landscape and offered a "Square Deal" to Americans, a promise that their government would serve not the "malefactors of great wealth" but the average citizen. At a time of intensifying clashes between the forces of progress and the armies of reaction, TR, personally and politically, embodied reform.

As what he called "chief lawmakers" in "the final seat of authority," the justices of the Supreme Court had the duty, in Roosevelt's view, to serve as allies in that cause of reform, to act as "great constructive statesmen" in bringing the law into harmony with the progressive political and economic forces of the day. Instead, the Fuller Court was reaction's citadel—the stronghold, TR wrote in his *Autobiography*, of "negative action against the interests of the people, ingeniously devised to limit their power against wrong, instead of affirmative action giving to the people power to right wrong." Roosevelt knew he could not change the court by force of will. He would have to wait the turning of the roulette wheel until he could put on it men of his own mind.

His first opportunity came in 1902, when Justice Gray retired, and he nominated Oliver Wendell Holmes, Jr. If Roosevelt was a professional politician and impassioned reformer, Holmes was nearly his opposite. He was nominally a Republican but lacked any interest in party politicking. He was an accomplished lawyer and judge—chief justice of the Massachusetts Supreme Judicial Court—but also a scholar, the author of *The Common Law*, a pioneering study of the formation of law. Even more, Holmes was a kind of Enlightenment philosopher, son of an eminent man of letters, acquainted with such literati as Emerson and Longfellow, one of the few Americans who could converse on easy terms in London with both John Stuart Mill and Prime Minister William Gladstone.

Though Holmes lacked the party standing and political connections usually needed to reach the high bench, Roosevelt admired his

Civil War sacrifices—he had been wounded three times in the desperate early battles of the war. Moreover, the Bostonian was, in TR's eyes, "one of us"—a fellow Harvard man and member of the university's elite Porcellian Club. It helped that Roosevelt's close adviser was Senator Henry Cabot Lodge of Massachusetts, another Porcellian and a friend of Holmes.

But perhaps most appealing to the president was Holmes's iconoclasm, his rejection of judicial shibboleths and dogmas. "The life of the law has not been logic," he wrote in *The Common Law*; "it has been experience," responses to "the felt necessities of the time." Though Holmes's modernizing pragmatism cloaked a temper that, so unlike TR's, was essentially conservative, even pessimistic—he was emphatically not a "goo-goo" reformer—Holmes promised a strong challenge to the outdated theories and prejudices that dominated the Fuller Court.

Roosevelt believed that Holmes met his elevated standard for Supreme Court appointments. "In the ordinary and low sense which we attach to the words 'partisan' and 'politician,'" TR wrote Lodge, a Supreme Court justice should be neither. "But in the higher sense, in the proper sense, he is not in my judgment fitted for the position unless he is a party man, a constructive statesman." The Supreme Court of the 1860s, TR added, "was good exactly in so far as its members fitly represented the spirit of Lincoln." "I should hold myself as guilty of an irreparable wrong to the nation," he concluded grandly, if he appointed "any man who was not absolutely sane and sound on the great national policies for which we stand in public life."

Yet Roosevelt's next appointment would seem to fall well short of such lofty standards. William Day was in the familiar grain of Republican justices, a railroad lawyer and McKinley's longtime ally in small-town Ohio. Steady and unspectacular, he rose through the ranks as a party fund-raiser, Ohio governor, and McKinley's secretary of state. TR appointed him in 1903 mainly to appease Old

Guardists ahead of the next year's presidential election. Day might have been, as Roosevelt believed, free of reactionary dogmas, but his long experience in local politics and state government had made him so wary of federal power that he became a reliable ally of the court's conservative phalanx.

Roosevelt's third and last appointment, in 1906, was cut from a different cloth. William H. Moody, a Harvard man and protégé of Lodge from north of Boston, was a fighting progressive who served two frenetic years as Roosevelt's attorney general and point man in the fight against the trusts, taking on monopolies in tobacco, lumber, drugs, fertilizer, paper, and groceries. He personally prosecuted the Beef Trust and targeted Standard Oil. He pushed through the Hepburn Act in 1906, which resurrected the Interstate Commerce Commission after the Supreme Court had stripped it of its regulatory powers. TR truly could say, "Moody is entirely our kind of judge. If they were all like him we would have no trouble."

BUT THEY WERE NOT all like Moody, not even Holmes. Shortly after Roosevelt took office in September 1901, his Justice Department brought an antitrust suit to block the merger of two big railroad companies. The *Northern Securities* case became a spearhead in TR's war on the trusts. By the time it reached the Supreme Court in late 1903, that battle was in full swing, getting a tremendous boost when the court, by the narrowest margin, 5–4, upheld the government. While Justice Day voted with the majority, the critical swing vote was not Holmes, but, surprisingly, David Brewer, who had come to fear that immense industrial empires threatened to crush individual liberty. In his concurrence, Brewer foresaw a time when "a single corporation whose stock was owned by three or four parties would be in practical control . . . of the whole transportation system of the country." Holmes disagreed. He thought too much was being made of trust-busting, creating a "kind of hydraulic pressure" before which "even well settled principles of law will bend." Chief Justice Fuller heartily assented. TR was furious. "Theodore went wild about it," Roosevelt's friend the historian Henry Adams wrote an acquaintance.

But trust-busting was about as far as the Fuller Court would go in acquiescence to reform. Confronted with demands to accommodate the modern economy, and especially when it came to the rights of workers, the Supreme Court continued to rely on what TR would call "a long outgrown philosophy, which was itself the product of primitive economic conditions." During his second term, the court, in *Lochner* v. *New York*, struck down a state law that limited working hours in the bakery industry. Reformers had in 1897 persuaded the New York legislature to pass the law as a health measure, to protect bakers from the effects of long days working in hot, dusty conditions. Joseph Lochner, owner of a bakeshop in upstate Utica, was twice convicted of forcing his bakers to work more than sixty hours a week. After two New York appeals courts ruled against Lochner, he turned to the Supreme Court in 1905, where he won full vindication. In the state law, Justice Rufus Peckham, writing for the majority, discerned the threat of the "all-pervading power" of legislative majorities that if left unchecked could make "wards of the State" of workers in every trade. What was really at stake in *Lochner*, Peckham wrote, was liberty of contract—the "freedom of master and employee to contract with each other" on equal terms, without government interference.

Actually at stake in *Lochner* was the baker's "treasured freedom" to work as many hours as his employer demanded. In a pithy dissent, Justice Holmes noted that "this case is decided upon an economic theory which a large part of the country does not entertain," charging the majority with writing private opinions into constitutional law. Law professor and reformer Ernst Freund bashed the court for overriding the judgment of the legislature, to which "the choice between the comparative benefits of the public welfare and private liberty of action" had constitutionally been committed. But the *Lochner* precedent would remain essentially intact for three decades.

So too would the court's decision three years later in *Adair* v. *U.S.*, when it rejected Congress's attempt to outlaw "yellow-dog" contracts that railroads forced on workers with the threat of being fired if they joined a union. Once again, liberty of contract was the issue, with the justices imagining that employer and employee could be on equal footing in negotiations. And in *Loewe* v. *Lawlor*, also decided in 1908, the court deployed the Sherman Anti-Trust Act against union organizers who orchestrated a boycott to pressure a company to accept unionization. This was a conspiracy in restraint of trade.

The one exception to the Supreme Court's hostility to workers' rights came three weeks after *Loewe*, when it upheld an Oregon maximum-hour law for women. What helped to make the difference in *Muller* v. *Oregon* was a novel presentation by the attorney defending the law, Louis D. Brandeis. The Bostonian prepared a one-hundred-page sociological treatise that demonstrated the ill effects of long hours on the well-being—moral as well as physical—of working women. But chivalry—or sexism—too played a part in the court's abandonment of the "liberty of contract" shibboleth in this case. The justices bowed to "the inherent difference between the sexes," conceding that "a female in a laundry" needed special legislation to rescue her "from the greed as well as the passion of man."

Apart from this single chink in its anti-labor armor, as well as a tolerance for trust-busting, the Supreme Court proved obdurate, still solidly stacked against progressive forces, impervious to TR's condemnations and insults, even when he publicly damned the court's rejection of a congressional attempt to increase employers' liability for injuries on the job as "a very slovenly piece of work." While Moody was almost always "safe and sound" in his votes on cases, as was Holmes usually and Day occasionally, the Supreme Court remained wedded to its long outgrown economic philosophy.

A CENTURY LATER historians still cannot fully explain the most fateful of Theodore Roosevelt's decisions—not to run for a second full term as president in 1908. It seemed to defy human nature—or at least TR's. He loved being president. He reveled in both the trappings and the essence of power. He believed he had been strikingly successful in the White House and knew that millions of Americans agreed. He had more work to do, more bills to be passed, still an array of enemies to be thwacked hip and thigh. Would he win again? He could have few doubts. William Jennings Bryan—who had been beaten twice by McKinley—again would be the Democratic nominee.

But, if not TR, who? This was no problem for the president—indeed, it was an advantage. He had already picked his successor, William Howard Taft. TR seemed almost in love with his plump, genial, comradely secretary of war. Writing to him once as "you beloved individual," he went on to say that he admired Taft more than any public man of past or present, excepting Washington and Lincoln. Repeatedly Roosevelt offered him a seat on the Supreme Court, almost begging him to take it. But while Taft always maintained that the court was his highest ambition, he had his eye on a bigger prize—the presidency. And Roosevelt in effect gave it to him.

Rarely has a benign presidential choice, though, ended up more personally destructive and politically catastrophic. For a time President Taft appeared to be carrying on TR's Square Deal, especially in antitrust actions that outnumbered Roosevelt's. But Roosevelt grew more and more disillusioned—even apocalyptic—as his successor turned to the right on key appointments, tariff revisions, and conservation. It became clear that Taft's presidency meant a restoration of the Old Guard conservatism Roosevelt had sought to banish from the Republican party. By midterm, TR was openly opposing his old friend, and in 1912 he plunged into the presidential race. When conservative Republicans controlling the GOP renominated Taft, Roosevelt led his "Bull Moose" faction out of the party and ran on a third-party Progressive ticket.

TR's platform was a ferocious onslaught against laissez faire and its defenders, especially Supreme Court justices whom he termed "a menace to the welfare of the Nation." At a time when criticism of the judiciary was reaching new intensity, no major political figure outdid Roosevelt in heat and radicalism. Central to his crusade was an inflammatory proposal for the popular recall, via referenda, of judicial decisions. Voters were to be empowered to strike down court rulings with which they disagreed. TR called on the states to enact such a measure, though he thought it should be extended to the federal judiciary and the interpretation of the national Constitution. Accepting the Progressive party's presidential nomination in August 1912, Roosevelt declared that the "people themselves must be the ultimate makers of their own Constitution."

Critics were quick to assail TR's recall proposal as dangerous, even revolutionary. Taft warned that it would permit "a suspension of the Constitution to enable a temporary majority of the electorate to enforce a popular but invalid act." The *New York Times* called it a "wild scheme" that, taken to its logical conclusion, could lead to the overturning of all Supreme Court decisions, beginning with *Marbury*—"the cause of all the trouble"—and then to the court's abolition and "the transfer of its business to the town meeting." The *Journal of Commerce* claimed it raised a "serious question" of the former president's "mental balance."

Yet Roosevelt strenuously defended his plan as a reasonable solution to the growing crisis created by a reactionary judiciary's contempt for popular legislation. Citizens, he said, could not be denied the means to "effectively control the mighty commercial forces which they have themselves called into being." Recall of judicial decisions was a safer course than either the recall of judges themselves, which would threaten their independence, or a piecemeal amendment of the Constitution. It was, he argued, a less radical alternative than proposals advocated by labor activists and others on the left to abolish judicial review, which TR saw as a needed check on legislative excesses. The problem was to check the extremism of the courts. Roosevelt maintained that his plan was soundly in the American vein—it would restore "the ultimate sovereign power— the people—to a position where it can decide" between the legislature and the judiciary.

Roosevelt's defeat in the 1912 election took the steam out of his drive for judicial reform. With Republicans bitterly split, Woodrow Wilson, an avowed progressive, became the second Democrat elected to the presidency since the Civil War. Outdoing Taft in the electoral vote, 88 to 8, was a small consolation to TR. There was little to show for his campaign against the courts. Only Colorado enacted a law modeled on Roosevelt's proposal—approved in a popular initiative in the November 1912 election. But no recall vote was ever held, and in 1920 the Colorado Supreme Court declared the law unconstitutional, giving the lie to TR's hopeful claim that "it is the people, and not the judges, who are entitled to say what their constitution means."

THE SUPREME COURT that Roosevelt had so savagely denounced was to a striking degree Taft's court. During his four years as president, Taft had had a remarkable streak of luck at the judicial roulette wheel—*six* appointments—and he exploited his good fortune to the hilt. His was a long-range strategy—to pack the court with relatively young conservative attorneys who would serve for decades. Even more, if he played his cards right, he might end up among them.

Melville Fuller's chief justiceship ended with his death in July 1910. Many had expected that Taft would offer the prize to Charles Evans Hughes, whom he had placed on the court as an associate justice two months earlier. Hughes had all the credentials—reform Republican, noted attorney, governor of New York. And Hughes had accepted the associate's spot in part because Taft dangled the top job in front of him. Indeed, until the last minute Hughes expected to succeed Fuller. But something seemed to stall the nomination. The president was doing some recalculating. Taft himself had long hungered for the chief justiceship. If he chose the forty-eight-year-old Hughes, the post might be filled for decades. Taft's own chance to reach the judicial pinnacle would be blocked. Better to pick an older man, and he did—the undistinguished, but sixty-six-year-old, Edward D. White, a sitting justice appointed by Grover Cleveland back in 1894. Hughes resigned from the court six years later to run for the presidency—unsuccessfully as it turned out—against Woodrow Wilson. Rarely has one man's age made so much judicial and presidential history.

In addition to Hughes and White, Taft had a bonanza of four more appointments. They formed a rough pattern: born in rural America, attended good colleges and law schools, started work as small-town lawyers, moved easily into party politics, and ultimately flourished in urban America. Most were brought up in strongly religious families, Catholic or Protestant. And they were all stout conservatives.

Horace H. Lurton, Taft's friend from Ohio, was a traditionalist like the president who saw the Supreme Court as the guardian of "the fundamental law which conducts and controls the otherwise uncontrollable legislative power," a check to "hotfooted action" by "impulsive majorities." Willis Van Devanter, a Wyoming railroad attorney, would serve on the court until 1937, becoming what a fellow justice called the commander-in-chief of judicial reaction. Joseph Rucker Lamar, born of a patrician family and another railroad lawyer, served only five years and somewhat indistinctly as a reliable part of the Taft "unit." Taft's last pick, Mahlon Pitney, a New Jersey railroad attorney and politico, was noted for his consistently anti-labor positions.

These men joined a court that was already heavily conservative. Their doctrinaire views left Oliver Wendell Holmes often isolated from his brethren, especially after John Harlan died in 1911. Holmes took on Harlan's mantle as the court's "great dissenter," pitting his pragmatism against conservative dogma, true to his early belief that the law must "modify itself in accordance with the will of the *de facto* supreme power in the community." Holmes saw all life as an experiment, a competition of ideas, and progress a matter of trial and error driven by "the felt necessities of the time." In the judgments of the Supreme Court, he wrote in his very first opinion in 1903, "Considerable latitude must be allowed for differences of view as well as for possible peculiar conditions which this court can know but imperfectly, if at all." Otherwise, a constitution "would become the partisan of a particular set of ethical or economical opinions."

WOODROW WILSON, the Democrat elected to the presidency in 1912 on the ruins of the GOP, was a truer heir to TR's progressivism than Roosevelt's handpicked successor had proved to be. A respected constitutional scholar before becoming governor of New Jersey, Wilson had been much impressed by TR's "enlargement" of the presidency, especially his use of the bully pulpit to build a constituency for reform by direct appeals to the people. But Wilson's populism went only so far. He opposed the demands of Roosevelt and others for the recall of judges or judicial decisions, dismissing the idea that "determinations of what the law is must respond to popular impulse." Instead, "the way to purify the judiciary," he said in 1912, "is to purify it at its roots," through the process of judicial selection.

Yet at his first opportunity to purify the nation's highest court, President Wilson selected a reactionary ideologue and a racist. In his private life, James McReynolds, a lifelong bachelor, was said to be gracious and considerate. But at work, Dr. Jekyll became Mr. Hyde. When he reached the Supreme Court, McReynolds was insufferably rude to his fellow justices, intolerant, sarcastic, and sexist, too. Once when he spotted a woman attorney in the courtroom, he grumbled, "I see the female is here again."

McReynolds, like Wilson, was a native of the South, born in an old Tennessee frontier town. Brought up by fundamentalist parents—his father was known as the "pope" for his confidence in his own infallibility—young McReynolds did well as a scholar and debater at Vanderbilt, and then went on to the University of Virginia Law School, where his favorite teacher was a stern moralist who taught Sunday Bible classes. In 1896, McReynolds ran unsuccessfully for Congress as a conservative Democrat with Republican support and in opposition to the "evil" populist platform of his party's presidential nominee, William Jennings Bryan. Through connections, he went to work for Roosevelt and then Taft as a trustbuster. This was anomalous for a man otherwise suspicious of government power, but it gave him the reformist gloss that prompted Wilson to appoint him his attorney general in 1913. A year later, Wilson evidently was so relieved to promote this increasingly irascible lone wolf out of the cabinet and onto the Supreme Court that he overcame whatever qualms he may have had about McReynolds's progressivism. For more than a quarter century, McReynolds reigned as the Supreme Court's most vociferous and aggressive reactionary.

Wilson's second nominee for a Supreme Court seat could scarcely have been more different from McReynolds, or better chosen to redeem the president's promise to purify the judiciary. Louis D. Brandeis also was a Southerner, born and raised in Louisville, but there the resemblance with McReynolds ended. The son of "Forty-eighters" from Prague who had fled the conservative reaction following the failed European uprisings of 1848, Brandeis grew up in an enlightened family devoted to music and literature. After two years of study in Dresden, he entered Harvard Law School at age eighteen and earned his degree in two years. With a fellow student, he founded a Boston law practice that biographer Alpheus Thomas Mason called a "laboratory for social and economic research."

Brandeis was an exquisitely tolerant, compassionate, and worldly man. The zeal for freedom was in his blood, grounded in the individual worth of each human being. He was a Boston reformer who did not loudly set forth to battle. No enemy of capitalism, Brandeis sought to extend its abundance to the downtrodden and to limit the power of big corporations to exploit them. Before long his soaring fame as the "people's attorney" and a legal philosophy that was both highly ethical and sociologically analytical, as demonstrated by his pioneering brief in *Muller*, won him a national reputation. A close adviser to Wilson in 1912, Brandeis was the president's first choice to be attorney general, but Wilson bowed to objections from conservative Bostonians and instead named James McReynolds. In 1916, though, the president tapped Brandeis for the Supreme Court.

Instantly the legal community exploded in outrage. Seven former presidents of the American Bar Association, William Howard Taft among them, deemed him "not a fit person" to join the high court. Fifty-five eminent Bostonians, headed by President A. Lawrence Lowell of Harvard, signed a petition stating that Brandeis did not possess "the judicial temperament and capacity" necessary for the high court and that his "reputation as a lawyer" was such "that he has not the confidence of the people."

Brandeis himself saw these objections as cloaking "the dominant reasons for the opposition," as he wrote in an unfinished brief defending himself—"that he is considered a radical and is a Jew." Hearings before the Senate Judiciary Committee labored on for nearly five months. With Wilson exerting maximum pressure, amid fears that defeat would turn the Democratic party back "into the wilderness for forty more years," the ten Democrats on the committee finally voted to confirm Brandeis; all eight Republicans were opposed. The Senate approved the nomination, 47 to 22. Among the many ironies in the whole dispute was that Brandeis—who had not followed the typical political track to the court and had voted in turn for the progressive Republican Roosevelt, the conservative Republican Taft, and the reform Democrat Wilson for president—should be elevated to the court by a straight party vote.

To THE DEGREE that opposition to Brandeis's nomination had been ideological, it was justified. He really was unlike most other lawyers, certainly unlike those appointed to the Supreme Court. As an attorney and then as a justice, Brandeis held freedom as his central value—freedom as an immensely complex dynamic of ends and means, of ideas and processes, that challenged the mind as well as the heart. No dogma, of the right or the left, could encompass it. To Brandeis, as Mason wrote, "Men are not necessarily made free when immune from rule; nor does freedom spring full grown when the state protects the poor against the rich. The life of freedom is self-wrought; not conferred; it can be aided by many social agencies—all functioning as means and never as ends."

Brandeis applied this conception of freedom to the gritty realities of American life—factory work, wages and hours, joblessness, unions, strikes, trusts. As a jurist, he would bottom his opinions in masses of statistics, to the boredom of his hero and collaborator, Holmes. Brandeis believed in the "presumption of constitutionality" of laws designed to protect workers and consumers. His belief in the virtues of private property was so strong that he wanted property to be shared broadly.

Brandeis joined Holmes on the high court in time to participate in momentous decisions arising from the Wilson administration's prosecution of opponents to American involvement in World War I. In *Schenck v. U.S.*, decided a few months after the war ended, Holmes, speaking for a unanimous court, sustained the conviction of Charles Schenck, a Socialist party official who had sent leaflets to men eligible for the draft urging them to resist conscription. *Schenck* established "clear and present danger" as the test for free speech. The old Civil War soldier wrote that it was "a question of proximity and degree. When a nation is at war many things that might be said in time of peace are such a hindrance to its effort that their utterance will not be endured so long as men fight." Brandeis later deeply regretted that he had gone along with Holmes because the "clear and present danger" standard might allow the government to restrict speech in peacetime, when Brandeis thought it should be limited only if it involved incitement to an immediate and serious crime. But, he explained to a friend, he was new to the court and new to the issue of free speech. "You must also remember," he added, "that when Holmes writes, he doesn't give a fellow a chance—he shoots so quickly."

Soon after, though, in November 1919, Holmes and Brandeis were the lone dissenters in *Abrams* v. *U.S.* In that case, the court ruled that arousing disaffection against the government in wartime—by distributing leaflets that opposed American intervention in Russia's revolution, as Jacob Abrams, an anarchist, had done on Manhattan's Lower East Side one August evening in 1918—was not protected by the First Amendment. Now Holmes, without admitting that he had erred in *Schenck*, poured scorn on the government's pursuit of "poor and puny" anarchists with their ignorant and immature creed.

"Persecution for the expression of opinions seems to me perfectly logical," Holmes wrote, in a swipe at the majority. "If you have no doubt of your premises or your power and want a certain result with all your heart you naturally express your wishes in law and sweep away all opposition. But when men have realized that time has upset many fighting faiths, they may come to believe even more than they believe the very foundations of their own conduct that the ultimate good desired is better reached by free trade in ideas—that the best test of truth is the power of the thought to get itself accepted in the competition of the market, and that truth is the only ground upon which their wishes safely can be carried out. That at any rate is the theory of our Constitution."

For the time being, this was the theory of Holmes and Brandeis alone, one they achieved only after their stumble in *Schenck*. It would be more than two decades before the Supreme Court would begin, again haltingly, to take up Holmes's challenge to create and defend a First Amendment marketplace of ideas.

ON JUNE 30, 1921, William Howard Taft's judicial realpolitik handsomely paid off. President Warren Harding, a fellow Republican who had succeeded Wilson, appointed him chief justice of the Supreme Court, at last to succeed his own appointee, Edward White. It had been a long wait for Taft, with many anxious moments. He had been so avid for the post that he had even harbored the vain thought that Wilson might give it to him. Each vacancy on the court spurred a campaign on his behalf as "the best qualified man in the country." It was perhaps not only outrage at the appointment of Brandeis that prompted Taft to the thought that "White will not end his judicial career with an apoplectic fit caused by the nomination." Though he was approaching his midseventies with failing eyesight and hearing, Chief Justice White outlived the Wilson administration.

While he was visiting President-elect Harding in Ohio shortly after the election, Taft got the promise of a justiceship, but he coolly made clear that he would accept only the *chief* justiceship. Harding put him off. A visit to White in mid-March 1921 was similarly discouraging. White appeared so well that Taft made inquiries about the chief justice's health with White's doctor. Taft began to wonder about his own condition and age. At sixty-four, if selected he would be the oldest man to become chief justice, except of course for White. Finally, in May, White died. But then other possible candidates surfaced. To Taft, it was all quite maddening. He was reduced to drafting a résumé of his qualifications—among them, "Four years president." At long last, Harding chose him. There was some fretting about confirmation, but only a handful of Senate progressives voted no. Taft basked in the thousands of congratulatory letters and telegrams that flooded in.

Happily ensconced at the center of the high bench, Taft could now concentrate on inducing Harding to choose the proper men for the court. Looking around at his brethren, Taft saw mostly deadwood— aged or infirm justices who would be obstacles to a chief anxious rapidly to leave a mark. Perhaps even Holmes might be persuaded to retire, ridding Taft of a "noisy dissenter."

Manipulating Harding on appointments was no arduous task, despite the chief justice's concern that the president would be tempted to load the Supreme Court, as he had most of the rest of the government, with old cronies. "Taft's *modus operandi* was very simple," historian Henry Abraham wrote in his study of court appointments. "Once a vacancy presented itself, he would literally bombard the president with firm recommendations and casual suggestions." Their first choice was an obvious one, George Sutherland, Republican from Utah, who would become the intellectual leader of the court's extreme right wing. Prospering as a corporate attorney, Sutherland had moved easily into Utah's conservative politics. Election to the

Senate had brought him close to fellow-solon Harding. Enthusiastically backed for the court by Republican colleagues in the Senate, he was unembarrassed to become a "brother" to Brandeis, whose appointment he had as senator vociferously opposed.

Strenuously backed and coached by Taft, Pierce Butler, a Minnesota Democrat, was Harding's next pick. One of nine children of Irish Catholic parents, Butler was a self-taught lawyer who had earned millions representing western and midwestern railroads. He had won some notoriety as a regent at the University of Minnesota for arranging the dismissals of faculty members who held allegedly radical or disloyal views. On the court, Butler would show no more regard for dissidents, or for blacks or workers. Though Harding's last nominee, Edward T. Sanford, a Republican millionaire from Tennessee, was not Taft's candidate, he turned out to be one of his most devoted followers among the justices.

So, after only a year and a half on the court, the chief justice had Taft men from the Harding presidency and Taft men who were holdovers from his own presidency, giving him a decisive conservative majority. And he had the kinds of cases he wanted—cases that would enable him to stand fast against the tide of social and economic reform that had swamped his presidency when he had been the unhappy heir to Theodore Roosevelt's activism. Taft believed that reform measures deserved the Supreme Court's special scrutiny, as he indicated when he struck down an effort by Congress to curb child labor through its taxing power. "The good sought in unconstitutional legislation is an insidious feature, because it leads citizens and legislators of good purpose to promote it, without thought of the serious breach it will make in the ark of our covenant, or the harm which will come from breaking down recognized standards." Taft's contempt for the legislature and its eagerness to pass "any law that seemed popular," resulting in an "overwhelming mass of ill-digested legislation," was shown in his court's unprecedented use of judicial review to knock down acts of Congress, state laws, and municipal ordinances. While the Fuller Court, which also styled itself a bulwark against revolution, vetoed nine such laws at its peak in 1898, the Taft Court invalidated two dozen in 1926 alone. Between 1922 and 1928, it *averaged* eighteen vetoes a year.

The chief justice laid the blame on "the hasty action of the majority," which it was his court's "high duty and function" to check, but many measures he struck down reflected decades of efforts by Congress and the states to overcome judicial obstructions. Reformers had been fighting for a congressional ban on child labor for at least twenty years when in 1922 Taft voided Congress's levy of a child labor tax in *Bailey* v. *Drexel Furniture*. Workers had struggled for more than half a century to secure their rights to organize and strike. The landmark Clayton Act of 1914 took direct aim at judicial obstacles to collective action by exempting labor unions from antitrust laws and by curbing injunctions. But Taft saw Clayton as nothing more than a capitulation by cowardly congressmen to "truculent labor leaders, intoxicated with their sense of political power," and in a series of decisions in the 1920s, the Taft Court eviscerated the act. Ever since *Munn* v. *Illinois* had in 1877 opened the door to the regulation of business in the public interest, conservative Supreme Court justices had sought to close it, most effectively by raising the barrier of substantive due process, which equated regulation with the infringement of property rights. Taft's court narrowed the public interest doctrine even further, exempting large and powerful sectors of industry and commerce— trivialized by the chief justice as "the business of the butcher, or the baker, the tailor, the woodchopper, the mining operator, or the miner"—from government regulation, especially of labor relations.

Yet when "hasty action" targeted alleged subversives, Taft was eager to rubber-stamp the impulses of majorities. In 1925, the Taft Court upheld a New York "criminal anarchy" law that was passed in 1902 in the furor following President McKinley's assassination by a self-styled anarchist and used to prosecute Benjamin Gitlow two decades later for publishing a "Left Wing Manifesto." Though, as Taft loyalist Justice Sanford conceded in his majority opinion, "there was no evidence of any effect resulting" from the manifesto's publication, "every presumption is to be indulged in favor of the validity of the statute." After all, "a single revolutionary spark may kindle a fire that, smouldering for a time, may burst into a sweeping and destructive conflagration." Two years later, in *Whitney* v. *California*, the Supreme Court again indulged every presumption in favor of a state "criminal syndicalism" statute passed in 1920 at the height of the postwar frenzy against "reds." The court ruled that the act of merely joining an organization accused of menacing "the public peace and security of the State" was to engage in a criminal conspiracy.

Brandeis and Holmes were the only dissenters in these two cases. Writing in *Whitney*, Brandeis alluded to the court's abuse of Holmes's "clear and present danger" standard. "Only an emergency can justify repression," he wrote, and then appealed to the Founders whose legacy conservatives like Taft professed to uphold: "Those who won our independence by revolution were not cowards." Unlike his conservative colleagues, Brandeis suggested, "they did not fear political change. They did not exalt order at the cost of liberty. . . ."

COMPARED TO Harding's four court selections in the three years before his presidency was cut short by his death, his successor, Calvin Coolidge, had only one pick in five years—Harlan Fiske Stone. That single appointment, though, would have an impact on the court rivaling that of Holmes and Brandeis. Long after, court watchers wondered how one of the most conservative of presidents could choose a liberal-minded justice who in the 1930s would become a leader of the resistance to the forces of reaction. At the time, though, it seemed a reasonable choice. Stone, like Coolidge, had deep New England roots, an old-line Republican father, and a degree from Amherst College. Stone attended Columbia Law and served as its dean, and practiced corporation law, acting as counsel to J. P. Morgan. After Coolidge won a full term in 1924, Stone joined the cabinet as attorney general and promptly cleaned house in the Justice Department, which had been the source of many of the Harding scandals.

Stone also had the right enemies for conservatives like Coolidge. Senator George Norris of Nebraska and five other progressives voted against his confirmation. Doubtless those progressives were surprised even more than Coolidge himself when Stone joined Holmes and Brandeis in many of their dissents. As for Taft, he became convinced that Stone had been seduced and corrupted by his two senior colleagues.

Stone's appointment scarcely diminished Taft's conservative majority. Yet the chief justice was fretful and frustrated. The truth was, he hated dissent. On the rare occasions when he was in the minority, he kept quiet about it, writing only three dissenting opinions in nine years on the court. Dissent, he believed, was a reflection on his leadership, and it weakened the court's authority, its power to make the law certain. Taft prized teamwork—all the justices pulling in harness. He paid close heed to the personalities of the brethren, attended to their comforts, tried to be scrupulously fair in assigning opinions. He encouraged a vigorous airing of views in conference, made concessions to bulk up a majority, and sometimes, especially early in his tenure, allowed himself to be persuaded by Holmes or Brandeis to change his mind. But unanimity proved to be an elusive thing.

Taft's curse was that in Holmes and Brandeis he faced two men whose "attitude of protest," as he called it, and hunger for combat were keen and unrelenting. The two were among the most probing, original intellects—and best writers—ever to sit on the Supreme Court. They did not merely disagree with the conservative majority.

Their dissents were annihilating. The skepticism and pragmatism of Holmes and the modernizing, sociological jurisprudence of Brandeis slashed at the intellectual roots of the conservatives—their theory and logic, their premises and evidence.

Those conservative roots lay deep in the nineteenth century, based upon what Holmes had as long ago as 1905, in his *Lochner* dissent, dismissed as an outdated minority view. Brandeis's fame as a lawyer had come from his campaign to persuade judges to confront modern facts and problems. Now every defeat, Taft said, "colors the rest of the day which follows and one despairs of the Republic." As a student of constitutional history, Taft well knew how dissenting opinions could in time become majority rulings. A man who had twice remade the Supreme Court—as president and as Harding's mentor—Taft understood the power of appointments to shape its direction. The reign of conservative justices had been ensured by a nearly unbroken line of Republican presidents stretching back more than half a century. Now even Herbert Hoover, the Republican elected in 1928, frightened Taft. He was convinced that, "if a number of us die, Hoover would put in some rather extreme destroyers of the Constitution."

Taft's was a striking display of doubt about his legacy, about the strength and viability of what the generations of conservatives had made of the Constitution. He knew that the Supreme Court stood outside the mainstream of public opinion, that people wanted and expected more from their government than the court would allow. But that was the court's purpose—to stand against the unwise demands of "the leviathan, the People," to preserve "the form of government as prescribed by our fathers." Especially as the nation's economy plunged into depression, Taft saw himself as the man who could "prevent the Bolsheviki from getting control."

When he retired in 1930, utterly spent and ill, he was little comforted that his successor would be Charles Evans Hughes, the man who had been his own first choice for the job in 1910 and had been waylaid by Taft's ambitions, or that Hughes, now at sixty-eight the oldest man to become chief justice, had indicated that in the war against the "era of regulation," the Supreme Court's ultimate weapon of judicial review "is likely to be of increasing value."

Two weeks after Hughes took his seat on the court, Taft died. After him, the deluge.

CHAPTER EIGHT

FDR's Boldest Gamble

———————

BY THE TIME Franklin Delano Roosevelt took the presidential oath of office on March 4, 1933, the Great Depression seemed to have no bottom. Beginning with the stock market collapse in late 1929, the nation had plunged into an economic catastrophe. Thousands of banks and businesses had shut down. Fifteen million Americans—a third of the workforce—were out of jobs. Agricultural prices had dropped below the costs of production, leaving millions of farmers on the edge of insolvency. The political climate had changed drastically, as the cataclysm swept the Republican party out of power. Now Congress was firmly in Democratic hands. President Hoover, denounced for doing nothing to meet the crisis, had suffered a nationwide defeat at the polls in 1932, crushed by an upstart New York governor vowing a "New Deal."

Franklin Roosevelt promised to attack the Depression with "action, and action now," in a spirit, as he said, of "bold, persistent experimentation." In his first hundred days in office, he initiated a wide range of measures that dramatically expanded federal intervention in the economy and challenged the rule of laissez faire. The new president launched the largest relief program in American history, extended federal regulation over the stock market, banks, and transportation, and mandated the restructuring of mortgage debt to save homeowners from foreclosure. The Tennessee Valley Authority was a grand foray into national planning, designed to develop a vast region's resources under public ownership and control. The Agricultural Adjustment Act sought to restore farm income by guaranteeing parity prices to farmers who agreed to cut production. The capstone was the National Industrial Recovery Act, passed in June 1933, which ambitiously sought to end the old conflict between capital and labor by promoting "a great cooperative movement throughout all industry." The NIRA would allow business to develop codes of fair competition, supervised by the president, and give government the authority to regulate labor relations. The aim, above all, was to put millions of Americans back to work.

These and a host of other measures passed over feeble Republican opposition in Congress, and then moved on to the federal courts, finally arriving at that bastion of the old economic order— the Supreme Court—where the lottery of appointments and tenure still prevailed. Charles Evans Hughes was entrenched as the high court's leader, a moderate, perhaps, by Taft standards, but nevertheless appalled by the New Deal onslaught. Alongside him on the court's right wing were the "Four Horsemen" of reaction: Willis Van Devanter, the Taft appointee in his third decade on the bench; James McReynolds, a veteran now of two decades; and two Harding/Taft men, George Sutherland and Pierce Butler. Louis Brandeis and Harlan Fiske Stone were a liberal minority, together with Hoover appointee Benjamin Cardozo, one of the most distinguished lawyers and jurists in the United States, universally acclaimed as a worthy successor to Holmes when the great dissenter finally retired at ninety in 1932. The ninth justice, another Hoover appointee, Owen Roberts, a Pennsylvania Republican with strong railroad ties, was allied with the Four Horsemen, though not always dependably.

For the court's right wing, the New Deal was an assault on all they held dear. They scoffed at the notion that the economic crisis justified "encroachments upon the sanctity of private and public contracts," as Sutherland, their most powerful spokesman, wrote in 1934, or that it demanded a new understanding of the Constitution. Its *"meaning* is changeless," said Sutherland, and the "whole aim of construction" was "to discover the meaning, to ascertain and give effect to the intent, of its framers and the people who adopted it." Apparently, in his researches into the Constitution's original meaning, Sutherland failed to notice the lack of a provision for the judicial power of review he was only too ready to wield against New Deal legislation. Unlike conservatives in Congress, who could only fulminate against FDR's "dictatorship" and "socialism," Sutherland and his three fellow Horsemen, along with Hughes and Roberts, could do something about it.

On "Black Monday," as May 25, 1935, came to be known, the Supreme Court delivered three major blows to the president. A farm bankruptcy bill designed to reduce foreclosures was vetoed as a violation of the due process rights of creditors. Then, the court rebuked FDR for his removal of an obstructionist Republican from the Federal Trade Commission. Finally, and stunningly, with *Schechter Poultry Corp. v. U.S.*, the court struck down the New Deal's centerpiece, the NIRA. A firm of New York kosher poultry dealers had appealed its conviction for violating NIRA codes by, among other things, selling "sick chickens" to the public and cheating workers of their pay. Hughes, writing for the court, objected to the "virtually unfettered" discretion Congress had given the president to oversee the industrial codes, and went further to rule that the codes themselves were an unconstitutional interference in commerce. "Extraordinary conditions," Hughes noted pointedly, "do not create or enlarge constitutional power."

Black Monday shook the administration. A few days later, FDR waved a sheaf of telegrams at the dozens of reporters crowded into his office for a press conference. The telegrams were, he said, "pathetic appeals" from citizens dismayed by *Schechter* and the demise of the NIRA. As he told the assembled newsmen, "The big issue is this: Does this decision mean that the United States Government has no control over any national economic problem?" The president seemed to answer his own question, saying, "We have been relegated to the horse-and-buggy definition of interstate commerce." But, reporters wanted to know, what was Roosevelt going to do about it? "We haven't got to that yet," the president replied.

The justices knew what they were going to do. They kept on the offensive against the New Deal. In January 1936, the Supreme Court struck down the Agricultural Adjustment Act in *U.S.* v. *Butler*, a case that arose from the government's attempt to collect the AAA's "processing tax" from a bankrupt Massachusetts textile firm. Denying that the agricultural crisis was a matter of the "general welfare," the court decided that the problems of farmers were a local matter, beyond the scope of federal power. Though the AAA had doubled wheat and cotton prices in three years, the court dismissed the processing tax, which raised money from mills, meatpackers, and other processors to pay farmers to reduce production, as a redistributionist scheme—"the expropriation of money from one group for the benefit of another," the court complained.

Five months later, in *Carter* v. *Carter Coal Co.*, the Supreme Court ruled the Guffey Coal Act unconstitutional. Passed after *Schechter*, with Congress attempting to meet the court's objections to the NIRA, the bill was intended to help revive the devastated coal industry while bringing labor peace to the notoriously violent mines.

But West Virginia's Carter Coal Company, a fierce opponent of the United Mine Workers, drew on *Schechter* and *Butler* to argue that a coal industry code protecting workers' rights to organize was unconstitutional. "Coal mining," a Carter lawyer argued, "is just as much a local activity as is farming or manufacture." The Four Horsemen plus Hughes and Owen Roberts agreed. Writing for them, Sutherland invoked a stack of nineteenth-century precedents to show that, apart from powers specifically delegated by the Constitution, Congress was powerless to "promote the general welfare." Despite the fact that almost all of Carter's coal was shipped out of West Virginia, Sutherland insisted that its mining was "a purely local activity," and thus "the relation of employer to employee is a local relation," exempt from federal meddling.

As the court rampaged through the New Deal, striking down more than a dozen federal and state laws in eighteen months, the conservatives created what the president, in June 1936, told the press was a "'no-man's-land' where no Government—State or Federal—can function." But when a reporter asked him, "How can you meet that situation?," FDR replied, "I think that is about all there is to say on it."

A MYTH would rise later that a maddened Roosevelt suddenly and recklessly attacked the Hughes Court after his reelection in 1936. History is not so simple. As the Supreme Court voided act after act, the president was less interested in "revenge" than in solving a seemingly intractable problem. "Clearly, it is running in the President's mind that substantially all of the New Deal bills will be declared unconstitutional," Interior Secretary Harold Ickes noted in his diary in the winter of 1935.

By then, the president, working closely with Attorney General Homer Cummings, was searching for means to empower the government "to intervene reasonably in the regulation of nation-wide commerce and nation-wide agriculture." One possibility was to override the court's decisions by giving Congress explicit constitutional authority to regulate business and labor. Another was to curtail the court's obstructionism by limiting its powers of judicial review. That approach was finding a strong echo in Congress as legislators filed dozens of bills in the spring of 1936 that ranged from restrictions on the court's appellate jurisdiction to the complete abolition of judicial review of federal laws. Progressive senator George Norris, who accused the justices of acting as "a continuous constitutional convention," proposed that only a unanimous court could kill legislation. "It takes twelve men to find a man guilty of murder," he said. "I don't see why it should not take a unanimous court to find a law unconstitutional."

Roosevelt and Cummings were particularly drawn to a proposal that would allow a new Congress to reenact a law that the Supreme Court had declared unconstitutional. As the momentum for action built—and even Herbert Hoover demanded, after the court vetoed a New York law setting a minimum wage for women, that "something should be done to give back to the States the powers they thought they already had"—the president floated a few trial balloons, suggesting to one reporter after Black Monday that he favored a constitutional amendment that "will lift the Dead Hand, giving the people of today the right to deal with today's vital issues."

But that was the great problem with many of the reform proposals mooted by the administration and in Congress and the press— they would require a constitutional amendment. As the president observed to a friend, "no two people agree both on the general method of amendment or on the language of an amendment." But even if an amendment could be drafted and won the needed two-thirds backing in both houses of Congress, the legislatures—indeed, one chamber of a two-house legislature—of only thirteen states could block it. Even more, if such an amendment somehow finally was ratified, it was the Supreme Court itself that would interpret—or misinterpret—it. And, in any case, it might come too late to save the New Deal.

It was hard to outwit the Framers. So Roosevelt reluctantly put aside the amendment route. If the New Deal was to survive, the Supreme Court must be changed by changing its personnel. After all, as Cummings wrote to FDR in January 1936, "The real difficulty is not with the Constitution but with the judges who interpret it." Roosevelt himself thought that the court's decisions were the product of the "private, social philosophy" of the justices. But how was that to be changed? The conservatives had the votes, a solid majority, and they seemed healthy and disinclined to resign. Mortality tables were consulted and the Metropolitan Life Insurance Company calculated that even the oldest of the justices might well outlive a second Roosevelt term.

The only practical solution appeared to be to change the court by—to use a term that FDR initially shunned—"packing" it; that is, by adding enough new justices to produce a New Deal majority. There was, after all, nothing sacred about a bench of nine. "The number of Justices has been changed several times before," the president would remind Americans, "in the Administrations of John Adams and Thomas Jefferson—both signers of the Declaration of Independence—Andrew Jackson, Abraham Lincoln and Ulysses S. Grant."

WHEN ROOSEVELT unveiled his court-packing plan to Congress on February 5, 1937, it exploded like a bombshell. Against expectations—and the advice of liberal allies—the president had not made the Supreme Court an issue in his 1936 reelection campaign. He had run against the old order, against such "enemies of peace" as "business and financial monopoly, speculation, reckless banking, class antagonism," and against "hear-nothing, see-nothing, do-nothing Government." But he had banked his rhetoric against the old order on the Supreme Court itself and offered no proposals for reform.

After his historic landslide victory in November, he and Cummings set to work shaping their court plan. To veil its intention, they made it part of a broader judicial reform package that would add an extra member to every federal court where a sitting judge failed to retire within six months of his seventieth birthday. But the high bench was the real target. If the plan was approved and none of the sitting justices retired, FDR would have six new appointments and, with the three liberals already on the bench, a solid New Deal majority within weeks or months.

President and attorney general plotted together in secrecy, involving few other aides. FDR revealed his determination to act in his January 1937 annual message to Congress, warning the court that "means must be found to adapt our legal forms and our judicial interpretation to the actual present national needs of the largest progressive democracy in the modern world." But it was not until the morning of the announcement, February 5, that Roosevelt briefed his cabinet and the Democratic congressional leadership. The men who would have to shepherd the controversial proposal through Congress were shocked and angered by FDR's failure to consult them. Senate majority leader Joe Robinson flushed crimson and stared down at the table. On the way back to the Capitol, the powerful chairman of the House Judiciary Committee, Hatton Sumners, said, "Boys, here's where I cash in." It was the first sign that FDR would be in for a hell of a fight.

The most crucial part of that fight would come from the Supreme Court itself. Rather than cast the motive for his plan in its true, ideological light—to combat the evisceration of the New Deal by the court's reactionaries—Roosevelt claimed it was simply a matter of efficiency, managing to sound almost paternalistic in his message to Congress as he lamented the burden of cases on aged justices. Few believed this rationale, and even his allies were dismayed by the president's deviousness. But it gave Charles Evans Hughes his opening.

Not many men looked more like a chief justice than Hughes, with his closely trimmed beard and stately manner. But he was also a political animal—a former New York governor and the Republican who had almost beaten Wilson in 1916, a member of both Harding's and Coolidge's cabinets in the 1920s. When Burton Wheeler, a Senate progressive who was leading the fight against the court plan, invited Hughes to comment with a letter to the Senate Judiciary Committee, Hughes knew exactly what to do. In a long, reasoned analysis of the court's work read to the committee on March 22, the chief justice destroyed Roosevelt's "efficiency" argument.

"The Supreme Court is fully abreast of its work," Hughes wrote. "There is no congestion of cases upon our calendar. This gratifying condition has obtained for several years." FDR's proposal would actually impair the court's efficiency, Hughes suggested. "There would be more judges to hear, more judges to confer, more judges to discuss, more judges to be convinced and to decide." Hughes implied that he was speaking for all his colleagues, but he had consulted only Van Devanter and Brandeis before giving Wheeler the letter. Stone, in particular, who was keeping his own views private—he opposed packing but saw a need for reform—made known his irritation at Hughes's extraordinary intervention. Stone told an editorial writer that he was unaware of Hughes's letter "until I read about it in the paper." Still, the letter had its impact. As Ickes noted, "shrewdly, Hughes chose to fight his skirmish where we were the weakest."

FDR had already realized that weakness. Overconfident at the outset of the fight, by early March he was trying to dampen the furor and rally his own faltering Democratic troops. The efficiency argument receded as the president brought his real motive into the open. With the court's conservatism as his foil, Roosevelt tried to resurrect the transforming leadership of his first term and the combativeness of the 1936 campaign. "We have begun to keep our promises," he proclaimed at a "Democratic Victory Dinner" on March 4, 1937, ". . . we have begun to move against conditions under which one-third of this Nation is still ill-nourished, ill-clad, ill-housed.

"We gave warning last November that we had only just begun to fight. Did some people really believe we did not mean it? Well—I meant it, and you meant it." One by one he listed and lashed out at the Hughes Court's "vetoes" of New Deal reform legislation. And in a radio address a few days later, on March 9, he told listeners that the Supreme Court had failed to pull together with the other branches in the "three horse team" of the national government. Instead, it had "improperly set itself up as a third House of the Congress—a super-legislature." It was time, he said, "to save the Constitution from the Court and the Court from itself."

But on these ideological grounds, too, FDR was soon outmaneuvered by Hughes. The chief justice would save the court from itself. Hughes, of course, would later deny that he or his fellow justices had been influenced to "the slightest degree" by the president's plan, but on March 29, a week after his letter was read out to senators, the Supreme Court announced four decisions that signaled an amazing shift in course. The key case was *West Coast Hotel* v. *Parrish*, where the court, by a 5–4 vote, upheld a Washington state minimum-wage law for women and minors that was substantially the same as a New York law the court had struck down by the identical 5–4 margin just the year before in *Morehead* v. *New York ex rel. Tipaldo*, a decision that had drawn a firestorm of criticism, including Herbert Hoover's. It was Owen Roberts who switched his vote in *West Coast Hotel*—"the switch in time that saved nine," as it came to be called. In fact, Roberts had decided to change his vote when the justices discussed the case in December 1936, before the president unveiled his plan. But that was after FDR's smashing reelection triumph and amid rumors that he intended to confront the brethren. Hughes denied that, in his determination to protect his court from another self-inflicted wound, he had pressed Roberts to change his mind. Twenty years later, Roberts acknowledged that he had been "fully conscious of the tremendous strain and threat" posed by FDR's challenge to the high bench.

Intent on leading the Supreme Court in a new direction, Hughes assigned the *West Coast Hotel* opinion to himself and took the opportunity to disavow the old "liberty of contract" dogma—it was not, he wrote, an "absolute and uncontrollable liberty," but must be "subject to the restraints of due process," including reasonable regulation. Hughes used language that had rarely been heard from the high bench, decrying the "exploitation of a class of workers" who were "defenceless" against their employers.

In a second reversal that same day, the Supreme Court upheld a farm bankruptcy law that Congress passed after the court had unanimously struck down the first one on Black Monday in 1935. The new act was almost the same as the old, and again the justices were unanimous—in reaching the opposite conclusion. They also sustained—again unanimously—new railroad labor legislation, though a few months before, a majority had ruled that labor relations did not fall under the commerce clause and were beyond the reach of federal power. Finally, the court unanimously approved a regulatory tax on firearms, though conservatives had long opposed taxes that were regulatory—rather than revenue-producing—in intent.

Two weeks after this "White Monday," the Supreme Court executed its most astonishing reversal by upholding labor's "Magna Carta"—the Wagner Act, a bill that gave a federal imprimatur to unionization and made the government the ultimate arbiter of industrial relations. The act had carefully been drafted to anticipate the justices' objections, but surveying the dismal field of anti-labor precedents, recent and ancient, most observers predicted a defeat for the New Deal in *National Labor Relations Board* v. *Jones & Laughlin Steel Corp.* Remarkably, the court simply cast aside those precedents, including its rulings in *Schechter* and *Carter*, and recognized, for the first time, "a fundamental right" to organize unions. Giving a broad reading to the commerce clause, Hughes, again writing for the court, acknowledged Congress's "plenary" power to "protect interstate commerce no matter what the source of the dangers which threaten it," including the regulation of labor relations to forestall "the paralyzing consequences of industrial war." Decades of contention over the federal government's authority to tackle the nation's economic problems were briskly put to rest as Hughes took the old jurisprudence to task. "We are asked to shut our eyes to the plainest facts of our national life and to deal with the question of direct and indirect effects in an intellectual vacuum."

The Four Horsemen, who in several of the White Monday cases had submitted grudgingly to Hughes's strategy of foxing FDR, were bitter in their opposition to *Jones & Laughlin*. A reporter in the courtroom described McReynolds "poking his pencil angrily at the crowd as he shouted his opinion" that now "a private owner is deprived of power to manage his own property" by being obliged to deal with unions.

With its decisions in the spring of 1937, the Supreme Court abandoned its historic devotion to laissez faire. If Roosevelt saw this "constitutional revolution" as a threat to his plan, he deftly concealed it. He told reporters that he had been "chortling all morning" about *Jones & Laughlin*. The conservative *New York Herald-Tribune*, he remembered, had carried in 1935 "a beautiful editorial called, 'Thumbs Down on the Wagner Act.'" And now, two years later, the *Trib* was lauding the court for "A Great Decision." "Today," the president said, "is a very, very happy day."

His happiness was short-lived. Harold Ickes thought that the reversals would "weaken the prestige of the Court in public estimation because when it was under fire, the Court ran to cover." In fact, almost the opposite happened. Public support for Roosevelt's court plan, as reflected in polls, had always been unstable. With many Americans torn between anger over the justices' obstruction of the New Deal and the president's tricky, radical proposal to overcome it, the Hughes counteroffensive produced spikes of opposition to packing. *Jones & Laughlin* helped to send support for the plan into a tailspin. Even FDR loyalists now asked, if the court was changing its views, why pack it? But having been trumped repeatedly by Hughes, the president mistrusted the chief justice. After the court had switched a few times, why should the reactionaries, with Hughes's support, not regain the upper hand when the danger had passed? And, as Assistant Attorney General Robert Jackson had told the Senate in hearings over the court bill before White Monday, "when the decision of crucial constitutional issues" could turn on "a single death, or resignation, or change of mind," it would seem "that our constitutional progress is governed by a blind fate instead of by human reason."

Fear of another reversal lessened when in mid-May one of the Horsemen, Van Devanter, announced that he would resign. Ironically, he was taking advantage of a retirement bill Congress had passed in late February in an attempt to deflect FDR's plan, encouraging aged justices to retire by guaranteeing them full pay. And again the question was asked: if the personnel were changing, then why pack the court? On the day Van Devanter resigned, the Senate Judiciary Committee, controlled by Roosevelt's fellow Democrats, condemned the president's plan as a threat "to make this Government one of men rather than one of law," with constitutional interpretation "to be changed with each change of administration." For FDR, who still refused to give in, the court fight was broadening—he now faced challenges to his leadership from within the ranks of his own party.

Then he suffered the climactic blow. In early June, Senate majority leader Joe Robinson had finally persuaded FDR that his plan
was doomed. But Robinson, who had his eye on a court seat, despite
his age and conservatism, promised to push through a compromise
that would allow the president to appoint new justices for each sitting justice over seventy-five, though it would limit him to only one
such appointment a year. While FDR would be denied his instant
New Deal majority, he could claim victory for his principle. But just
as Robinson was loyally leading Senate debate on the compromise,
he suddenly died of a heart attack. All hope for court reform died
with him.

IN OCTOBER 1935, midway in its onslaught on the New Deal,
the Supreme Court had moved into its new home, a stunning edifice
confronting Congress across Capitol Hill. The court had led such
a "nomadic existence" from the start, in political scientist Barbara
Perry's words, that the justices seemed fully deserving of their new
magnificence. The court had first met in a humdrum commercial
building in New York City in 1790; then in Philadelphia the next
year, the court was housed like an afterthought in a succession of
small rooms. From there it moved to Washington, D.C., and a cubby-
hole in the new Capitol, until renovations produced chambers in the
building's basement. Those rooms were wrecked in the burning of
the Capitol by the British in the War of 1812. In 1860, the justices
moved upstairs to a larger room vacated by the Senate when the
solons took over their present chamber.

The idea that "the legislative and judicial branches would share
quarters was anathema to a system of separated powers," Perry
wrote. It was even humiliating in the crowded areas. "For example,
when rooms were at a premium, justices initially had to robe in public before oral argument; when they finally did procure their own

robing room in the Capitol, it was barely large enough for all nine justices and their assistants."

The new courthouse was comfortable, convenient, and commemorative. Its arresting west pediment included, above the inscription EQUAL JUSTICE UNDER LAW, the sculpted faces of chief justices of the Supreme Court, among them William Howard Taft, who had launched the campaign for the new building in 1925. Yet it was by abandoning Taft's militant jurisprudence that the Hughes Court helped to defeat FDR's plan and secure for itself the independent status and power its new shrine represented.

DECADES AFTER THAT defeat historians were still puzzling over Roosevelt's handling of his ill-fated proposal. Why did he prepare his plan in secrecy and spring it on congressional leaders without consultation? Why did he not make court reform a key issue in his 1936 campaign so that he could claim an election mandate for it? Why did he initially offer the plan only as an "efficiency" measure, ignoring the transcending issue of the Supreme Court's extreme negativism and conservatism? Why, in brief, did he fail to offer transformational leadership?

One answer is that the 1936 election had empowered Roosevelt psychologically as well as politically. He had just brought off a stunning personal campaign victory. After winning two gubernatorial and two presidential elections he had a palpable—and justifiable—confidence in his own political judgment, and in the support of the American electorate.

During the election campaign he had rejected—rightly, as the outcome indicated—suggestions that he moderate both his proposals and his oratory. He was determined to offer voters a clear choice between his New Deal and those Republican policies that had triggered—and then failed to cope with—the Great Depression.

The Supreme Court's conduct was implicit in his assaults on the old order—it was, after all, the last federal stronghold of the extreme right—yet he sensed the regard many Americans had for it despite its anti–New Deal decisions. Hence he was reluctant to take it on directly until his reelection was secured.

But having won that overwhelming mandate, he hobbled himself by grasping the anemic and devious cause of "efficiency," instead of bluntly attacking the Supreme Court's hard-right verdicts. FDR calculated at first that the cause of adding "fresh blood" to the judiciary would trigger the least controversy. He neither expected nor wanted the proposal to become the center of a raging ideological, political, and personal dispute that would spin out of his control and blight his second term. Strangely for a leader who had appealed so widely to voters in elections, he sought to narrow the struggle rather than broaden it. He displayed a lack of courage in sharp contrast to the audacity he demonstrated in many fights before and after the court battle.

Did Roosevelt have other options? Could he have risen above the turmoil that dragged him down into a personality fracas, where the issue became his "dictatorial" ambitions? Could he have raised the struggle to the supreme issue of judicial *rule*? Remarkably, FDR at times seemed to be flirting with a strategic possibility that would have dwarfed his court-packing tactics.

In his radio talk early in March 1937, at the height of the court fight, he brought his listeners back to 1803, when the Supreme Court in *Marbury* v. *Madison* held that a law passed by Congress "violated an express provision of the Constitution," Roosevelt said. "The Court claimed the power to declare it unconstitutional and did so declare it. But a little later the Court itself admitted that it was an extraordinary power to exercise and through Mr. Justice Washington laid down this limitation on it: 'It is but a decent respect due to the wisdom, the integrity and the patriotism of the legislative body, by which any law is passed, to presume in favor of its validity until its violation of the Constitution is proved beyond all reasonable doubt.'

"But since the rise of the modern movement for social and economic progress through legislation, the Court has more and more often and more and more boldly asserted a power to veto laws passed by the Congress and State Legislatures in complete disregard of this original limitation.

"In the last four years the sound rule of giving statutes the benefit of all reasonable doubt has been cast aside. The Court has been acting not as a judicial body, but as a policy-making body."

One hundred and thirty years after *Marbury*, Roosevelt was counterattacking John Marshall, charging that judicial review was in fact judicial *rule*, since the court's "policy-making" was subject to no check or limitation from the elected branches.

Six months later, in September 1937, on the 150th anniversary of the Constitution's signing at the convention in Philadelphia, after he had lost the battle over the court, Roosevelt was even more explicit and confrontational.

"The Constitution of the United States was a layman's document, not a lawyer's contract," he declared. "*That* cannot be stressed too often. . . .

"Contrary to the belief of many Americans, the Constitution says nothing about any power of the Court to declare legislation unconstitutional; nor does it mention the number of judges for the Court. Again and again the Convention voted down proposals to give Justices of the Court a veto over legislation. Clearly a majority of the delegates believed that the relation of the Court to the Congress and the Executive, like the other subjects treated in general terms, would work itself out by evolution and change over the years.

"But for one hundred and fifty years we have had an unending struggle between those who would preserve this original broad concept of the Constitution as a layman's instrument of government and those who would shrivel the Constitution into a lawyer's contract."

Roosevelt spoke with such passion and so militantly that listeners might have expected him to proclaim a new plan that would attempt what his packing proposal had not—to challenge the Supreme Court's power at its roots by calling into question the constitutional underpinnings of judicial review, contesting the court's exclusive hold on constitutional interpretation, and mobilizing the "lay rank and file" to wrest that authority from the "highest-priced lawyers." But he offered no new program or strategy. In the parlance of the day, the Constitution Day speech ended not with a bang but a whimper—a history lesson.

The truth was that the president was stymied. He had lost a power showdown with the right. His court plan had mobilized not the "lay rank and file" of the grand coalition that swept him to victory in 1936, but battalions of hard-core Republicans, the GOP press, Southern Democrats, and a host of other foes. Even worse, his own coalition lay in splinters. He could see no way out.

CHAPTER NINE

"Wild Horses": The Roosevelt Court

SUDDENLY, with the resignation of one of the Four Horsemen, Willis Van Devanter, in May 1937, at the height of the court-packing fight, the wheel of fortune began to spin again, with a vengeance. For Franklin Roosevelt, still simmering over defeat, it was a consoling time—he would now pack the court the old-fashioned way, by presidential appointment, and as thoroughly as he could have wished. In six short years of his second and third terms, 1937 to 1943, FDR would make nine appointments to the high bench, more than any president since George Washington, and by the end of it, only Harlan Fiske Stone and Owen Roberts would remain from the old court.

In 1945, his last year before resigning his seat in frustration, Roberts filed fifty-three dissents, a measure of how utterly Roosevelt had transformed the court. The old guard was swept away, replaced by stalwart and even partisan New Dealers. There was nary a railroad lawyer among them, and few had previous judicial experience. They were mostly young, dynamic men of diverse backgrounds, a perfect counterimage to their crusty Republican predecessors. FDR could enjoy a sweet measure of revenge for the failure of his court-packing bill as he turned the old order upside down.

Roosevelt started with Senator Hugo Black of Alabama, whom he named to replace Van Devanter in August 1937, when the gun shells of the court fight still reverberated. FDR relished the surprise appointment of what reporters described as an "absolute anomaly—an intellectual leftist liberal from below the Mason and Dixon line." Black was a leading New Dealer and an outspoken supporter of the court plan. But Roosevelt reckoned that senators would support one of their own, whatever their misgivings. "They'll have to take him," the president blithely told Democratic party boss Jim Farley. He was right. Conservatives fulminated—a Georgia congressman denounced the nomination as "the worst insult that has yet been given to the nation"—but five days after FDR sent his name up, the Senate duly endorsed Black, 63–16.

Then, a month later, the bombshell. Opponents to Black's nomination had pointed out that he had run for office with the backing of the Ku Klux Klan. A Pittsburgh newspaper now revealed that in the 1920s Black had actually been a *member* of the Alabama Klan, sworn to defend "white supremacy." African-American leaders were enraged, along with Catholics who had long been targeted by the Klan, fellow Democrats in the Senate, and liberals across the country. Black feebly rebutted the charges in a radio talk that lacked even a repudiation of the Klan. However surprised and embarrassed Roosevelt might have felt—and angered by Black's failure to level with him before the nomination—he was outwardly imperturbable. Black's defense "did the trick," he told Farley, "you just wait and see." What actually did the trick was FDR's unwillingness, after months of charges of tampering with the court, to remedy what a Washington newsletter termed a "prime presidential boner" by trying to push Black out of his seat. Nor did the Senate have the stomach for a fight over racism. But it was an ugly start to Black's long tenure as a justice.

If Black was controversial, FDR's second nominee, Stanley Reed, appeared almost bland. Still, he was a man of parts. After studying law at the University of Virginia, Columbia, and the Sorbonne, he returned to his county seat in Kentucky, plunged into local Democratic politics, and at age twenty-eight won a seat in the state's General Assembly. After moving to Washington, he managed the feat of serving in major posts under both Hoover and Roosevelt, who appointed him solicitor general in 1935. In that job, Reed was one of the few insiders to help the president prepare the court plan. He had also argued—and lost—major New Deal cases before the court whose foremost reactionary, George Sutherland, he was now replacing.

FDR liked to tease his appointees before offering them the nomination. "Well, Stanley," he said in an unexpected phone call to Reed in January 1938, "I'm afraid I'm going to have to ask you to resign the Solicitor Generalship." The president paused. "Yes, I've just sent your name up in nomination for the vacancy of Justice Sutherland on the Supreme Court. Won't you come over and have lunch with me today?"

Felix Frankfurter, Roosevelt's third pick for the court, to replace Cardozo, who died in July 1938, could hardly have contrasted more in background with either Black or Reed. Born in Vienna of a well-to-do Jewish family, he emigrated to the United States while still a boy. After graduating from Harvard Law School in 1906, he spent a few years in legal work in Washington, but he yearned for the academic life of Harvard, where shortly he joined the law faculty and never left it—until FDR placed him on the high bench. Like Brandeis, to whom his relationship was "half brother, half son," Frankfurter had never run for public office. Still, he was a liberal activist, the mentor to a host of young New Dealers, and had become a close and frequent adviser to FDR himself.

By the late 1930s, Frankfurter's reputation as scholar and activist and his White House entrée had made him a much-mentioned candidate for the Supreme Court. But for Roosevelt there were three problems, about which he was candid with "Felix." The Harvard professor was viewed by conservatives as a foreign-born radical; he was not a westerner when the court needed more geographical balance; and by replacing the Jewish Cardozo, he might, in the words of the publisher William Allen White, a friend of both Frankfurter and FDR, "give the Jew baiters a chance to say that the Jews have pre-empted a seat in the Court." Roosevelt also might have had misgivings about Frankfurter's attitude during the court fight. The Harvard professor had been a leading critic of justices who "identified the Constitution with their private social philosophy" and had even favored a constitutional amendment to override the Supreme Court's restrictions on federal power. FDR's plan, though, struck Frankfurter as a reckless assault on the court's independence, and he was unwilling to speak up for it publicly.

Eventually the pressure from Frankfurter's friends—many close to the White House—forced the president's hand. Frankfurter finally got the call on January 4, 1939, while in underwear, changing for dinner in his Brattle Street home in Cambridge.

"You know," the president began, "I told you I don't want to appoint you to the Supreme Court. . . ."

Roosevelt had to wait only a few weeks to get his westerner, when Brandeis retired after twenty-three years on the court. William O. Douglas was the real thing, growing up in Washington state in a village of one hundred people thirty miles north of the Columbia River. He had a Horatio Alger life, working in orchards and packing fruit, but later graduating from Whitman College and then teaching school. Still impecunious, he took a freight train east, paying his way by tending the sheep aboard. In New York, he managed to enter Columbia Law School, graduating second in his class. After only a year or two as a working lawyer he secured a post at the Yale Law School, where he made connections with movers and shakers who were in turn connected with New York and Washington. In the process he became an expert in securities law, leading to his appointment in 1937 as head of FDR's recently established Securities and Exchange Commission. He joined the White House inner circle in both politicking and poker.

Summoned one day in March 1939 to the Oval Office, he was greeted by the president, who told him, "I have a new job for you. It's a mean job, a dirty job, a thankless job. . . .

"It's a job you'll detest. . . .

"This job is something like being in jail. . . .

"Tomorrow I am sending your name to the Senate as Louis Brandeis' successor."

The very morning Justice Pierce Butler died in November 1939, giving FDR his fifth vacancy in two and a half years, Roosevelt told his attorney general, Frank Murphy, that he would name him as Butler's successor. Described as motivated by a "blend of Catholic piety and Progressive idealism," Murphy had a sweetness of nature that some saw as bordering on sanctimoniousness. As mayor of Detroit and Michigan governor during the turbulent Depression years, Murphy became a leading New Dealer at the grassroots. As governor, he weathered the violent 1937 sitdown strikes in the auto industry, but fell afoul of the nationwide electoral swing against Democrats in 1938. As FDR's attorney general, Murphy would give concise expression to the New Deal's conception of the judicial role, embracing what he called the "broader view that the law is properly a positive instrument for human betterment."

WITH MURPHY'S NOMINATION, FDR now had a solid court majority of New Dealers who broadly shared his latest appointee's view of the law. But the president wasn't done yet. Roosevelt's successful run in 1940 for an unprecedented third term as the nation faced a new emergency—the global threat of militaristic fascism—would soon give him the opportunity to continue his overhaul of the Supreme Court.

The judicial wheel of fortune was still spinning. Early in 1941, a few weeks after Roosevelt's reelection, Justice McReynolds at last announced his retirement. He had fought the good conservative fight to the end, denouncing the Social Security Act as illegal, standing up for the purity and sanctity of property rights and liberty of contract, damning the new court's betrayal of the Constitution. And he had been personally obnoxious to his fellow justices—especially his Jewish colleagues—to the end.

Strange to say, FDR's man to replace the last of the Horsemen was no liberal activist, but the most conservative of New Dealers—James F. Byrnes. His life was the classic rags-to-riches tale: His father died shortly after his birth in Charleston, and Byrnes left school at fourteen to help support the family. After passing the bar, he made a successful run for a seat in the House, and then won a Senate seat on his second try. Despite his conservatism, Byrnes was an early FDR loyalist, and though their relations had cooled slightly in the president's second term, Roosevelt had given him reason to hope for the vice-presidential slot on the 1940 ticket. Perhaps it was partly to assuage that disappointment—and to eliminate a potential rival for the presidency in 1944—that FDR, after a delay of some months, named him to the court in June 1941, though, as a reporter observed, "he was losing the smoothest, most effective worker he ever had in the Senate, at the same time acquiring an unknown quantity for the Court."

If Byrnes was a slightly mystifying appointment, it proved to be less than momentous. It turned out that Byrnes was not happy on the court. The deliberative and cloistered world of the justices was uncongenial to his activist temperament. He also had unslaked political ambition. With the administration mobilizing the country for war after the attack on Pearl Harbor and new fields for action and achievement opening up, Byrnes declared, "I don't think I can stand the abstractions of jurisprudence at a time like this." After little more than a year, he bolted the bench to become what FDR called the "assistant President" with oversight of the domestic war economy.

Robert H. Jackson, appointed at the same time as Byrnes, was much more FDR's type of guy. He was a fellow New Yorker with roots in Jamestown in the western reaches of the state. After a year at Albany Law—he never really attended college—he became a small-town attorney. He first hooked up with Roosevelt during World War I, when as a county Democratic leader, he looked to FDR, then assistant secretary of the navy, for help with federal patronage. Jackson joined the New Deal in 1934 as a tax reformer in the Treasury Department and soon moved over to Justice, where he defended the court plan and would produce one of the most influential critiques of the old court and its politicized use of judicial power to block democratic movements and reduce governments to helplessness. Jackson's devotion to the New Deal won him the gratitude and admiration of FDR, who began to think of him as a possible successor in the White House. Early in 1938, he urged Jackson to run for his old job of governor of New York, as a step toward the presidency. When Jackson declined—he thought of himself as a man of law more than of politics—FDR put him on an upward trajectory for the Supreme Court. He succeeded Reed as solicitor general in 1938, where, as the government's chief advocate, he had the luck to argue the New Deal's case before a more sympathetic bench than Reed had faced. Two years later, he followed Murphy as attorney general and two years after that, onto the Supreme Court.

Byrnes's resignation in October 1942 gave the president a ninth— and last—appointment. He turned to a man he had first considered for the Supreme Court in 1939, Wiley Rutledge, a native Kentuckian and legal academic who had held senior positions at several universities. Asked in the 1930s to describe his legal philosophy, Rutledge said, "I am not a radical in any sense of the word, but I cannot remain blind to the ills of the present system, and I am interested in seeing them remedied as far as possible." This qualified him as a liberal in legal circles; while at the University of Iowa, moreover, he was one of the few prominent academics outspokenly in favor of the court plan. His stand led Iowa legislators to threaten to withhold faculty salary raises—and brought him to FDR's attention. The president appointed him to the U.S. Court of Appeals for the District of Columbia Circuit, where he delivered reliably pro–New Deal opinions and became a natural choice for the high bench.

"WHILE THE chief justice has only one vote," Charles Evans Hughes had written in 1928, "the way in which the Court does its work gives him a special opportunity for leadership." He had used that leadership potential to save the Supreme Court's independence by beating back FDR's offensive in 1937. When the president went on to take over Hughes's court by his powers of appointment, the chief justice made the most of his authority, even when confronted by FDR's headstrong appointees, by dominating the court's weekly conference and tactically assigning opinions to his colleagues. He won praise from Felix Frankfurter for his "mastery" of the business of the court. To see him preside, Frankfurter effused, was "like witnessing Toscanini lead an orchestra." Not that all the associates submitted to the maestro's baton. "I don't work for Hughes," McReynolds was heard to mutter when a messenger came to summon the tardy old man to conference.

Like John Marshall, as Robert Steamer, a student of Supreme Court leadership, would conclude, Hughes "was not a philosopher but a practitioner of the first rank." And as practitioner, his greatest contribution was the recognition, pressed upon him most forcefully by the perils of 1937, that with the Depression and the New Deal's response to it, laissez faire was dead, and that denial of that reality had led the court into discredit and danger. So Hughes adapted. In fact, he recovered some of his own early moderate progressivism, often siding in significant cases with the court's young New Dealers, even sometimes leading them, while the remaining Horsemen huddled in angry dissent.

Hughes retired from the Supreme Court in July 1941 and died seven years later. Most court observers assumed that Roosevelt would choose a Democrat to succeed him, given FDR's party loyalty, but the president had other thoughts. With Adolf Hitler rampaging through Europe, and Japan challenging the United States across the wide Pacific, he was more intent on unifying the country. Leading Democrats as well as Republicans were calling for a liberal Republican such as Justice Harlan Fiske Stone.

After 1937, Stone's role on the Supreme Court had grown. As the personnel changed, Stone felt liberated from the burdens of chronic dissent and eagerly seized opportunities to write his convictions into law. "With Sutherland off the Court," he wrote in 1938, "I have been getting rather more interesting opinions." At the same time, he undertook to serve as balance to the more doctrinaire of his new colleagues, especially Hugo Black, who appeared to Stone to rival George Sutherland for dogmatism. Each adopted "a fatal way of interpreting an instrument of government," he believed, and lacked the flexibility to treat it as "a living instrument." By the time of Hughes's retirement, Stone had become an unofficial spokesman for the court and its most respected figure. Roosevelt expected that as chief justice he would continue to support New Deal economic reforms—and he did.

Less expected was Stone's pioneering support of civil liberties, which he did not trumpet in a newsworthy opinion but revealed in a *footnote*—perhaps the most consequential footnote in American judicial history. He inserted it into a run-of-the-mill opinion for the court, *U.S. v. Carolene Products*, a 1938 case involving the interstate transportation of milk. After setting a high threshold for judicial review of regulatory laws—as long as they had at least a "rational basis" they would pass constitutional muster—Stone added, in footnote 4, that "more exacting judicial inquiry" should be applied to laws that restricted civil liberties and civil and political rights or were directed at "discrete and insular minorities." Thus, economic legislation would, as New Dealers had demanded, be given the presumption of constitutionality, but laws affecting individual rights would face "a narrower scope for operation of the presumption of constitutionality." In a phrase Stone later coined and the court eventually adopted, Bill of Rights liberties were to have a "preferred position" in constitutional law.

The significance of the *Carolene* footnote was not only in its privileging of civil rights and liberties. It signaled a dramatic shift in the Supreme Court's agenda. For decades, the court's focus had been on economic legislation, creating a long conflict over the powers of government to regulate industry and commerce. But, as Stone's *Carolene* opinion itself affirmed, that issue was settled. Now a new set of issues would move to the fore—the powers of an ever larger and potentially more intrusive and controlling government to limit individual rights and liberties. As Stone's *Carolene* footnote forecast, the court would take on the role of the arbiter, an assertion of judicial power over acts of the legislature and executive that would prove at least as fertile a source of conflict as property rights and the liberty of contract had been. At stake was nothing less than how, in diverse ways, Americans lived their lives as private and public citizens.

One of the first civil liberties decisions under Stone's chief justiceship exemplified the divisions such cases could spawn as well as the

Supreme Court's willingness to exert its authority in this new realm. California had passed an "anti-Okie" law designed to stop the stream of indigent immigrants uprooted by the Depression. In considering *Edwards* v. *California*, in 1941, some justices held that the California act abridged a "fundamental right" to move freely among the states that was protected by the Fourteenth Amendment, and stigmatized the indigent as an inferior class of citizens. Others believed that the law could be invalidated for interfering with interstate commerce. After lengthy negotiation by Stone, the court divided three ways— but the offending statute was unanimously invalidated. Reflecting on the decision, Stone said he was getting "the job" so organized that "it will run on smoothly if I can get my team of wild horses to pull together."

That remained to be seen. The *Wall Street Journal* noted the justices' "tendency to fall into clamorous argument even on the rare occasions when they agreed on the end result." In Stone's first term as chief justice, nonunanimous opinions ran to 36 percent of the total, the highest in the court's history to that time. The justices broke their own record the next year with 44 percent of opinions nonunanimous. By 1943, Stone was not referring to a "team of wild horses" but lamenting his "collection of fleas." He was, he acknowledged, having "much difficulty herding" them.

How had FDR's fully packed court split so bitterly? At first that bench had seemed a center of harmony for liberal members. Black was pleased by Frankfurter's nomination, and Frankfurter and Douglas started out with mutual respect. But as old and new problems confronted the Supreme Court, differences simmered and finally boiled over. The justices divided in myriad ways; inchoate factions formed, only to disappear and reappear again. But the most persistent blocs massed around the court's dominant personalities, Black and Frankfurter, and their conflict over the fundamental issue of judicial power.

Each man had taken a different lesson from the reactionary activism of the old court. For Frankfurter, this meant that the justices should not be assertive policy-makers, but approach issues with restraint and balance and give the political branches the benefit of the constitutional doubt. And so Frankfurter and his followers—usually Reed, Byrnes, and Jackson—believed that the Supreme Court should have mainly a negative role, intervening only in clear-cut cases of unconstitutionality and limiting its intervention to narrow, incremental steps. For Black and his bloc—most notably Douglas, with Murphy and Rutledge as regular allies—the trouble with the old court was that it was reactionary, not that it was activist. For liberal causes—social and economic reforms, civil liberties, especially free speech—the Supreme Court should act assertively, marking out clear and bright lines to mandate or restrict government action. Thus, in the case of civil liberties, Black embraced the "preferred position" doctrine with a fervor and rigor that far surpassed Stone's commitment. But to Frankfurter, "preferred position" was just a "mischievous phrase," and he scorned the use of a footnote as the "way of announcing a new constitutional doctrine."

That neither side had a stable majority of justices only intensified the conflict. Even Frankfurter and Black voted inconsistently, especially as the darkening world scene and the American response to it made issues of individual rights and liberties more urgent and complex.

RISING BELLICOSITY abroad in the late 1930s inevitably set off a rush of American patriotism. Many states, for example, compelled children to salute the flag at the start of the school day. But for the religious sect of the Jehovah's Witnesses, to salute the flag was to violate God's commandment against bowing down to graven images. In 1936, in his Pennsylvania town, a Witness named Walter Gobitis challenged the law. When *Minersville School District* v.

Gobitis reached the Supreme Court four years later, the justices rallied behind Frankfurter's patriotic opinion that "national unity is the basis of national security" and that the Gobitis children could not be excused "from conduct required of all other children in the promotion of national cohesion." All the justices signed on but one—Stone dissented, convinced that the court should strike down the law.

Frankfurter was shocked and pleaded with Stone that the Supreme Court must not hold "with too tight a rein the organs of popular government." Stone replied that the "vulgar intrusion of law into the domain of conscience" thrust a larger responsibility on the court. In his dissent, Stone cited his own footnote in *Carolene* to remind Frankfurter of "the importance of a searching judicial inquiry into the legislative judgment in situations where prejudice against discrete and insular minorities" led the government to attempt to compel "conformity of belief and opinion." But Stone stood alone. Frankfurter conducted no searching inquiry. Behind his mantle of judicial restraint, Frankfurter ratified a law whose purpose he approved. The choice, he wrote to Stone, was "between legislatively allowable pursuit of national security"—the flag salute!—"and the right to stand on individual idiosyncracies." Frankfurter's decision for the flag triggered a wave of attacks on "idiosyncratic" Witnesses.

But two years later, in 1942, Witnesses in West Virginia renewed the challenge to flag-salute laws. By then, Black, Douglas, and Murphy had come to regret siding with Frankfurter in *Gobitis*. In yet another Witness case, *Jones* v. *Opelika*, decided in June 1942, the majority had sustained a licensing tax on the sale of goods, including religious tracts, on the street or from house to house. Black, Douglas, and Murphy had dissented, agreeing with the Witnesses that the tax infringed their religious liberty. The three had added a note to their dissent, writing that *Gobitis* had been "wrongly decided." Echoing Stone's *Carolene* footnote, they argued that under the Bill of Rights, the government had "a high responsibility to accommodate itself to the religious views of minorities, however unpopular and unortho-dox those views may be." It was in his own dissent in *Opelika* that Stone coined the phrase "preferred position."

In the never-ending roulette of judicial appointments, Jackson and Rutledge had joined the court in time to hear *West Virginia Board of Education* v. *Barnette*, the new flag-salute case. Frankfurter's usual ally, Robert Jackson, surprised him by voting to overturn the *Gobitis* flag-salute decision, and in fact he authored an opinion that tore Frankfurter's earlier holding to shreds. Announcing the court's decision in June 1943, Jackson zeroed in on Frankfurter's extreme portrait of the flag as a symbol of national unity, concluding that "if there is any fixed star in our constitutional constellation, it is that no official, high or petty, can prescribe what shall be orthodox in politics, nationalism, religion, or other matters of opinion or force citizens to confess by word or act their faith therein." Five justices concurred with Jackson. Stung, Frankfurter lectured his colleagues on restraint, writing that "this Court's only and very narrow func-tion" was to decide whether a legislative act had merely "reasonable justification." The court could not serve as "the primary protec-tor" of liberty, striking down laws by some "undefined destructive power" that "was not conferred on this Court by the Constitution." He threw at his brethren the charge New Dealers had leveled at the old court—they were acting like a super-legislature, restricting "the powers of democratic government."

Frankfurter suffered further reversal the same year when new justice Rutledge joined the four *Opelika* dissenters—Stone and the repentant trio—to overturn that decision by a 5–4 margin in another licensing case involving Witnesses, *Murdock* v. *Pennsylvania*, with Douglas writing that "freedom of press, freedom of speech, freedom of religion are in a preferred position."

On the controversial issue of free speech for "reds," in *Schneider-man* v. *U.S.*, a case decided in 1943, Frankfurter voted to approve the

Justice Department's effort to strip citizenship from a naturalized citizen because of his activities as an outspoken Communist. Again the principle was judicial restraint—Congress should be allowed to set conditions for citizenship and the executive to enforce them—but Frankfurter's instinct was deeply personal, based in his own experiences as a naturalized American. Loyal citizenship, Frankfurter said, could not be reconciled with commitment to the "holy cause" of communism. "No man can serve two masters," he told his colleagues. But he was in the minority, along with Roberts and—surprisingly— Stone, who not long before in *Gobitis* had stood alone for nonconformity in belief and opinion. For the majority, Justice Murphy held that the government had not proven that a belief in ideas was incompatible with loyalty to the Constitution. "Criticism of, and the sincerity of desires to improve, the Constitution," Murphy wrote, "should not be judged by conformity to prevailing thought."

But in other cases, Frankfurter had the votes. On the divisive issue of labor picketing, he wrote for the majority in 1941 that in violent situations, free speech lost its meaning "as an appeal to reason" and became "an instrument of force." Black, Reed, and Douglas blasted him for using the violent acts of a few individuals to suppress the speech rights of thousands of union members.

Such a sharply divided court producing wildly inconsistent opinions underlined the novelty of the Supreme Court's immersion in issues of civil liberties. The justices had relatively few precedents to guide them—and those too were often inconsistent. With the court lurching between restraint and activism, at stake was whether it would indeed use its powers of judicial review to assume guardianship of the rights and liberties of Americans.

IN 1944, the Supreme Court faced its most daunting human rights issue and ended up with a moral disaster. Two years before, early in

1942, as Japanese naval forces were advancing relentlessly east across the Pacific, President Roosevelt had asked Congress for authority to move Japanese Americans, both foreign and native born, out of restricted military areas in California and other states. Over 100,000 Americans—men, women, and children—were forced out of their homes and transported to remote areas, where they were confined in so-called relocation centers by armed guards behind barbed wire.

Roosevelt was responding to a public aroused by fear and racism that was fed by demagogic commentators like Westbrook Pegler, who wrote, "to hell with *habeas corpus* until the danger is over." Even the magisterial columnist Walter Lippmann threw his prestige behind the rising hysteria, opining that "nobody's constitutional rights include the right to reside and do business on a battle field." The official reason of course was the Japanese threat to the West Coast. But the lengthy and distant Hawaiian Islands stood in the path of such an invasion—and, even though the naval base at Pearl Harbor was attacked, authorities made no proposal to "relocate" tens of thousands of Japanese Americans living in Hawaii.

In an early case, *Hirabayashi* v. *U.S.*, that challenged a curfew aimed at Japanese Americans before they were interned, a unanimous Supreme Court accepted the military's justification of the curfew's necessity, holding that in wartime, the government should be given "wide scope" in "every phase of the national defense."

In 1944, Fred Korematsu, who had been convicted of disobeying the relocation order, charged that the entire program violated the Constitution by depriving citizens of their liberty without a shred of due process. Now the court divided. Stone wanted narrowly to affirm the *Hirabayashi* holding that the justices would not second-guess the military. But Black, while he was ready to rule against Korematsu, bowing once more to the "military imperative," wanted to make clear in his opinion for the court that only "the gravest imminent danger" justified detention. Meanwhile, Murphy, Jackson, and Roberts all regretted their concurrence in *Hirabayashi* and planned to dissent, while Douglas was on the fence, even drafting a four-page dissent, before Black, Frankfurter, and Stone teamed up to persuade him to join the majority and to put the Supreme Court's great authority, here expressed as judicial modesty, behind a racist policy and the creation of American-style concentration camps.

Black never disavowed his holding in *Korematsu*, but Douglas wrote in his memoirs that he "always regretted that I bowed to my elders." He eased that burden somewhat by authoring, late in 1944, an order for the release of a Japanese-American woman, Mitsuye Endo, from a Utah concentration camp. That case was an easy one, as the court's unanimity showed. It did not challenge the internment program but asked whether Endo could be detained even after the government had conceded her loyalty. Douglas's answer was clear: "once loyalty is shown, the basis for the military decision disappears—this woman is entitled to a summary release." But with the war approaching its end and the Japanese threat to the West Coast long since recognized as a chimera, *Ex parte Endo* could not erase the court's fateful deference to military authority at the expense of the rights of thousands of loyal Americans. It was, as Murphy wrote in his *Korematsu* dissent, the "legalization of racism" and would remain a huge blot on the court's standing.

STRICKEN IN COURT on a late April day in 1946, Chief Justice Stone died at home a few hours later at the age of seventy-four. For all his qualities as a jurist, Stone had failed to lead his court. Unlike his predecessors Taft and Hughes, Stone was reluctant to use high-pressure tactics to marshal his colleagues or to push them to decision. His mild style allowed the court's stronger personalities— notably the antagonists Black and Frankfurter—to dominate. As a result, divisions deepened and personal animosities festered.

Columnist Max Lerner thought it salutary that the Stone Court, with its sharp, noisy divisions and conflicting judgments, could make no pretense to "Olympian infallibility," but inasmuch as it retained its power as the ultimate constitutional authority, the Supreme Court's erratic course, especially in the new domain of civil liberties, made it an uncertain guardian of the people's rights and freedoms. That was reflected in its fading prestige. By 1946, the court's disharmony was public and notorious, and when President Truman sought Stone's successor, he looked for a man who would "smooth over the discords on the highest bench."

Two months after Stone's death, Truman chose Fred Vinson for the center chair. Vinson was a natural choice for the Missouri politician who had succeeded FDR only a year before. Born in a Kentucky hamlet fifty-six years earlier, Vinson had served six terms in the House and five years as a federal judge before taking key positions overseeing the wartime economy. Earlier, in a bipartisan spirit, Truman had named Republican senator Harold Burton to the Supreme Court, following Justice Roberts's resignation. In 1949, Truman appointed two more justices, both Democrats—his attorney general, Tom Clark, a protégé of the Texans like Sam Rayburn who presided over the House, and Sherman Minton, senator from Indiana.

The new justices had much in common. They were all close friends of the president—Vinson and Clark were his poker-playing pals—and became his personal picks, made with little consultation. They all supported stronger, more effective government while urging judicial self-restraint. In general they did not like to challenge presidential and congressional authority. In his seven years as chief justice, Vinson never voted to hold a congressional statute unconstitutional. The new justices produced, for the first time, a stable majority for Frankfurterian restraint. At a time of increasing conflict over domestic communism, this brought a series of victories in the government's campaign to suppress Communists and their fellow travelers, cast in Frankfurterian terms of deference to Congress's determination that, as the 1950 McCarran Act declared, the "secret, conspiratorial" Communist party was a "clear and present danger to the security of the United States and to the existence of free American institutions."

Still, the arrival of the Truman justices did little to curtail the court's divisions. None of them—certainly not Vinson—was a match for the powerful personalities of the Roosevelt Court, whose feuds were fed by a vicious circle of doctrinal differences and personal hostility. And Frankfurter, with his cautious balancing, was often at odds with his Truman colleagues, who were inclined almost invariably to rubber-stamp the actions of the elected branches. He would not endorse, as Vinson did in *Dennis* v. *U.S.* in 1951, the prosecution of twelve Communist leaders for violating the 1940 Smith Act, which made it a crime to advocate violent revolution; all he would say was that "Congress was not forbidden by the Constitution to pass" that law. He showered his new brethren with harangues and snide remarks as he had his fellow New Dealers, once nearly provoking amiable Fred Vinson to fisticuffs. This would lead to a tentative—and temporary—rapprochement with Black by the early 1950s, but Frankfurter continued to give Black's ally, William Douglas, the silent treatment for long stretches of time.

The temper of the Vinson Court appeared glaringly in the most fraught of the Cold War cases, the convictions of Julius and Ethel Rosenberg for espionage. Julius was a Communist who had transmitted sketchy information about the American nuclear weapons program to the Soviet Union for a brief period in 1944–45—it was never established that he played a significant role in the Soviet Union's development of the atomic bomb. Ethel was charged to pressure her husband to cooperate with the government—she was never shown to have been an active spy. But the Rosenbergs became scapegoats in the national security hysteria of the early Cold War. Their trial

judge blamed their "diabolical conspiracy" for fifty thousand casualties in the Korean War, and "who knows but that millions more of
innocent people may pay the price for your treason."

Sentenced to death in 1952, the Rosenbergs repeatedly petitioned
the Supreme Court for review. Black and Frankfurter favored hearing the case, but Douglas's was the crucial vote. Twice he voted
against review and also cast a decisive vote against a stay. But on
June 17, 1953, the day before the scheduled execution, Douglas issued
his own dramatic stay, writing that "before we allow human lives
to be snuffed out we [must] be sure—emphatically sure—that we
act within the law." Frankfurter was disgusted; he felt it was typical Douglas "grandstanding." With the court having adjourned for
the summer, Vinson summoned the justices to convene for a "special term" within twenty-four hours, in what Black called "a race for
death." After a brief hearing, the stay was lifted—with only Black,
Frankfurter, and Douglas voting no—and the Rosenbergs were sent
to their deaths. It was, a Frankfurter clerk noted, the climax of the
Vinson Court's submission to "the loyalty-security mania and the
xenophobia of the day."

Two years earlier, upholding the conviction of the Communist
leaders in *Dennis*, Frankfurter had written, "History teaches that the
independence of the judiciary is jeopardized when courts become
embroiled in the passions of the day and assume primary responsibility in choosing between competing political, economic and
social pressures."

This was a noble lesson of judicial restraint drawn from the sear-
ing trials of 1937, but also strangely obtuse. Frankfurter seemed to
take for granted that his own stance of restraint would insulate the
Supreme Court from choice among competing pressures, that it was
a position of neutrality detached from political decision-making.
Not only the court's long history but Frankfurter's own experiences
should have taught him that nothing could have been further from

the truth. His own perceptions as to what was necessary for "national cohesion," what constituted loyal citizenship or a threat to national security, conditioned—even determined—the extent of "deference" he would show to political leaders. Frankfurter, after all, never forswore the Supreme Court's assumed power to review the acts of the political branches. If the justices did not have "primary responsibility" for policy, they retained an ultimate supremacy over it. Frankfurter's restraint was merely a question of degree, and the answer to that question in particular cases involved choices that inevitably were political. As the wavering course of the Roosevelt Court in the field of civil liberties showed all too dramatically, justices—whether activists or practitioners of restraint—could not avoid embroilment "in the passions of the day."

CHAPTER TEN

Leadership: The Warren Court

AFTER THE 1930s collision between the FDR steamroller and the old Republican court ended with the triumph of the New Deal, some expected the Supreme Court to settle back into a stable and even mundane existence. This was not to be. The court swung sharply to the left, then zigzagged, as New Dealers divided and clashed, and some carefully selected appointees turned out to be surprises. Felix Frankfurter, the young Harvard professor and New Dealer who had been a close friend to FDR, turned into one of the most conservative justices, as did FDR's protégé Robert Jackson.

In the game of judicial roulette, though, such surprises weren't confined to Democrats. After Dwight Eisenhower in 1952 became the first Republican elected president in a quarter century, he named to the Supreme Court a party stalwart who had run a failed campaign for the GOP's presidential nomination and had once been its candidate for the vice presidency, Governor Earl Warren of

California. Warren had also spearheaded the wartime removal of Japanese Americans from the West Coast, warning that they could bring a "repetition of Pearl Harbor" to the American mainland. But he would, as chief justice, metamorphose into the most liberal leader of the Supreme Court in American history. Under his leadership, the court would move deeply into such controversial areas as black rights and civil liberties and voting power, and assert itself as the most dynamic branch of American government. By making the Supreme Court a center of progressive reform, Warren would forge a luminous exception to the court's historic role as the bulwark of anti-democratic, anti-egalitarian conservatism.

Dwight Eisenhower promised to modernize the GOP, to rid it of bitter-enders who still sought to overturn the New Deal, while replacing Democratic liberal crusades with moderate "good government." His long career in the army had taught him to disdain partisanship and extremes right or left. Both parties had courted the victorious commander of the Allied armies in the years after World War II—Truman had offered to back him for the 1948 Democratic presidential nomination—and it was only months before he began his campaign for the 1952 Republican nomination that he declared his party affiliation. He went on to beat Robert Taft, son of the former president and chief justice and the leader of the Republican right, at the GOP convention, and then, in the general election, he crushed Adlai Stevenson, heir to New Deal liberalism.

When Chief Justice Vinson died suddenly of a heart attack in September 1953, aged only sixty-three, Eisenhower had an unexpected chance to reshape the Supreme Court in his own centrist image. He wanted a nominee of national stature, wide experience in government, and integrity. There was such a man, one who had just days before announced his retirement from politics and, moreover, one to whom Ike had given a hostage to fortune, a "personal promise" made a month after the 1952 election that he would name him to the "first vacancy on the Supreme Court"—Earl Warren. Eisenhower was grateful to the "big man" for using his control of the large California delegation to help Ike defeat Taft at the convention, and he was impressed by Warren's administrative experience and statesmanlike qualities, notably the bipartisan appeal of the governor both Republican and Democratic Californians had nominated for a third term in 1950. "Earl Warren's a Democrat and doesn't know it," Harry Truman said of the Republican vice-presidential candidate who had opposed him in 1948.

But when Ike had made his promise, he had not anticipated that the first open seat would be the chief justiceship, and he thought Warren would understand that. So the president and his attorney general, Herbert Brownell, discussed other candidates, most notably Robert Jackson, whose elevation from associate justice would open up a seat for Warren. The promotion of a New Dealer who had become a leader of the court's conservative wing attracted Eisenhower, but he had to face political reality: after their long drought, Republicans would rebel at the nomination of a Roosevelt "crony," especially one so closely identified with FDR's attack on the old Republican court. Moreover, Earl Warren *didn't* understand: he made it clear to Brownell that the president would be "breaking his word if he wasn't named to the Court immediately."

Eisenhower was irritated by gossip that Warren's appointment was merely a political payoff. "The truth was," he insisted in his memoirs, "that I owed Governor Warren nothing." If that was not entirely the truth, neither did Ike have an inkling that he would come to regard Warren as one of the two worst mistakes of his presidency. The president wasn't wrong in judging Warren a man of "high ideals and a great deal of commonsense." But he failed to foresee how those qualities would combine with Warren's passionate, determined activism to revolutionize constitutional law. The new chief justice had never met a problem without a solution, and the bolder the solution, the better he liked it. And the Supreme Court, with its authority over the Constitution and accountable neither to voters nor to elected officials, offered a matchless field of opportunities for that activism.

As had long been his way, Felix Frankfurter at first warmly welcomed his new colleague to the bench and undertook to tutor him, sending over articles and memoranda and copies of his own opinions that might be "helpful as direction for dealing with specific cases as they arise." But as the new chief began to shed his initial caution and restraint to reveal an activism in line with that of the Black-Douglas camp, Frankfurter turned against him, resenting his growing friendship with Black, and characteristically making doctrinal differences personal. He directed bitter, provocative remarks at the chief even in open court, but behind the scenes, he could be brutal. Once in conference, he shouted at Warren, "Be a judge, god damn it, be a judge!" Another time, when Warren interrupted one of Frankfurter's interminable lectures to the brethren, Frankfurter was said to have retorted, "You're the worst Chief Justice this country has ever had." They were "just uncongenial personalities," one of their colleagues would tell the historian Bernard Schwartz—the intellectual versus the man of action. Relentless argumentation "was a recreation for Felix and this sort of attitude the Chief Justice just couldn't understand. He had all his life been a peacemaker and, if you will, a compromiser and to get people working together—not to argue, to avoid confrontations, and Felix liked them." Still, in Warren's early years as chief justice, Frankfurter's conservative "restraint" was the dominant tenor of the court's decisions, with the activist bloc weakened by the losses in 1949 of Murphy and Rutledge.

IT WAS THIS conservative, cautious Supreme Court that confronted an egalitarian revolution sweeping across much of the country, spearheaded by the National Association for the Advancement of Colored People, whose strategy was to bypass the unresponsive political branches and to challenge racial discrimination aggressively through the courts. The Vinson Court had already faced up to specific cases of racial bias, in 1948 barring judicial enforcement of racially restrictive property covenants intended to prevent the sale of homes in white neighborhoods to African Americans. Two years later, in three cases decided on the same day, June 5, 1950, the court struck down segregation in an Oklahoma graduate school of education, a Texas law school, and in railroad dining cars. But hanging over these decisions was the grim visage of *Plessy* v. *Ferguson's* "separate but equal" doctrine—the "South's Magna Carta," some called it—whose denial that "the enforced separation of the two races stamps the colored race with a badge of inferiority" had for decades distorted race relations in every aspect of Southern life.

So far the justices had evaded the broader issue of Jim Crow, agreeing with Frankfurter's insistence that they "should not go out and meet problems." The two school opinions had been unanimous because they were limited to barring segregation from graduate schools and because of the gross inequality of the facilities available to blacks. The justices could order desegregation not by overturning but by applying the "separate but equal" rule. But late in 1952 five cases from school districts around the country arrived at the court to challenge *Plessy* directly, by contending that even if black schools had equal resources, segregating children in public education violated the Fourteenth Amendment's equal protection clause. The cases were consolidated as *Brown* v. *Board of Education*, the suit filed against the Topeka, Kansas, school district, where, because white and black schools were relatively equal in quality, the focus was on the fundamental principle of segregation. With *Brown*, the justices knew that the showdown had come. Vinson, who indicated that he was unwilling to overturn "long continued interpretations," remarked enigmatically that "boldness is indispensable but wisdom is essential."

Before the badly fragmented court could decide *Brown*, Vinson died, succeeded by a chief justice who did not think boldness and wisdom were irreconcilable. While new to the court, Warren was an experienced politician with an instinctive ability to herd fleas. At the start, with no more than five solid votes among the justices to abolish segregation in schools, he realized that only a unanimous court could make such a momentous verdict stick. In conference, he put the case against *Plessy*, pointing out that segregation was based on "a concept of the inherent inferiority of the colored race," an idea that "in this day and age" was morally and constitutionally repugnant. He assuaged fears of upheaval in the South by promising an opinion that would produce "a minimum of emotion and strife." The decision would apply only to schools, leaving the rest of Jim Crow, for the moment, intact. To meet Frankfurter's fears that the Supreme Court would be drawn into the quagmire of enforcement, Warren agreed to delegate that task to the federal district courts. And he responded to concerns about the South's reaction to an order for immediate desegregation by approving flexibility in implementation, permitting "different handling in different places."

On Monday, May 17, 1954, Chief Justice Earl Warren read *Brown* to a hushed Supreme Court chamber. In a firm but calm voice, Warren abruptly dismissed *Plessy*—in public education, "the doctrine of 'separate but equal' has no place." To separate black children "from others of similar age and qualifications solely because of their race generates a feeling of inferiority as to their status in the community that may affect their hearts and minds in a way unlikely ever to be undone." Separate schools were "inherently unequal" and therefore violated the equal protection clause.

It was a brief and not resplendent opinion. Warren had done what he could to minimize the drama. No announcement had been made that the decision was imminent. To avoid a big crowd or excited radio commentators, reporters had been led to expect a routine day at court. Warren hoped that by downplaying the ruling he might make it more acceptable to the country as a whole, but especially to the South.

That strategy—especially the decision to impose no definite deadline for desegregation—was surprisingly successful. "The end of the world has not come for the South or for the nation," wrote the Louisville *Courier-Journal*. Equally important was the court's unanimity behind Warren's opinion. When he announced that solidarity in the courtroom, there was audible astonishment. As *New York Times* columnist Arthur Krock noted, "a familiar prophecy" had been that "there would be nine opinions written" and "close division on the central finding."

Still the test would come when the decision began to be implemented in communities across the South. Already calls were going out for "massive resistance," while Mississippi senator James Eastland declared defiance of this "legislative" decision by a court that "sits as a Constitutional Convention in judicial robes." As Eisenhower remained silent, the chief justice felt deserted by the president, who would bear the ultimate responsibility for enforcement. Although he allowed that "the Constitution is as the Supreme Court interprets it," Eisenhower believed that the court should never have tampered with *Plessy*. Desegregation, if it was to occur, would come through "a change in spirit," not by judicial fiat. At a White House dinner while the justices were considering *Brown*, the president had taken the opportunity to explain to Warren that Southerners were not bad people. All they were concerned about "is to see that their sweet little girls are not required to sit in school alongside some big overgrown Negroes."

If Warren was frustrated by Eisenhower's repeated refusals to endorse *Brown*, Ike was disappointed in Warren. The president had no weapon to challenge him except one—the lottery luck of four more appointments to the court. John Marshall Harlan, Ike's first pick after Warren, to take Robert Jackson's seat in 1954, had impeccable credentials—a degree from Princeton and a Rhodes scholarship to Oxford, and years of experience as a Wall Street lawyer and chief counsel to the New York State Crime Commission. He was also an old friend of Herbert Brownell's. His confirmation was delayed by Southern Democrats irate over *Brown*. Much was made of the fact that Harlan was the grandson and namesake of the great *Plessy* dissenter. And indeed Harlan would take progressive stands on civil rights, though on most other issues he was a Frankfurter loyalist, highly reluctant to overrule the political branches, and known more as a technician than as a legal philosopher. If he was called the Warren Court's "most principled" conservative, it was a conservatism far distant from that of the Four Horsemen.

William Brennan, named by Ike to replace Sherman Minton in 1956, was a sharply contrasting figure. Born of an Irish immigrant father whose first job was in a Newark brewery but who ended up as a prominent Democratic politico in that city, Brennan was a scholarship student at Harvard Law who practiced labor law in Newark before taking a lead role in the reorganization of New Jersey's judiciary, becoming a judge himself, and rising in a few years to the state's Supreme Court. Eisenhower, facing a reelection campaign, was receptive to nominating a Catholic who had support in the church hierarchy. And by tapping a Democrat, the president could buff his prized "nonpartisan" image. Brownell—who claimed to have read all of Brennan's judicial opinions, perhaps overlooking some outspokenly liberal ones—pronounced his record "outstanding."

Brennan would have the honor of becoming the second of what Eisenhower called the two biggest mistakes of his presidency. The justice began as a skilled consensus builder, able to construct majorities, often on narrow grounds, from a fragmented court. Gradually he emerged as a leader of the liberal bloc and, with Black, its foremost libertarian. Brennan took such advanced stands, indeed, that Frankfurter, who had taught him at Harvard, reportedly said, "I always wanted my students to think for themselves, but Brennan goes too far." As the years passed, Brennan became close to Warren personally, giving him solace as the chief grew old and more dependent on friends and admirers.

Eisenhower's last two justices would give the president little cause for disappointment. Charles Whittaker, named to replace Stanley Reed in 1957, was a "self-made man" who grew up on a hardscrabble Kansas farm where he augmented the family income by trapping animals for their hides. Even though he never received a high school diploma, Whittaker worked himself into a Kansas law school, a Kansas City law firm, and the Republican leadership of the state. In his scant five years on the court, he closely aligned with the conservatives.

Potter Stewart, who replaced Harold Burton in 1958, had sterling GOP roots—his father was a popular Republican mayor of Cincinnati. Stewart attended Hotchkiss, Yale, and Cambridge, then worked as a Wall Street lawyer. After serving in World War II, he joined a leading Ohio firm and dabbled in politics before Eisenhower appointed him to a federal appeals court in 1954. Only forty-three when he reached the Supreme Court, he quickly won the reputation of a "swing voter," though he swung most often with the conservatives. He was, above all, a pragmatist who preferred to avoid constitutional questions and, when they were unavoidable, to decide them on narrow grounds.

BY THE END of the 1950s, Earl Warren's court was not yet completely the Warren Court. Much to the dismay of the Republican right, as well as Southern Democrats opposed to *Brown*, Eisenhower's nominees were, as a whole, more liberal and activist than the Roosevelt and Truman justices they replaced. Southern senators delayed even Potter Stewart's confirmation because of his support for *Brown*, with South Carolina's Strom Thurmond charging that Stewart "believes that the Constitution of the United States can be amended by the Supreme Court." Still, through much of the 1950s, the conservative majority remained in the ascendant. Black and Douglas expressed their increasingly absolutist libertarian views most forcefully in dissent, scoring the Frankfurter-Harlan "balancing test" of security and liberty as "closely akin to the notion that neither the First Amendment nor any other provision of the Bill of Rights should be enforced unless the Court believes it is *reasonable* to do so."

Yet Black's tenacity, Warren's leadership, and the government's extremism in the pursuit of security won several crucial victories for civil liberties and established the Supreme Court's resolve to confront government power in defense of the Bill of Rights. On June 17, 1957, which the right wing would call "Red Monday," the court struck blows at four key pieces of the apparatus used to ferret out the "disloyal": the abusive inquisitorial powers of the House Un-American Activities Committee; a state attorney general acting as a one-man committee to investigate academics and other alleged subversives; the anti-Communist Smith Act, which the Vinson Court had upheld against party leaders in *Dennis*; and the State Department's inquiries into the loyalty of its own employees. To defend civil liberties in these cases, the Supreme Court turned the powers seized by John Marshall and extended by generations of conservative justices to progressive purposes, asserting its authority over both federal and state proceedings and over the actions of both the legislative and executive branches of the national government.

Red Monday raised the biggest anti-court furor in Congress since the 1930s, only now it was conservatives who were decrying liberal excesses, Republicans who introduced legislation targeting the Supreme Court's power. Senator William Jenner of Indiana proposed the elimination of the court's jurisdiction over cases of loyalty or subversion, denouncing "the spectacle of a Court constantly changing the law, and even changing the meaning of the Constitution." The Supreme Court had become "a legislative arm of the Government; and many of its feats are subject to no review." Only by a feverish effort were Democrats, thrust into the role of defenders of judicial supremacy, able to block the flood of court-curbing bills.

NOT LONG AFTER the adoption of the Fourteenth Amendment in 1868, the Supreme Court had narrowed the broad promise of its due process and equal protection clauses to little more than a defense of property rights. Almost a century later, *Brown* and other desegregation cases signaled a dramatic shift, with the court moving, for the first time, to apply equal protection in its intended form, as a shield for African-American rights against state power. But that clause, as the Reconstruction Congress had framed it, had a wider potential to secure *all* constitutional guarantees fully and equally to *all* citizens. Such rights were to be asserted against the states, a principle the court had promptly undermined in the *Slaughterhouse Cases* with its pinched construction of national citizenship, which insulated the states from most rights claims based on the federal Constitution.

For decades after *Slaughterhouse*, conservative justices, over the objections of dissenters like the first Justice Harlan and Brandeis, had monotonously spurned opportunities to broaden the "privileges and immunities" of United States citizenship by "incorporating" the guarantees of the Bill of Rights into the Fourteenth Amendment, which would make them enforceable on the states. Only in 1925, in its *Gitlow* decision, did the Supreme Court acknowledge, almost in passing, that freedoms of speech and press were *national* rights under the Fourteenth Amendment—even while it upheld Benjamin Gitlow's conviction for publishing dangerous words. Since then, the court had slowly extended federal protections on a piecemeal, case-by-case basis, resisting Hugo Black's calls for total incorporation of the Bill of Rights as, he argued, the Fourteenth Amendment's framers had intended.

While not written in the Constitution's first ten amendments, no right was more fundamental to democratic self-government than the right to cast an effective vote. Over time more and more Americans had moved into cities, only to find themselves grossly underrepresented in their state legislatures. In Tennessee, a rural county with 2,340 voters had a full seat in the legislature, while Memphis, with 300,000 or more voters, had only seven. Similar dire examples had long abounded across the country, including California. There, when liberals and laborites in 1948 had sponsored a measure to align voting power more closely to population, Governor Warren had opposed it. But now on the court it was clear to him that such "misdistricting" had a strong anti-democratic impact, with special damage to minority representation. Moreover, the ill was self-enforcing and self-perpetuating—legislators who overrepresented rural voters would hardly choose to abandon their built-in advantage by empowering urbanites.

Since the 1930s, over a dozen suits against malapportionment had been filed in the federal courts. In 1946, one of them, *Colegrove* v. *Green*, had reached the Supreme Court, which dismissed the action. Relying on a tradition with roots in Roger Taney's 1849 *Luther* v. *Borden* opinion that the court should not involve itself in "political questions," Frankfurter had argued then that malapportionment was a problem of "a peculiarly political nature," and courts "ought not to enter this political thicket." The remedy was beyond the competence of the judiciary—it must ultimately be "the vigilance of the people in exercising their political rights." But how could "the people" practice that vigilance when they were so grossly underrepresented as to be effectively disenfranchised?

Sixteen years later, under Earl Warren's leadership, the Supreme Court was prepared to make another malapportionment case, *Baker* v. *Carr*, what the chief justice would later call the most important decision of his tenure. Even as Harlan echoed Frankfurter in urging that the court's "aloofness from political vicissitudes" had "always been the mainspring of its stability and vitality," Warren was convinced that the court's timidity had "made change hopeless." The chief justice built a fragile coalition, then saved it from collapse when conservatives nearly bolted in the face of Frankfurter's counterattack. Brennan, writing for a 6–2 majority, held that federal courts had jurisdiction over cases of alleged malapportionment and could order state legislatures to redraw district lines on a fair basis. "A citizen's right to a vote free of arbitrary impairment by state action" was guaranteed by the Constitution, Brennan wrote; when "state power is used as an instrument for circumventing a federally protected right," the issue was not political but constitutional. A year later, in *Gray* v. *Sanders*, the court laid down the principle for fairness: political equality, equal representation—"one person, one vote." In victory after *Baker*, the chief justice wrote Brennan, "It is a great day for the Irish," then thinking again, Warren crossed out "Irish" and wrote in "country."

Baker v. *Carr* was also Felix Frankfurter's swan song. In his dissent, he lamented the "massive repudiation of the experience of our whole past" in the Supreme Court's assertion of a "destructively novel judicial power" and feared that the court would sacrifice its authority "as the ultimate organ of 'the supreme Law of the Land'" by abandoning its "complete detachment, in fact and in appearance, from political entanglements." Within five months of this climactic appeal for restraint, the old justice, disabled by a stroke, retired from the high bench.

. . .

RARELY HAS THE arrival of a single new justice given a more decisive tilt to the Supreme Court's balance than that of Arthur Goldberg, named by John Kennedy as Frankfurter's successor in August 1962. By taking Frankfurter's seat, Goldberg unleashed the Warren Court's activism. A labor lawyer from Chicago who had served as JFK's secretary of labor, the new justice would give almost unvarying support to civil liberties and civil rights claimants and become the decisive fifth vote in the activist bloc that included Black, Douglas, Brennan, and Warren himself.

But John Kennedy, who paid little attention to the workings of the Supreme Court, was really not that kind of passionate, committed liberal. His first appointment to the court, five months earlier, better reflected his personality and interests. Byron "Whizzer" White, named in April 1962 to replace Charles Whittaker, was a former All-American football player from Colorado and a vigorous supporter of JFK in the 1960 campaign. He was rewarded with a job in the Justice Department as a deputy to the president's brother, Attorney General Robert Kennedy, with mainly administrative duties. Like JFK, White was young, vigorous, and pragmatic. Kennedy knew little about White's judicial philosophy—or whether he even had one. White himself, when asked by a reporter after his nomination whether he would be a liberal or a conservative justice, replied, "I never know what people mean by those words." As Robert Kennedy recalled the decision-making, "You didn't think how he would vote in a reapportionment case or a criminal case. You wanted someone who, in the long run, you could believe would be doing what you thought was best. You wanted someone who agreed generally with your views of the country." White would prove a staunch foe of racial and sexual discrimination, but on the civil liberties issues that would define the Warren Court's peak, he most often sided with the conservative bloc that, after Frankfurter's retirement, was made up of Tom Clark, Harlan, and Stewart.

But with Goldberg's appointment, the activists were in the saddle and the court set off on an era of constitutional innovation unmatched since the days of John Marshall. "With five votes, you can do anything around here," Brennan liked to say. Like the Marshall Court, Earl Warren's bench vigorously asserted judicial power in order to reshape the Constitution to its specifications. But where Marshall voided only one act of Congress on constitutional grounds in his thirty-five-year career—albeit momentously in *Marbury* v. *Madison*—the Warren Court struck down 16 federal statutes between 1963 and 1969. And while Marshall aggressively wielded judicial review to secure federal supremacy over the states, between 1789 and 1864, the Supreme Court nullified only 39 state and local statutes. Between 1963 and 1969, the Warren Court did so 113 times, at a rate approached only by the Taft Court between 1921 and 1930.

The Warren Court's unprecedented use of judicial review inevitably provoked intense controversy, and not only from Southern racists and anti-Communist fanatics with their "Impeach Earl Warren" placards and handbills. Since the 1790s and especially since the Civil War, conservatives had praised the Founders' wisdom in supposedly establishing a judiciary empowered to block rampant majorities and cheered when the Supreme Court used that authority to defend the rich and powerful. Now that the court was, for the first time in its long history, consistently using that power to expand liberty and equality, conservatives angrily pointed out that judicial review had no basis in the Constitution. Some of the most trenchant criticism of such activism came from within the court itself, with a frequent dissenter like Justice White charging that the liberal majority was exploiting the power of review to invent "new law and new public policy."

Much of what the Supreme Court achieved was indeed new, but

liberals, defending a power they had once condemned, argued that the justices were simply making explicit constitutional guarantees of equal rights that politicians and the court itself had long ignored or betrayed. The Warren Court was defining those rights with rigor and applying them to government at all levels. In cases like *Brown* and *Baker*, the court ventured into areas of simple justice where elected officials feared—or never wished—to tread. Far less hesitantly than the Roosevelt Court, the Warren Court challenged the high bench's long conservative legacy in civil rights and civil liberties. For the first time, the Supreme Court was in the vanguard of change, driving the forces of reform both in government and at the grassroots in the 1960s. Decisions like *Brown* gave impetus to African-American activism that in turn pressured the political branches to finally deliver on the promise of civil and political equality for blacks. The Warren Court's championing of equality and individual liberty galvanized a host of other "liberation" movements that won key legislative victories against public and private discrimination. Its dedication to free speech widened the potentialities of political argument and protest, most notably in the campaign against the Vietnam War. So sweeping was the Warren Court's commitment to reform, so bracing its leadership for change, that many liberals not only forgot their past objections to judicial power, but were seduced into the belief that the court, not the political branches, with their fickle, opportunistic politicians and swayable constituencies, was the best constitutional vehicle to extend and protect progressive gains into the future.

But looking to the Supreme Court for continuing liberal leadership was always a bad bet. Legal scholar Alexander Bickel, who had clerked for Felix Frankfurter and was no friend to judicial activism, warned that what he termed the Warren Court's results-oriented "subjectivity" in decision-making could easily, with a switch in personnel, be turned against the precedents the court's liberals were so forcefully laying down. After all, the Warren Court itself overturned forty-five precedents during the chief justice's sixteen years on the bench. In the absence of "durable principles," Bickel doubted that "judicial supremacy can work and is tolerable in broad areas of social policy." The combination of the Supreme Court's institutional conservatism, temporarily overridden by Brennan's omnipotent "five votes," and the instabilities promoted by the judicial roulette of court appointments all but ensured that Warren Court liberalism would be threatened with backlash and reversal. The Warren Court's progressive advances were indeed luminous but they were also, emphatically, exceptions to the historical rule of a conservative supreme judiciary. To secure and broaden those advances would require not lawsuits but the hard work of political organizing and persuasion. It would require political, not judicial, leadership.

IN THE MEANTIME, the Warren Court of the 1960s continued to break new constitutional ground. During those years, the justices enlarged the scope of speech and press freedoms until it approached, though it did not yet reach, William Douglas's ideal "that the First Amendment allows all ideas to be expressed—whether orthodox, popular, offbeat, or repulsive." The Warren Court also recognized rights that were not stated explicitly in the Constitution. In 1965, in *Griswold* v. *Connecticut*, which struck down a state law that banned birth control—a relic of the nineteenth century and the Society for the Suppression of Vice—Douglas found that the law violated a woman's "right to privacy." That right, he conceded, was nowhere mentioned in the Constitution, but—pointing to the First, Third, Fourth, Fifth, and Ninth Amendments—he maintained that "specific guarantees in the Bill of Rights have penumbras, formed by emanations from those guarantees that help give them life and substance." Six other justices, including White, Harlan, and Clark, joined the court's judgment, though all but Clark departed from

Douglas's reasoning. Goldberg's concurrence located the right to privacy in the Ninth and Fourteenth Amendments, while Harlan's relied exclusively on the Fourteenth's due process protection of liberty.

For the leading activist of the old Roosevelt Court, all this was too much—or nowhere near enough. Hugo Black was a civil liberties absolutist but constitutional fundamentalist, and he was growing disenchanted with the freewheeling activism of the Warren Court. "I like my privacy as well as the next one," he wrote in a dissent to *Griswold* that echoed the views of his former antagonist, Felix Frankfurter, "but I am nevertheless compelled to admit that government has a right to invade it unless prohibited by some specific constitutional provision." Without that, the court was arbitrarily using "the federal judiciary power to invalidate any legislative act which the judges find irrational, unreasonable or offensive" in an attempt to "keep the Constitution in tune with the times."

But Black fully supported the Supreme Court's stepped-up nationalization of the Bill of Rights, its use of the Fourteenth Amendment to make a panoply of constitutional guarantees binding upon the states. In the historian Peter Irons's words, the justices turned "the Bill of Rights into a powerful weapon against government officials—from police officers to presidents—who failed to treat people fairly and equally." Most controversial was a long series of decisions that defined, expanded, and nationalized the procedural rights of suspected or accused criminals. The decisions addressed specific violations of due process too common in the states: evidence seized by unlawful entry or without probable cause, forced confessions, poor men and women defending themselves in court. In *Mapp* v. *Ohio* in 1961, the Fourth Amendment right against illegal search and seizure was nationalized, and the court developed rules to exclude from trials evidence obtained illegally. In *Gideon* v. *Wainwright* in 1963, the court held that the Sixth Amendment right to counsel was fundamental, requiring the states to appoint lawyers for indigents in criminal trials. The next year, in *Escobedo* v. *Illinois*, the court decided that the right to counsel became operational when police began to interrogate a suspect. *Miranda* v. *Arizona*, in 1966, made the constitutional requirements for police specific: before a suspect could be questioned, he had to be advised of his rights to counsel and warned against self-incrimination. If he was not given what came to be known as the Miranda warning, anything he said could not be used against him in court.

THE WARREN COURT'S campaign to ensure equal rights and due process—to criminal suspects, to members of minorities, to voters, to dissident voices, to people of faith or no faith—continued unaffected by Arthur Goldberg's resignation, in June 1965, to become the U.S. ambassador to the United Nations. There was only one man President Lyndon Johnson would consider for the opening—his close friend and adviser Abe Fortas. The youngest son of a Jewish cabinetmaker in Memphis, Fortas went to Yale where he became editor-in-chief of the law review and protégé of William Douglas, whom he followed to Washington. In 1942, the precocious New Dealer became, at the age of thirty-two, under secretary of the interior. After the war, he cofounded what became one of the capital's best-connected law firms. Fortas relished his role as a consummate insider and confidant to powerful men—none more powerful than Lyndon Johnson. He was reluctant to give it up for the Supreme Court, but Johnson would not take no for an answer. "He's going to wear him down," Goldberg told his clerk. "He'll wait until the end of time." On the court, Fortas followed in Goldberg's footsteps as the fifth vote for the liberal majority.

The promise of equality held out by the Warren Court became, for the first time in American history, embodied on the bench itself with Lyndon Johnson's next appointment, to fill the seat vacated by Tom Clark in 1967. Thurgood Marshall may already have had more influence on American constitutional law as an attorney than he would later as an activist justice on the Supreme Court. Born in Baltimore to middle-class parents, Marshall was an exceptionally bright student in school and college but knew that, even so, the University of Maryland Law School would not admit blacks. He instead attended law school at Howard University, graduating first in his class in 1931. At Howard, he met black activists who were building the legal foundation for assaults on pervasive discrimination.

After becoming counsel to the Baltimore branch of the NAACP, Marshall began long trips through the South, stopping off in small dusty towns to meet some of the most destitute blacks in America. A tall, gregarious backslapper, he quickly made friends as he inspected the impoverished schools where African-American children were segregated and assessed local voting rights—or the lack thereof. Promoted to special counsel for the NAACP at its New York headquarters, Marshall began extensive litigation of civil rights cases emerging from the racist towns he had visited.

Throughout these years, Marshall faced the seething issue of whether black leaders like himself should fight for equality through the judiciary, with lawsuits challenging segregation in transportation, education, labor, public facilities, and the armed forces, or through civil disobedience—lunch-counter sit-ins, boycotts, mass protests, action in the streets—in order to provoke the political branches into enacting civil rights. Inevitably Marshall and the NAACP, with their pursuit of justice through the courts, came into conflict with Dr. Martin Luther King, Jr., the spokesman and strategist for nonviolent direct action. Marshall chose to carry on his kind of protest, establishing legal landmarks and providing the courts with the ideas and methods to rewrite constitutional law, most notably in *Brown*. He was just the kind of activist—militant but operating through established channels—that Lyndon Johnson admired. In 1965, LBJ named him the first African-American solicitor general, then in 1967 he nominated him to become the first African American on the Supreme Court. The Senate confirmed him, 69–11.

For Johnson this was a crucial act of transforming leadership at the climax of the civil rights struggle. But Johnson's next move did sharp and enduring damage to that and other liberal causes. In June 1968, the president received a letter from the chief justice that declared Warren's intent to retire, "effective at your pleasure." Warren said he was not ill or unhappy in the job. The only reason he gave was his age, but, though he never acknowledged it, the real explanation was the likelihood that his old nemesis in California Republican politics, Richard Nixon, would be elected president in November 1968. Warren wanted to thwart Nixon and ensure the appointment of a successor who would continue his activist legacy.

Johnson, by then a lame duck, was eager to secure his own legacy. He turned immediately to the man he had put on the court three years before and who had, while on the bench, continued to act as his valued adviser, Abe Fortas. Elevating the associate justice would give Johnson a second seat to fill. Rejecting advice to pair Fortas with a nonpartisan Republican, the president chose Homer Thornberry, a Texas judge of little distinction apart from his close, decades-long association with LBJ.

Even before an announcement could be made, aroused Republicans, who like Warren expected Nixon to take the presidency, mobilized to fight tooth and nail to block the nominations. Southern Democrats were little more welcoming, and when Fortas became the first nominee for chief justice to testify before the Senate Judiciary Committee, they used the opportunity to lambaste the Warren Court's record on race and "law and order." More harmful were Fortas's repeated denials that he had continued to advise the president while on the bench, though White House logs showed dozens of face-to-face meetings, and the justice had on the desk in his office a red telephone with a direct line to LBJ. After four damaging days, the committee dismissed Fortas and the Senate adjourned for the summer. During that break came the revelation that Fortas had, while a justice, received a $15,000 lecture fee that was raised from clients of his old law firm. When the Senate reconvened in September, opponents staged a six-day filibuster, and after a motion for cloture failed, Fortas asked the president to withdraw his nomination. Johnson agreed, "with deep regret."

LBJ had seized at an opportunity for a "two-fer" that would have assured liberal domination for years into the future—and had come away with nothing. Even worse, the furies would continue to pursue Fortas until, within a year, new scandalous revelations that he had taken money from a convicted stock manipulator would drive him off the bench.

After Fortas's withdrawal, on October 10, 1968, Johnson issued a statement that Earl Warren "has indicated his willingness to serve until his successor qualifies." The president also announced that he would not "send another name to the Senate for this high office." Earl Warren's resignation would become effective at the pleasure of Richard Nixon.

CHAPTER ELEVEN

Republicans as Activists

WHEN RICHARD NIXON tapped Warren Burger for chief justice of the Supreme Court in the spring of 1969, he launched the pick with a hastily summoned press conference to explain how high-minded his search for Earl Warren's successor had been. He told reporters that he had not cleared the nomination politically—"the Supreme Court must be above politics," he declared. He would not consider racial, religious, or geographical balance. He would not pick a crony like his attorney general, John Mitchell. He named other men he would not appoint—two-time GOP presidential nominee Tom Dewey, because he was too old; Justice Potter Stewart, because promotions from within rarely succeeded; Herbert Brownell, because of his "controversial" service as Eisenhower's attorney general.

What kind of person, then, would Nixon select? A leader, he said—someone like Stone or Hughes or even Warren himself. The president singled out Felix Frankfurter as the kind of "strict constructionist" he wanted on the court—a judge who would "be very conservative in overthrowing a law passed by the elected representatives of the people."

Reporters rarely had seen Nixon so enjoying himself, as he preached appointment ethics while settling various political scores. It was a bit difficult, though, to connect his lofty tests of leadership with the man he was proposing for the Supreme Court's center seat. Warren Burger was hardly a Marshall or Warren or even a Stone. Born of a Swiss immigrant family in St. Paul, Minnesota, in 1907, Burger spent much of his childhood helping his father run a truck farm on the outskirts of the city. His athletic and scholarly achievements won him a Princeton scholarship, but one not large enough to live on, so he attended the University of Minnesota and then the St. Paul College of Law. As a young attorney, he became a Republican activist and in 1952 backed Eisenhower against Taft in the fight for the GOP presidential nomination. The next year he joined the Justice Department as an assistant attorney general, until his appointment by Ike to the federal appeals court for the District of Columbia.

For all of his pious talk about keeping the Supreme Court above politics, Nixon had made public dissatisfaction with Earl Warren's activist leadership a centerpiece of his 1968 campaign. And despite Nixon's call for "strict construction" from the Supreme Court, he was less concerned about the niceties of the Warren Court's jurisprudence than with its results, especially its expansion of individual rights, which Nixon translated for voters as "permissiveness." At a time of rising crime, with urban riots and disorderly protests against the Vietnam War, Nixon blamed the Warren Court for a breakdown of "law and order." In one of his favorite applause lines, repeated in speech after speech, Nixon charged that the judiciary had "gone too far in weakening the peace forces as against the criminal forces." Burger's tough positions on criminal procedures as an appeals court judge had brought him to Nixon's attention. That was the kind of "strict constructionist" the president wanted, one who would unleash the police.

Nixon's campaign against the Supreme Court also fitted into his broader strategy to attract into the Republican fold Southern conservatives rebelling against Democratic party liberalism. Ever since *Brown* and the court's order the following year that desegregation proceed "with all deliberate speed," enforcement had caused unrest— and occasional violence—in the South. In 1957, President Eisenhower had sent federal troops to Little Rock, Arkansas, to quell bloody resistance to the integration of Central High School. "Our personal opinions" about *Brown*, he told the country, could "have no bearing on the matter of enforcement; the responsibility and authority of the Supreme Court to interpret the Constitution are very clear." Five years later, John Kennedy sent troops to put down a riot protesting the integration of the University of Mississippi. By the late 1960s, the flash point was the court-ordered busing of black children to white schools and white children to black schools. While Nixon claimed to support integration, the candidate had complained about federal meddling in local schools and told a group of Southerners that "busing the child . . . into a strange community—I think you destroy that child." As president, he would drag his feet on enforcement— passive, not massive, resistance.

When he appointed Burger, Nixon had claimed that "the Court will not be used" for geographical balance, but the president was determined to promote his "Southern strategy" by naming a conservative from the South. After Abe Fortas resigned under pressure on May 15, 1969, a week before Nixon announced Burger's nomination to replace Warren, no Northerner made Nixon's short-list. His choice was—almost inevitably given the GOP's historic weakness in the South—a Democrat, Judge Clement Haynsworth, a distinguished old-line South Carolinian. After graduating from Harvard

Law School, Haynsworth joined a family law firm back home and "Democrats for Ike." Always seeking to win support in the South, Eisenhower in 1957 had made him an appellate judge.

Haynsworth's conservative record on the appeals court drew quick opposition from labor and civil rights leaders. While the caricature of the judge as a racist was unfair, it was a pair of ethical lapses, when he presided in cases where he had a financial interest, that gave opponents a lever, especially after Fortas's downfall over conflict-of-interest charges. As battles raged day after day in the Senate, the president was urged to withdraw the nomination, but Nixon stuck to his man. Haynsworth's defeat, with only 45 ayes to 55 nays, cut across party lines, as 17 Republicans, including some who had led the rush against Fortas, voted no.

While his stalwart backing of Haynsworth meant that the administration had "politically probably come out ahead" in the South, Nixon was stung by the rejection. Determined, as he said, to "play it very tough," the president responded with a classic "spite" nomination, putting up what a Nixon official called a "real Southern judge"—Georgia native G. Harrold Carswell, another Democrat Ike had appointed to the federal bench. But Carswell was no Haynsworth. Senate hearings soon proved that he was a lifelong segregationist, on and off the bench, and an incompetent judge—an "absurd constructionist," as a law professor concluded after examining his opinions. Despite a stirring defense of mediocrity from Republican senator Roman Hruska of Nebraska—"Even if he were mediocre, there are a lot of mediocre judges and people and lawyers. They are entitled to a little representation, aren't they, and a little chance? We can't have all Brandeises and Frankfurters and Cardozos and stuff like that there"—the Senate rejected Carswell too.

Nixon seethed. It was John Mitchell and his Justice Department vetters who had failed to unearth Carswell's long racist trail, but the president aimed his fire at the Senate. "I have reluctantly concluded that it is not possible to get confirmation for a judge on the Supreme Court of any man who believes in the strict construction of the Constitution, as I do, if he comes from the South." A month later, he found, as he had promised, a "judge from the North," Harry A. Blackmun, who seemed capable and safe—a summa cum laude Harvard graduate, a resident counsel at the famed Mayo Clinic, and a "Minnesota twin" to his longtime St. Paul friend, Warren Burger. Despite some liberal opinions on the federal appeals court, he appeared to be a dependable conservative, especially on law and order. The Senate confirmed Blackmun unanimously, one year after Fortas resigned.

In the fall of 1971, another seat opened up with the retirement of Hugo Black. Now Nixon got his Southerner. After closely considering Representative Richard Poff, a Virginia Democrat whose long record of opposition to civil rights laws would trigger a new confrontation with the Senate, Nixon turned to another Virginian, Lewis F. Powell, Jr., a man of impeccable credentials, including past presidency of the American Bar Association. A prosperous corporation lawyer in Richmond, he appeared to be a "strict constructionist" in the mold of the second Justice Harlan, with little taint of racism in his background. By the South's standards, he was a moderate on segregation. The Senate confirmed him unanimously.

In ideology, Nixon's first three justices cleaved to the moderately conservative Eisenhower wing of the Republican party. For some years, however, potent new forces had been gathering in the GOP. A right-wing base, emerging out of Robert Taft's three failed attempts to win the party's presidential nomination, had mobilized behind Barry Goldwater's ideological campaign for the presidency in 1964. Lyndon Johnson's crushing defeat of Goldwater only stimulated this "New Right," which made the Warren Court a particular target for its promotion of equality above such other values as security, states' rights, and the rights of property. By the 1970s, young enthusiasts were flocking to the GOP, many from universities such as Yale, Chicago, and Stanford. Soon the New Rightists were creating their own journals and organizations—notably the Federalist Society, which vowed to overturn the liberal legal and judicial establishments.

It was to reach out to this hard-right wing, which included activists in the White House itself, that Nixon tagged William Rehnquist to take the place of the retiring John Harlan late in 1971. The Milwaukee-born Rehnquist had graduated at the top of his Stanford Law School class and clerked for Justice Robert Jackson, then moved into private practice in Arizona, where he was an outspoken foe of integration and equal rights. In 1969, he became director of the Office of Legal Counsel in the Justice Department, taking part in the administration's crackdown on antiwar protesters and even proposing a constitutional amendment on behalf of law enforcement, to counter the Warren Court's failures to protect "the right of society to convict the guilty."

Still, Nixon had to be persuaded. For one thing, he was inclined toward Senator Howard Baker of Tennessee, yet another Southerner and one who would be easily confirmed by his colleagues. For another, his first meeting with Rehnquist in 1971 left him with the lingering impression of a man dressed like a "clown," wearing a pink shirt and "psychedelic necktie." When an aide spelled Rehnquist's name, Nixon asked, "Is he Jewish?" Later he couldn't remember the name—"Renchburg"? "Renchquist," an aide replied. "Yeah," the president said. "Renchquist."

But Baker was slow to make up his mind, and as an adviser pointed out, since Rehnquist was only forty-seven years old, the president could "salt away a guy that would be on the Court for thirty years" as "a rock solid conservative." Rehnquist's confirmation was a battle, as evidence surfaced of his harsh opposition to civil rights, especially a 1952 memo for Justice Jackson in the *Brown* case, urging that *Plessy*'s racist doctrine "was right and should be reaffirmed." Twenty-six senators voted no. Afterward, the president gave the new justice a last bit of advice: "Just be as mean and rough as they said you were."

BY THE END of his first term, Nixon had put on the bench four justices who broadly shared his views on the issues that most preoccupied him politically: law and order and school desegregation. The Supreme Court's solid liberal majority had been decimated by the departures of Warren, Black, and Fortas. Even so, the evils of the Warren Court remained a target for Nixon. In his 1972 reelection campaign, he told voters that he needed "4 more years to strengthen the courts so we can have the peace forces strong, backed by the judges of this country."

The trouble was that despite the president's hopes and the pressures he applied, the new Nixon men produced no "counterrevolution" against the liberal Constitution. They succeeded in blunting the court's broad activist thrust, but with the exception of Rehnquist, none of them had a genuinely revolutionary temper, an eagerness to discard precedents or to supplant liberal activism with an activism of the right. They did little more than chip away while leaving the massive core of liberal jurisprudence intact.

Ironically, the early Burger Court was to be remembered not for its judicial restraint or its rulings on crime or race, but, despite the chief justice's best efforts, for an aggressively activist and "policy-making" decision on an issue new to the Supreme Court that would transform judicial politics for decades to come.

In the 1960s, challenges to state laws barring abortion intensified in legislatures and courts, many of them powered by *Griswold*'s recognition in 1965 of the constitutional right to privacy. A challenge to a Texas law that forbade abortion except when necessary to save a woman's life first reached the Supreme Court in 1971. With only seven justices sitting—Black and Harlan had yet to be replaced—a tentative majority formed to strike down the Texas abortion ban, but Warren Burger assigned the opinion to his old Minnesota friend Harry Blackmun, though the chief justice was in the minority and Blackmun's own position was not yet solid. When Douglas, who as the senior justice in the majority should have had the power of assignment, objected, Burger replied disingenuously that in his view the positions of several justices as expressed in conference were so unclear that the case "would have to stand or fall on the writing, when it was done"—that is, it depended on whether Blackmun's opinion could attract a majority. At the same time, Burger maneuvered for delay, arguing that the court's eventual ruling would have more weight if a full complement of justices heard the case. He expected that Nixon's new appointees, Powell and Rehnquist, would join him in upholding the law—and by then, Blackmun might be persuaded to do the same.

But the chief was in for a surprise. After the case was reargued in October 1972, Blackmun and Powell indicated that they would join Douglas, Brennan, Stewart, and Marshall to strike down the Texas restriction. Blackmun would, in fact, write the opinion for the court—but it would be to recognize abortion as a constitutional *right*, as a dimension of a woman's right to privacy. His maneuvers having backfired, the chief justice switched to the majority at the last minute. Warren Burger was unwilling to stand in dissent to a landmark ruling of the Burger Court. But he issued a brief concurrence to insist that the decision had no "sweeping consequences": "Plainly, the Court today rejects any claim that the Constitution requires abortion on demand."

Blackmun's opinion in *Roe* v. *Wade* was in fact not anything as blunt as that. It included a lengthy history of abortion practices and laws, an expression of the "sensitive and emotional" controversy surrounding it and his own conflicted feelings, and then a venture into the sort of judicial policy-making conservatives so often decried, as he meticulously laid out a calendar that progressively limited the woman's right to choose an abortion as her pregnancy advanced.

But in the stormy aftermath of *Roe*, Blackmun's painstaking handiwork seemed almost beside the point. The simple recognition of abortion as a constitutional right became *the* polarizing issue in national politics, a rallying cry for liberals who were "pro-choice" and for conservative "pro-lifers" who echoed Justice White's angry dissent that, in an "exercise of raw judicial power," the court had created a "constitutionally protected right" to "exterminate human life." *Roe* would haunt every nominee to the Supreme Court for decades.

THE ABORTION ISSUE never engaged Richard Nixon. By the time *Roe* was announced, January 22, 1973, two days after the president was inaugurated for a second term, he was deeply involved in a conspiracy to protect what mattered most to him—his power, threatened by investigations into the break-in at Democratic National Committee headquarters in June 1972 by men connected to his reelection campaign. Fatally, the president's aggressive—and criminal—role in obstructing the investigations was captured by tape recorders he had ordered installed in the Oval Office and elsewhere in the White House. When Nixon, citing the doctrine of "executive privilege," refused to turn over tapes of relevant conversations to the courts for use in a trial of former aides, the Supreme Court agreed, in July 1974, to hear the case on an expedited basis.

The stakes could hardly have been higher: on the court's decision rested the fate of a president. If the tapes were released and provided conclusive evidence of the president's wrongdoing, Nixon was finished. Many observers feared he would resist anything less than a unanimous opinion. Would not his own appointees—at least one or two of them—come out for judicial restraint and deference to the executive? But with its reaffirmation of John Marshall's famous claim to power in *Marbury*—"it is emphatically the province and duty of the judicial department to say what the law is"—the decision in *U.S. v. Nixon* was an assertion of judicial supremacy. While acknowledging the president's need for confidentiality in his decision-making, the court insisted that, in disputes between a federal judge and a president over the disclosure of evidence, it was the judge who had the final word.

And that decision was unanimous. Nixon had hoped for some "air," some way to evade compliance, but during several tense hours after the decision came down, his lawyers could find none. Seventeen days later, August 8, following the release of an especially damning tape, the president resigned. Law and order, it turned out, cut both ways.

NIXON HAD NO MORE justices to name after Powell and Rehnquist in 1971. Gerald Ford, his appointed successor, had but one vacancy to fill as he served out the rest of Nixon's second term. As a Republican leader in the House, Ford had been a vitriolic critic of the Warren Court, and in 1970, after the Haynsworth debacle and egged on by a vengeful Nixon, he had targeted William Douglas for impeachment. The charges were insubstantial and brusquely dismissed by the House Judiciary Committee; Ford's real aim had been to strike at the legacy of liberal judicial activism through a surviving New Deal justice. Douglas swore to stay on the court "until the last hound dog had stopped snapping at my heels." He achieved the longest tenure in the Supreme Court's history—more than thirty-six years—but ill health forced his retirement in 1975, at the age of seventy-seven. That gave his old tormentor the chance to name his replacement. The surging Republican right wing, which threatened to mount a challenge to his nomination in 1976, pressed Ford to appoint a hard conservative to the court. But as a president with no electoral mandate facing an aggressive Democratic Congress, he needed a "nonpartisan" nominee able to win confirmation. That led him to John Paul Stevens, a scholarly Chicago Republican with little background in party politics and a reputation for legal craftsmanship and independence won in five years as a federal appeals judge. The Senate confirmed him unanimously.

Decisions like *Roe* underscored the failure of two Republican presidents, with five justices between them, to pack the Supreme Court with ideologues single-mindedly committed to reversing its liberal activism. The fact that Democrat Jimmy Carter, who defeated Ford in 1976, had no appointments—the first president in history to serve a full term without at least one—only whetted New Right appetites. The roulette wheel was bound to turn their way, if only they could get one of their own into the White House.

That made Ronald Reagan's first nomination, when Potter Stewart decided to retire not long after Reagan took office in 1981, a crushing disappointment. Unlike Nixon, Reagan was a true believer, an ideologue committed to shifting the Republican party far to the right. Ever since his emergence on the national scene in 1964 as an eloquent Goldwaterite, the retired actor had made criticism of "judicial lawmaking" and "social engineering" by unelected judges staples of his oratory. A onetime New Deal Democrat, President Reagan identified with FDR, not least in his determination to defeat a hostile judiciary. But the new president also had a political debt to pay: his campaign promise to name "the most qualified woman I can find" to "one of the first Supreme Court vacancies in my administration."

Reagan's White House vetted the leading candidate, Sandra Day O'Connor, with exquisite care. After growing up on a ranch with 200,000 acres and 2,000 head of cattle on the Arizona–New Mexico border, O'Connor attended Stanford Law School, served as a civilian lawyer with the army, and won election as a Republican state senator in Arizona, before serving on the state's court of appeals. But was she conservative enough? Did she share the White House view that judges should "interpret the law, not enact new law by judicial fiat"? Was she sound on abortion? For the first time that issue was playing a crucial role in a Supreme Court nomination. After *Roe* was decided, anti-abortion crusaders began to press state legislatures to impose restrictions on women's right to choose. But their aim was not merely to limit *Roe*. They hoped to pack the Supreme Court with justices who would vote to overturn it.

Scouring O'Connor's record, the vetters found a few question marks, including reports that while in the state senate she had favored liberalization of Arizona's abortion laws. In July 1981, O'Connor met in the White House with Reagan and staffers. There she evidently assured the president that she would be no judicial activist on the court and that abortion was "personally repugnant" to her. But anti-abortion leaders were not assured. One warned the president that her nomination would ignite a firestorm of opposition across the country. Reagan stuck to his choice—she was, one official said, "the most conservative woman we could find"—and O'Connor won unanimous backing in the Senate.

O'Connor disappointed abortion foes on her very first major encounter with the issue, *Akron* v. *Akron Center for Reproductive Health*, in 1983. She did dissent from the court majority that struck down a battery of state obstacles to abortion—but O'Connor did *not* call for *Roe* to be overturned. The crux of her dissent was that the Ohio restrictions did not impose an "undue burden" on a woman's exercise of her abortion right. Narrowing *Roe*'s scope was a compromise—anathema to those who considered abortion murder.

The O'Connor disappointment made Reagan's next picks critical, but the opportunities were slow in coming. Conservatives inside the administration used the time to construct an elaborate screening process that rated candidates against the ideal Supreme Court nominee, who would exhibit a "refusal to create new constitutional rights for the individual," a "disposition towards 'less government rather than more,'" an "appreciation for the role of the free market in our society," and a "respect for traditional values." Attorney General Edwin Meese hit the road to campaign for a "jurisprudence of Original Intention" that would limit constitutional interpretation to discerning the motives of the Framers two hundred years before. Justice Brennan responded directly to Meese, maintaining that it was "arrogance cloaked as humility" to pretend to apply the Founders' intent to specific modern problems. "The genius of the Constitution," he said, "rests not in any static meaning it might have had in a world that is dead and gone, but in the adaptability of its great principles to cope with current problems and current needs."

The man to whom Ronald Reagan turned with little hesitation to lead the Supreme Court when Warren Burger stepped down in May 1986 was no more an "originalist" than Brennan. William Rehnquist did not believe there was a single, discoverable meaning to the Constitution. He liked to point out that he and Brennan might study the "original intent" of the First Amendment and come to opposite conclusions. Like his patron, Richard Nixon, Rehnquist was more realist than ideologue. The Supreme Court could never be above politics, in his view, either in the appointment process or in the conflicts on the bench, as justices fought to have their views prevail.

Such realism made Rehnquist a results-oriented activist of the right—and in all the ways that counted, what Rehnquist wanted, the Reaganites wanted, too. He was the "paradigmatic example" of judicial conservatism, the ideal man to direct "a generally rudderless Court." Senate Democrats, now in the minority, saw it differently. As Rehnquist acknowledged, had they been in control of the Senate, he might have well and fairly been rejected. As it was, he collected 33 negative votes, the most ever for a successful chief justice nominee.

His promotion gave Reagan a second seat to fill. Shadowing the

White House was the O'Connor "mistake." After five years on the court, she continued to give conservatives reason to doubt what administration lawyers called "her commitment to principles of judicial restraint and fundamental constitutional values." Though far more often than not she voted the "right" way, she frequently filed separate concurrences that undermined conservative cohesiveness. Looking for the anti-O'Connor, the vetters fell hard for Antonin Scalia. Born in Trenton to an elementary school teacher mother and an Italian immigrant father who became professor of romance languages at Brooklyn College, Scalia was described by a classmate at the Catholic military school he attended as an "archconservative Catholic" at age seventeen. After a few years of practicing law in Cleveland, Scalia taught at the University of Virginia Law School, became an assistant attorney general under Nixon, a scholar at the conservative American Enterprise Institute, and a Reagan appointee to the U.S. Court of Appeals for the District of Columbia, sometimes called the nation's "second court" and now becoming a training ground for Supreme Court justices.

To conservatives, Scalia's jurisprudence was "perfect." He touted "originalism" and deference to the political branches and to the states, but did not scruple to cross over into activism in pursuit of conservative results. And unlike so many of the Republican appointees, he had no hang-ups about precedent. If he disagreed with a past decision, he would not hesitate to overturn it—for instance, *Roe*, which as both a judge and a devout Catholic he felt was ripe for review. For such a militant conservative, his confirmation was, curiously, a breeze. He checked his temper—the one thing about him that had worried the vetters—and evaded controversies. Moreover, Democrats had spent most of their fury on Rehnquist's earlier confirmation. Scalia was approved unanimously.

Reagan's next nominee was, in the eyes of the vetters, almost Scalia's ideological twin, another "perfect" conservative, but their fates could scarcely have been more different. Justice Powell's retirement in June 1987 put the Supreme Court into play as it had not been for decades. Powell had evolved into a "determined moderate," who held the deciding vote in a wide variety of important cases, including abortion. Swinging left and right, he more than anyone had defined the inconsistent, middle-of-the-road jurisprudence of the Burger Court.

With a golden opportunity to tip the court decisively rightward, Reagan picked a man he insisted on describing as another Powell, "evenhanded and openminded." No terms so ill defined Robert Bork, whose long career as a reactionary academic and judge had put him in the vanguard of the right wing's legal counterrevolution. His voluminous paper trail exposed a nominee who would, in the name of originalism and restraint, sweep away the precedents of half a century. Democrats erupted. On the Senate floor, Ted Kennedy roared that "Robert Bork's America is a land in which women would be forced into back alley abortions, blacks would sit at segregated lunch counters, rogue police could break down citizens' doors in midnight raids, schoolchildren could not be taught about evolution, writers and artists could be censored at the whim of government."

Bork's confirmation hearing proved a disaster. For days, the judge lectured the senators, eagerly entertained hypotheticals, and almost leapt into traps Democrats set for him, even while jettisoning some of his most extreme views in a "confirmation conversion." Enough remained, though, to make Kennedy's remarks seem less like an intemperate, partisan outburst than a chilling prophecy. The Senate killed the Bork nomination, 58 to 42.

Reagan responded swiftly with a "spite" nomination, determined to force on the Senate a nominee "they'll object to just as much" as they had to Bork. But while Douglas Ginsburg, a federal appeals judge for the D.C. circuit, passed the in-house ideological litmus tests with flying colors, his private life fell short in the "traditional values" department. Within a week after Reagan named him, Ginsburg acknowledged that he had smoked marijuana while a student and law professor. Three days later, Ginsburg was out.

Embarrassed, Reagan now sought a moderate conservative who could get confirmed. Judge Anthony Kennedy of the federal appeals court in California had long been mentioned for the high bench, but "disturbing aspects" of his jurisprudence—a sympathy for privacy and other "new" rights, a lack of deference to the political branches— damaged his standing among true believers. But now, even though aides feared Kennedy would prove more a Powell than a Scalia, Reagan needed him. At his confirmation hearings, the nominee adroitly distanced himself from Bork, especially on privacy, and after three days of routine testimony, the Senate confirmed him unanimously.

WITH KENNEDY'S CONFIRMATION, a cohesive conservative majority seemed to take shape. Voting together 80 percent of the time in the Supreme Court's 1988 and 1989 terms, Rehnquist, O'Connor, Scalia, Kennedy, and White challenged key liberal precedents in civil rights and civil liberties. In *City of Richmond* v. *Croson*, they required states to prove past discriminatory acts in order to justify affirmative action, which would be limited only to those who were shown to have suffered the discrimination. They weakened protections against warrantless searches in two cases involving drug testing and, in a case involving peyote rituals, against invasions of religious liberty by secular laws.

The critical test was abortion, and in *Webster* v. *Reproductive Health Services*, the five conservatives substantially weakened *Roe* by approving a Missouri law that severely limited the use of public resources for abortions or for abortion counseling and required doctors to determine the "viability" of fetuses before performing the procedure after twenty weeks of pregnancy. Four of the conservatives seemed ready to discard *Roe*—Scalia most explicitly—but O'Connor resisted because *Webster* did not directly challenge its constitutionality. When such a case came to the court, she wrote forebodingly, "there will be time enough to reexamine *Roe*. And to do so carefully." In his dissent, Blackmun wrote, "I fear for the future. . . . I fear for the integrity of, and public esteem for, this Court."

Blackmun's fears must have intensified when the last liberal stalwarts of the Warren Court retired—William Brennan in July 1990 and Thurgood Marshall a year later. The power of appointment was now in the hands of President George H. W. Bush, Reagan's vice president and successor. Bush was mistrusted by the hard right and eager to appease it, while avoiding a Bork-like confirmation mess. To replace Brennan, Bush picked David Souter, after minimal vetting. In fact, there was not much to vet. Souter was scarcely known in the legal community. He had spent most of his career as a state court judge in New Hampshire. Bush put him on the federal appeals court in April 1991—three months before he named him to the Supreme Court. The president relied on the assurances of Souter's powerful New Hampshire patrons, his chief of staff, John Sununu, and Senator Warren Rudman. Indeed, Bush met Souter only an hour before he introduced him to the press. Worried conservatives were told by Sununu that Souter was a "home run" for them—they could neither confirm nor deny that. Nor did Democrats have more to go on than Rudman's word that the nominee would be fine on privacy and civil rights.

Souter's confirmation hearings were no more revealing. The judge made conservatives uneasy by his failure to take up their invitations to expound on strict construction, while Democrats wondered if his moderation was a pose to avoid being Borked. And what was all that praise Souter uttered of his predecessor, William Brennan— mere politeness, or something more? A puzzled Senate confirmed Souter overwhelmingly, with only nine votes, all liberal Democrats, in opposition.

There was no chance that Bush's second nominee, to replace

Thurgood Marshall, could have been a "stealth candidate." Forty-three-year-old Clarence Thomas was well known in conservative circles, not least because he was that rare phenomenon, a black Reaganite. A Georgian of humble origins who had worked his way into a Catholic college, Holy Cross—he had once dreamed of becoming a priest—and then Yale Law School, he rose in Washington to become head of the Equal Employment Opportunity Commission under Reagan. His success in weakening enforcement of antidiscrimination laws won him appointment to the federal appeals court for the D.C. circuit in 1990, where he was presumed to be in waiting for Marshall's "black seat" on the Supreme Court.

Bush thought Thomas's race would mute liberal opposition, but Democrats were dismayed by the fierce, almost Borkian conservatism in the nominee's many writings and speeches. At the hearings, Thomas tried to slide through, tempering his conservatism and dismissing some of his more extreme opinions as so many thought experiments. Evasion reached an absurd pitch when he denied that he had discussed *Roe* with anyone, *ever*. Then, ten days after the hearings ended, the Senate Judiciary Committee abruptly reconvened to hear charges by Anita Hill, who had been a young lawyer on Thomas's EEOC staff, that he had sexually harassed her. Denying any wrongdoing, Thomas denounced this "high-tech lynching for uppity blacks" who "deign to think for themselves." It was an ugly public spectacle that ended inconclusively. The Senate confirmed Thomas, but by the narrowest margin—six votes—of any successful nominee in the twentieth century.

The arrivals of Souter and Thomas signaled the peak of Republican court-packing. All of the justices except Byron White were Republican appointees, and the conservative majority of Rehnquist, O'Connor, Scalia, Kennedy, and White was now apparently augmented by the Bush nominees. The chief justice himself sensed that the long-deferred counterrevolution was at hand. In a 1991 case,

Payne v. *Tennessee,* he had announced that the court would not be bound by precedent "when governing decisions are unworkable or are badly reasoned. . . . *Stare decisis* is not an inexorable command." Thurgood Marshall, on the edge of retirement, had struck back hard at this "radical new exception" to the Supreme Court's traditional respect for its prior rulings. "The majority declares itself free to discard any principle of constitutional liberty . . . with which five or more Justices *now* disagree." This signaled, Marshall wrote, that "power, not reason, is the new currency of this Court's decisionmaking." The chief justice would not have disagreed: decision-making among the justices was driven by the votes of a majority. Votes were power—with five of them you could do anything, as William Brennan had said—and Rehnquist had the votes.

Or so he thought. A funny thing happened on the way to the counterrevolution. Not long after the Bush nominees joined the court, conservative cohesion began to dissolve. As Republicans had feared, Souter was the first to go, beginning to vote more often with the liberals than with the conservatives. More surprising were the defections of O'Connor and Kennedy. Disturbed by the aggressiveness and overreaching of their allies, especially Scalia and Thomas, they made a turn toward moderation. The two became—and would remain—a tag team of swing voters, giving their decisive votes now to the liberal bloc, now to the conservatives. By 1991, according to political scientist Thomas Hensley's analysis, over half of the court's decisions in civil rights and liberties cases were "liberal," compared to 33 percent in 1989. By 1992, the conservative core had shrunk to Rehnquist, Scalia, Thomas, and White—a minority.

With the acid test still abortion, *Planned Parenthood* v. *Casey,* in 1992, proclaimed the conservative crack-up. At issue was a Pennsylvania law that mandated a twenty-four-hour waiting period for women seeking abortions. It also required that women notify their spouses and that minors obtain their parents' consent before having the procedure. The chief justice began to draft what he assumed would be the majority opinion. He would uphold all of Pennsylvania's restrictions and effectively overturn *Roe*, writing, "The Court was mistaken in *Roe* when it classified a woman's decision to terminate her pregnancy as a 'fundamental right.'"

But unknown to the chief justice, Souter, O'Connor, and Kennedy were collaborating on an alternative opinion. They were appalled by the chief's eagerness to dismiss *Roe*. O'Connor was also offended by the Pennsylvania statute's spousal-notification provision—it struck her as sexist and patriarchal—and she wanted to write the "undue burden" standard she had invented for *Akron* into law. The biggest surprise was Kennedy. Only three years earlier, he had gone along with Rehnquist's *Webster* call for *Roe* to be overturned. Now, in a talk with Blackmun, whose gradual leftward drift had been moved in part by the right wing's unrelenting assault on his work in *Roe*, Kennedy told the old justice that he would uphold the right to abortion. In a direct hit at Rehnquist's *Payne* opinion, the "troika" spoke up for stare decisis: "A decision to overrule *Roe*'s essential holding under the existing circumstances would address error, if error there was, at the cost of both profound and unnecessary damage to the Court's legitimacy, and to the Nation's commitment to the rule of law." Blackmun and Stevens signed on to the core of their decision that "the essential holding of *Roe* v. *Wade* should be retained and once again reaffirmed." Suddenly, Rehnquist didn't have the votes.

CONTROVERSY OVER Republican court-packing had risen to such a heat during the Reagan-Bush presidencies as to become a defining issue in the 1992 presidential campaign. Bill Clinton criticized the Republican use of ideological litmus tests and promised that his appointees would be "unquestionably qualified by reason of training, experience, judgment." To these bland criteria, he added that his nominee would be "someone who believed in the constitutional right to privacy." In fact, he finally said, "I would want people on the Supreme Court . . . who were pro-choice." Six weeks into his presidency, with the retirement of Justice White after his thirty-one years on the high bench, Clinton looked forward to making the first appointment by a Democratic president since Lyndon Johnson chose Thurgood Marshall twenty-six years earlier.

Astonishingly, it was hard to peddle the job. The president's first choice, Governor Mario Cuomo of New York, declined. Clinton's secretary of education, Richard Riley, also declined, twice. After Clinton floated the name of his interior secretary, Bruce Babbitt, as a trial balloon, Babbitt withdrew in a storm of controversy ignited by anti-environmentalists. Two high-ranking judges in lower courts—both women—also asked to be removed from consideration. Then, finally, the president's eye fell on Ruth Bader Ginsburg, who had served for over a dozen years on the potent federal appeals court for the D.C. circuit. Raised in Brooklyn, she had won her law degree from Columbia, tied for first in her class. Clinton felt a quick "emotional connection" with a woman who had said she had three strikes against her, as a woman, a Jew, and "a mother to boot."

The Senate approved her 96 to 3. While her background as a leading advocate for women's rights pleased Democrats, her restrained jurisprudence on the appeals court convinced Republicans that she was as she described herself—a judge who would "decide the case before her without reaching out to cover cases not yet seen." She fit comfortably into a liberal bloc made up of Republican appointees.

A year later, when Justice Blackmun announced that he was retiring at the age of eighty-five, President Clinton had a second appointment—only to find once more that the gift was hard to give. Again, his first choice—Senate majority leader George Mitchell of Maine—turned down the honor. Other names were floated and shot down. Finally, at the urging of Senator Ted Kennedy, Clinton approached another federal appeals court judge, Stephen G. Breyer. A Harvard Law School graduate, Breyer had clerked for Justice Goldberg, served as counsel to the Senate Judiciary Committee, and was appointed to the appeals court by Jimmy Carter in 1980. As with Ginsburg, Breyer's appeals court record, along with his unfeigned respect for "the people's representatives" in Congress, won over Republicans. He was praised by both parties as a "principled moderate" and "moderate pragmatist," and after winning easy confirmation, he gravitated smoothly to the Stevens-Souter-Ginsburg axis.

Losing out in the grand roulette of judicial appointments, Clinton would have no further picks in his remaining six years in the White House. But if there would be no Clinton Court, whose court was it? The chief justice's grip had weakened even further with the arrival of the Clinton appointees and the loss of White. John Paul Stevens emerged as the liberal leader after Brennan's retirement; he and his allies voted together as consistently as the conservative trio of Rehnquist, Scalia, and Thomas. But even though the liberals held their own—and sometimes more—in the battle for dominance of the court, they were one vote short of a Stevens Court.

If leadership on the Supreme Court were measured by being on the winning side in key cases, then it might be called the O'Connor Court. Recoiling from the unbound extremism of Rehnquist et al., O'Connor forged a centrist—actually, moderately conservative— path that, term after term, put her in the majority in 90 percent of the decisions. Because she was the quintessential swing vote who had constantly to be wooed, her own jurisprudence came to characterize the court's: case-by-case decision-making on narrow grounds, often achieved by splitting the difference. If the court took few large leaps left or right, that was O'Connor's influence. The court was not exactly quiescent—indeed, its polarization and the inability of either bloc to gain the upper hand created strong and angry turbulence— but it tacked back and forth on a narrow track.

Yet rarely had the court been so supreme. For decades, conservatives had inveighed against the liberal activism of the judiciary and required their nominees to pledge allegiance to restraint and strict construction. But none of the conservatives on the Supreme Court would pass muster with Felix Frankfurter. Whether it was pushing for the principle of absolute "colorblindness" in law or the devolution of power to the states or checks on regulations, the conservatives all were activists, equal, at the least, in that with the liberals. After all, counterrevolutions, even in the cause of "restraint," could not be conducted with hands folded. Because she sometimes sided with conservatives in their activism and sometimes with liberals in their activism, O'Connor, despite her careful, step-by-step jurisprudence, her refusal to endorse broad principles, was the most activist judge of all. As a result, beginning in 1994, the Supreme Court struck down federal statutes at a higher rate than ever before, more than twice as often as had the Taft Court, almost twice as often as the Hughes Court before 1937, and half again as often as the Warren Court at its activist peak in the 1960s. It was simply, in political scientist Thomas Keck's phrase, "the most activist Supreme Court in history."

That record reflected a distrust of, not a deference to, "the people's representatives" in the legislative branch. In 1993, Congress tried to override a decision of the Supreme Court that religious groups saw as a threat to their right to freely exercise their faith, with a law that explicitly criticized the court's use of judicial review. Rejecting the new law, the justices slapped the legislators down hard, reminding them that only the judiciary could define the rights guaranteed by the Constitution and that "the courts retain the power, as they have since *Marbury* v. *Madison*, to determine if Congress has exceeded its authority." Nor were the justices reluctant to leap into what Frankfurter had called "political thickets," injecting themselves into a wide variety of controversial matters that might have been left to the political branches. This included the ultimate thicket of legislative apportionment, with the justices repeatedly overturning the decisions of governors and state legislatures and, by drawing and redrawing political boundary lines, determining the fate of elected officials.

Polarized and fragmented as it was, this imperious court reigned supreme over the political and constitutional landscape.

CHAPTER TWELVE

Hard Right: The Cheney-Bush Court

IN THE END, the story of *Bush* v. *Gore* was very simple. After all the complex, jostling political action—local, state, and national—that riveted the country for more than a month in the wake of Election Day 2000, the Supreme Court had the power to break the electoral college deadlock between George W. Bush and Al Gore and to settle the presidential election—and it did. Five conservative Republican justices—Rehnquist, O'Connor, Scalia, Kennedy, and Thomas— had the bare majority of votes they needed to settle it for their fellow conservative Republican, George Bush. They insisted in their majority opinion that resolving the disputed vote in the state of Florida was an "unsought responsibility" they were "forced" to confront, but they seized it with fervor and speed, issuing their decision less than thirty-six hours after the two sides made their arguments.

In order to elect George Bush, the conservative justices had to cast aside principles that had for decades powered the New Right's campaign against liberalism in law and justice. They had to suspend their "respect for federalism" to override the Florida Supreme Court in a matter historically left to the states—the way elections are conducted. They had to invent a new constitutional right—a "fundamental right" for each voter to have his or her ballot counted by a uniform standard. To do so, the conservatives, who had shown little but hostility to claims of unequal treatment in a wide range of cases, used the equal protection clause of the Fourteenth Amendment as daringly as the Warren Court ever had, but they left themselves an out: that "fundamental right" was good for this case only, "for the problem of equal protection in election processes generally presents many complexities." It does: Florida's crazy quilt of election procedures and technologies was the rule in the United States. Rarely were two polling stations anywhere alike—especially damaging to voters in poor and minority areas, where the lack of resources and official indifference reduced voter access and made for confused ballots and haphazard vote counts. But no court—certainly not this court—had ever before suggested that all voters were constitutionally entitled to have their ballots cast and counted the same way.

The five justices decided that Florida could not carry out a count of ballots that would meet their new standard by the deadline they imposed—it happened to be the very day of their decision, December 12—so they ordered an immediate halt to the counting, ensuring that none of the contested ballots would be counted by their—or any other—standard. That in turn ensured that George Bush's lead of 537 votes—out of almost six million cast by Floridians—hastily certified in November as final by Florida's secretary of state, who was cochair of Bush's state campaign, would be locked in. All of the state's 25 electoral votes would go to Bush and put him over the top in the electoral college.

The alternatives, the justices suggested, were too dreadful to contemplate. Florida, which constitutionally had the responsibility for determining how presidential electors were selected, might have completed its recount, following its own standards, and then delivered the results to the House of Representatives, which, under the Constitution, was the final arbiter in disputes over the certification of electors. But that constitutional procedure, Justice Scalia wrote in announcing the court's decision to hear the case, would "threaten irreparable harm" to George Bush "by casting a cloud upon what he claims to be the legitimacy of his election." The harm to Bush was that, in a recount, he might lose. So the justices made sure that the only votes that counted were their own.

Justice Stevens feared that the real harm might lie elsewhere. He and his fellow dissenters were disturbed by the Florida deadlock and all the controversies over balloting. Indeed, Souter and Breyer agreed on the need for the Florida Supreme Court to set improved standards. While for the conservative majority this was an excuse to halt all counting, Souter and Breyer wanted it to continue. Had the Supreme Court not "interrupted" it, Florida might have solved these problems on its own, Souter said, "and if not disposed of at the state level it could have been considered by Congress in any electoral vote dispute." As Breyer pointed out, "Congress, being a political body, expresses the people's will far more accurately than does an unelected Court."

Stevens and Ginsburg agreed that the Supreme Court should never have intervened. Bush's attack on Florida's procedures, Stevens wrote, was "wholly without merit" and the majority's decision "effectively orders the disenfranchisement of an unknown number of voters whose ballots reveal their intent—and are therefore legal votes under state law"—but that now would never be counted.

"Although we may never know with complete certainty the identity of the winner of this year's Presidential elections," Stevens concluded, "the identity of the loser is perfectly clear. It is the Nation's confidence in the judge as an impartial guardian of the rule of law."

By all lights, Stevens should have been right. Yet such was the authority of the Supreme Court that the five justices got away with their nakedly partisan decision. Al Gore, who had won a half million more votes nationally than Bush, but whose chance for the presidency was now abruptly erased, made a meek concession. "Now the U.S. Supreme Court has spoken," he said in a televised address. Florida did not rebel against the court's invasion of states' rights. Congress made no move to overturn the decision. There was no explosion of court-curbing proposals as controversial decisions had provoked in the past. There were no marches on Washington. Liberal scholars assailed the decision, as did many conservatives. "Desirable result aside," wrote political scientist and Bush backer John J. DiIulio, Jr., "it is bad constitutional law," an expression of "judicial imperialism." And yet, public confidence in the Supreme Court was remarkably unshaken, even, after a dip in the immediate aftermath, among Democrats. Some political scientists suggested that doubt about the fairness of the ruling was more than offset by the unusual exposure to the "legitimizing symbols" of the court—"the marble temple, the high bench, the purple curtain, the black robes"—all conveyed to the public by a media that spoke of the justices "with the greatest deference and respect."

For its part, the court resumed business-as-usual, revealing little of the turmoil and bitterness that gripped it in December 2000. The 2001 term featured the court's by now accustomed tacking left and right, here mandating tougher enforcement of environmental laws, there immunizing states from federal discrimination suits by disabled employees; here allowing mothers to be handcuffed and taken to jail for failing to buckle their children's car safety belts and there upholding campaign finance laws. As usual, O'Connor or Kennedy or both provided the swing votes in a term that saw an unusually high proportion—one third—of 5-4 decisions.

Observers could only guess at the impact of *Bush* v. *Gore* on the justices. An immediate sign, much commented upon, was Justice

Ginsburg's omission, in her opinion, of the customary "respectfully" when she concluded, "I dissent." O'Connor made occasional defensive remarks in public, pointing out that some informal recounts conducted after the court had ruled showed that Bush would have won anyway. Kennedy, it was noticed, seemed to travel more, spending time abroad. Justice Souter was said to have been the most deeply affected by the case, shocked by the partisanship and lawlessness of the decision, even to the point of considering resignation. More than any of the other justices—more than most Americans—his faith in judges as "impartial guardians of the rule of law" was shattered.

THE MAN THE Supreme Court thrust into the presidency was not tormented by doubt. From the outset, George W. Bush governed as though he had earned a clear mandate for his sharply conservative agenda. The new president saw himself as heir not to the mushy, incoherent conservatism of his father, George H. W. Bush, but rather to the conviction politics of Ronald Reagan. His base was an inherited one of economic libertarians, social conservatives, especially his fellow Christian evangelicals, and hawks who demanded an assertive American posture toward the world. Despite the power of this awkward coalition early in the twenty-first century—their dominance within the Republican party, in Congress and at the grassroots, as well as in its presidential wing—all three factions continued to style themselves insurgents against a hostile establishment, and since the Reagan years, they had become, if anything, more aggressive and demanding. It took a rare politician like George W. Bush to harness all three behind his ambitions.

The interests and goals of the factions clashed in many ways. Economic libertarians were uncomfortable with the values of evangelicals, while evangelicals in turn were more often victims, not beneficiaries, of the free market. Hawks tended to disdain them both.

One thing they did share, though, was hostility to judicial liberalism and an eagerness to complete the conservative takeover of the courts. For the free marketers, this meant lifting regulations and other interferences with property rights. For social conservatives, it meant banning abortion, gay rights, and other outrages against "traditional values," while dismantling the historic barriers between church and state. Hawks sought, above all, to unleash presidential power by removing the constraints they believed the courts, with Congress, had put on the executive in the aftermath of Vietnam and Watergate.

The closely divided Supreme Court represented both frustration and opportunity to conservatives. Decades of dedicated court-packing had failed to give them undisputed control of the high bench. But now they were perhaps one vote away from tipping the balance decisively on issues such as affirmative action and federal power over the states. A pair of new justices—to replace, say, Stevens and O'Connor— might yield the grand prize: *Roe*'s overthrow.

And George W. Bush seemed dedicated to giving them what they wanted. It was not so much his campaign rhetoric, promising judges "who will strictly interpret the Constitution and will not use the bench to write social policy." They had heard that before, at least since 1968, when Richard Nixon had made it a cliché through endless repetition. They were only slightly more impressed by Bush's claim that Antonin Scalia and Clarence Thomas were his favorite judges. The president showed his real commitment by packing the White House legal staff, where judicial candidates were born and made, with hard-core right-wingers drawn from the conservative legal network.

With its hundreds of chapters at law schools and in cities, its 35,000 members—including Justices Scalia and Thomas, as well as Robert Bork—and its $5 million budget, the Federalist Society was at the heart of that network. The group was much more than the "forum for ideas, discussion, and debate" it claimed to be. Its members lobbied state and federal government for changes in laws and regulations. They provided pro bono legal support for conservative causes. They served on boards and as counsel for the anti-abortion National Right to Life Committee, the Christian Coalition, and the Center for Individual Rights, which was active in fighting against the rights of women, minorities, the disabled, and the elderly. Most important, the Federalist Society was central in recruiting, grooming, and promoting young activists for policy-making positions, legislative staffs, and judicial offices in state and federal government.

Presided over by the president's counsel, Alberto Gonzales, a Bush loyalist from Texas, White House lawyers quickly prepared a database of potential Supreme Court nominees and drafted memos—some as long as one hundred pages—detailing the pros and cons of the best candidates. And then they waited. And waited.

Annually, as the summer end of the court's term—the traditional retirement time for justices—approached, rumors spread of possible vacancies and candidates who might fill them. In the White House, a retirement betting pool would form—Rehnquist and O'Connor were the regular favorites. Lobbying groups mobilized and clashed. In June 2003, pro-choice leader Kate Michelman called on the Senate to filibuster any nominee who refused to commit to upholding *Roe*. Anti-abortion lawyer James Bopp, Jr., fired back that demanding commitments meant "the destruction of an independent judiciary." It was all moot—there was no vacancy that year. But the anticipation produced some bizarre moments. Evangelist Pat Robertson asked his vast television flock to join him in a "prayer offensive" aimed at three unnamed justices—apparently Stevens and Ginsburg, with the third unclear—so that God would put it in their minds "that the time has come to retire."

The Lord did not respond immediately. Bush's first term passed without a single departure from the high court. Both he and John Kerry, the Democratic contender in 2004, pointed to that as evidence of what was at stake in the election. The message was driven home when, a week before the vote, the court announced that Rehnquist had been stricken with thyroid cancer. No prognosis was given, but soon after Bush's narrow reelection, both sides prepared for the inevitable.

Now the right-wing rallying cry was, No more Kennedys! Even more than O'Connor, Anthony Kennedy had come to represent betrayal. In his earliest years as a justice, he had been tightly bound to the court's right wing. That made his "conversion" to a more moderate course all the more bitter. And far more than O'Connor, he was given to sweeping, even grandiose, judgments that made his activism more visible than O'Connor's incremental approach. In recent years he had authored some of the opinions most hateful to social conservatives—the 1996 *Romer* v. *Evans* decision that permitted localities to protect homosexuals from discrimination, demanding that government "remain open on impartial terms to all who seek its assistance"; the 1997 *City of Boerne* v. *Flores* decision blocking an attempt by Congress to protect the free exercise of religion from government interference; the 2003 *Lawrence* v. *Texas* decision that explicitly rejected a 1986 precedent by striking down a state law that barred homosexual sodomy. Kennedy ended *Lawrence* with a flourish that had "originalists" seeing red: the Framers, he wrote, "knew times can blind us to certain truths and later generations can see that laws once thought necessary and proper in fact serve only to oppress." Every generation, he added, sounding like William Brennan, could invoke the Constitution "in their own search for greater freedom." Scalia accused Kennedy of signing on to "the so-called homosexual agenda," and Focus on the Family dubbed him "the most dangerous man in America."

BY MAY 2005, with Rehnquist's health rapidly declining, the White House was refining its list of candidates for the job of chief justice. The administration's most powerful right-winger, Vice President Dick Cheney, was now in charge. His selection committee, which included the president's chief political aide, Karl Rove, culled the prospects to five, who each endured an hours-long grilling at the vice president's residence.

Cheney was preoccupied with rehabilitating the presidential power he believed had been crippled by Congress and the courts in the 1970s. After the 9/11 attacks on New York and Washington in 2001, he had shaped the administration's position that the president had the authority to wage the "war on terrorism" without interference or review by the other branches. Already the Supreme Court had struck blows at that claim. In two cases decided on June 28, 2004, *Rasul* v. *Bush* and *Hamdi* v. *Rumsfeld*, the court rejected the administration's indefinite detention of "enemy combatants" without any impartial process to establish whether their imprisonment was justified. Citizens and noncitizens were entitled to access to federal courts or other "neutral decision-makers." Condemning Bush's effort "to *condense* power into a single branch of government," O'Connor wrote for the court in *Hamdi* that "a state of war is not a blank check for the President."

In the wake of these decisions, the vice president sought assurances from court candidates that they shared his views of executive power. But what was the conservative position? The administration's extremism had cost it the support of the court's right wing. In *Hamdi*, only Clarence Thomas had accepted the claim that *an American citizen* could be held indefinitely without legal process. Rehnquist had joined the majority, and Scalia thought O'Connor had gone too easy on Bush. While Scalia backed Bush with a dissent in *Rasul*, which involved a foreign detainee, in *Hamdi* he condemned the very idea that American citizens could be held as "enemy combatants" and demanded that they be immediately charged with a crime or released. In an "originalist" twist, he wrote that the "Founders well understood the difficult tradeoff between safety and freedom" and quoted Alexander Hamilton's warning that "to be more safe," nations "at length, become willing to run the risk of being less free."

FINALLY, in July 2005, President Bush had the opportunity he had awaited for more than four years. A few days after the end of the term, as cameramen stalked the ailing Rehnquist's house, awaiting word of his retirement, a Supreme Court messenger delivered a letter to the White House. It was from Justice O'Connor, announcing that she would leave the court when her successor was confirmed. The Bush people were stunned, as were her colleagues, except for Rehnquist himself, who had maneuvered her into quitting before he did.

When the two Arizonans had talked of retirement a few months earlier, O'Connor had been impressed by the chief justice's point that two vacancies on the court at the same time would be disruptive. Assuming that Rehnquist, desperately sick with cancer, would leave at the end of the 2005 term, she decided that she would serve one more year before retiring to care for her husband, ill with Alzheimer's disease. But shortly before the term ended, Rehnquist told her that he wanted to stay another year, adding, "And I don't think we need two vacancies." The implication took O'Connor aback: if she did not retire immediately, she would have to remain for two more years. "Well, okay," she said. "I'll retire then."

O'Connor's retirement changed the administration's calculus, but only slightly. After a half-hearted effort to find an acceptable female, Bush resorted to Cheney's short-list. The man he chose, though, was not the hard-liners' favorite. That would have been Michael Luttig, a federal appeals judge. Luttig was brilliant and exquisitely well-connected, but had a combative, difficult personality. He was an extremist who sounded like an extremist, an unsuitable candidate for O'Connor's seat. John Roberts, another appeals court judge who had clerked for Rehnquist and worked in Reagan's White House before Bush the elder named him to the federal appeals bench for the D.C. circuit in 1992 at the age of only thirty-seven, was an equally brilliant but far less truculent conservative. His reticence, in fact, had raised doubts for Cheney's team. In his appeals court confirmation hearings, Roberts had denied that he had a "comprehensive philosophy" or an "all-encompassing approach" to constitutional interpretation. Was that true? the vetters demanded. Roberts was not entirely reassuring when he pointed out that conservative icons Scalia and Thomas were themselves inconsistent. Sometimes they wrote as strict constructionists, sometimes not—it depended on the case.

Cheney was won over when, two weeks after O'Connor's retirement, Roberts's appeals court upheld the military tribunals that the administration had created to try detainees in response to O'Connor's *Hamdi* opinion the year before, even though those tribunals did not meet the standards of the Geneva Conventions for fairness and due process. With his oft-expressed contempt for international obligations, Cheney was gratified to read that the "Geneva Convention cannot be judicially enforced." Moreover, Roberts's "soft" conservatism and the fuzziness of his views on issues like abortion were a plus if he was to replace O'Connor rather than Rehnquist. Then, too, he hit it off with the president, who liked his easy manner and thought he would make a "good colleague."

But on September 3, a few days before Roberts was to go before the Senate Judiciary Committee, William Rehnquist finally succumbed to cancer. Bush did not hesitate. Before Rehnquist could be laid to rest, the president announced that he would nominate Roberts as his successor. As he pointed out, in the six weeks since he was named to O'Connor's seat, Roberts had made a good impression. The release of tens of thousands of pages of documents from his work in the White House pleased conservatives with evidence of his staunch Reaganism, while exposing no "smoking gun" to terrify liberals. And in private meetings with Democratic senators, he projected modesty and restraint. On *Roe*, he found a line that sounded good while telling inquisitors nothing. *Roe* was, he would say, "settled law," entitled to respect "under the principles of *stare decisis*"—meaning it was settled until the Supreme Court decided it wasn't.

Modesty and blurriness carried Roberts through his hearings. He opened with an appealing, but misleading, comparison of judges to umpires. They don't make the rules, he said. "They make sure everybody plays by the rules. But it is a limited role." Supreme Court justices, though, *do* make the rules, as the Rehnquist Court had shown to an unprecedented degree. Roberts neatly evaded the question of what kind of rulemaker he would be. Edward Kennedy thought he discerned in the nominee's paper trail "a narrow and cramped and, perhaps, even a mean-spirited view of the law," but what journalist Janet Malcolm described as Roberts's "invincible pleasantness" and "armor of charm" deflected every attempt to pin him down. In the final vote, more than a score of Senate Democrats backed Roberts, reckoning that at least he didn't seem to be as radical as Rehnquist— or any of a number of other candidates Bush might have sent down. Judiciary Committee member Herbert Kohl, a Wisconsin Democrat, said he was voting his hopes and not his fears.

Bush still had one more seat to fill. The Cheney short-list sat on his desk, but with Roberts safely installed as chief justice, the president was ready to make a bolder choice—to replace O'Connor with a woman, something the retiring justice herself had hoped for. But the women most favored by conservatives were far to the right of O'Connor, bait for a nasty confirmation fight. Encouraged by a talk with the Senate's Democratic minority leader, Harry Reid, who claimed to have been impressed by her in a meeting before the Roberts appointment, Bush decided to nominate his White House counsel, Harriet Miers. She had served Bush loyally for years in Texas and now in Washington. That Miers had no judicial experience or background in constitutional law—she had practiced corporate law in Dallas for twenty-four years and served a term on the city council—mattered less to Bush than his conviction that they saw eye-to-eye on all things that mattered. This included Bush and Cheney's expansive views of executive power, which Miers had spent years in the White House defending. It also included faith. Like Bush, Miers was a convert to evangelical Christianity, which had given her, her minister said, "a servant's mentality."

For Bush it was a personal pick. As he said when he announced the nomination, "I know her heart, I know her character." But movement conservatives didn't know her, and they had felt betrayed too often in the past to take nominees on trust. What if she turned into a replica of the woman she was replacing? Moreover, the pick was a slap in the face. For decades, they had groomed a deep team of brilliant young lawyers with sterling credentials, and now "the president's secretary"—as some mistook Miers—had been parachuted in to seize the grand prize.

For the first time in his presidency, Bush faced open rebellion on the right. Though conservatives painted Miers as almost comically ignorant of constitutional law and the role of the court, their real concern was her lack of ideological credentials. It was critical that they cut her down fast. If the nomination came to a vote in the Senate, Democrats would likely vote aye—and why not, considering the potential alternatives?—while Bush would bring along enough Republican loyalists, and Harriet Miers would become a Supreme Court justice! The conservative attack was swift and merciless. Mauled by her boss's "base," Miers withdrew, just three weeks after the president's proud announcement.

Chastened, Bush retreated to Cheney's short-list, where he found a judge his right-wing base could embrace as one of their own. Much would be made of similarities in the careers of Samuel Alito and John Roberts. Alito too had been among the eager young Federalist

Society lawyers to burrow into the Reagan administration. Like Roberts, he had been appointed to the federal bench by Bush's father. But unlike with Roberts, there was no fuzziness about Alito's views. What he described as his "deep interest in constitutional law" had been triggered as an undergraduate at Princeton "in large part by deep disagreement with Warren Court opinions." In 1988, after Robert Bork's nomination had gone down in flames, Alito praised him as "one of the most outstanding nominees of this century." As a federal judge, Alito was dubbed "Scalito" by liberals but his opinions were less those of a slashing partisan than of a relentlessly solid technician. "He was on the bench for fifteen years," said a White House official, "and he never got a case wrong." When *Casey* had come before his appeals court, Alito voted to uphold all of Pennsylvania's restrictions on abortion, including its spousal-notification provision, a position the woman he was nominated to replace called "repugnant."

Conservatives were ecstatic. Federalist Society members coordinated a "grassroots" campaign in support of their longtime colleague. Legislative strategy was run out of Cheney's office. The opposition was not so well organized. Senate Democrats could not sustain an early filibuster threat when moderates declined to join in. Though liberal advocacy groups painted Alito as part of the "radical right legal movement," Judiciary Committee Democrats, with their scattershot questioning, could not Bork him. Recent revelations that Bush had conducted illegal surveillance of Americans raised crucial questions about presidential authority. Despite a background that suggested Alito would endorse sweeping executive power, Democrats were unable to draw blood. While not as smooth as Roberts, the soft-spoken nominee answered questions cautiously and methodically, daring even to be boring. The committee approved his nomination by a party-line vote. After a last-ditch filibuster push sputtered, the full Senate confirmed Alito, with 42 Democrats opposed.

. . .

AFTER THE long frustration of awaiting vacancies, the Cheney-Bush imprint on the Supreme Court soon was evident enough. In John Roberts's first three terms as chief justice, 2006 through 2008, the conservative "phalanx," as legal scholar Ronald Dworkin christened Roberts, Alito, Scalia, and Thomas, and with the indispensable help of Anthony Kennedy, delivered a series of decisions that read like planks from a Republican party platform. Fifty years after *Brown*, the conservatives hobbled efforts to desegregate public schools by making it nearly impossible for districts to use racial considerations except where schools had been segregated by law, thus striking down the integration plans of hundreds of schools districts around the country. They undermined the exclusionary rule by allowing unconstitutionally obtained evidence to be used against criminal defendants. Overturning two precedents, they ruled that an inmate could not be excused for missing an appeals filing deadline because a federal judge had given his lawyer the wrong date. They limited the free speech of government employees and of high school students and blocked court challenges to the constitutionality of Bush's grants of federal money to religious institutions providing social services under his "faith-based initiative."

The conservatives gave Republicans satisfaction on two issues the party had long exploited for financial and electoral gain. The court for the first time approved the criminalization of a specific abortion procedure, so-called "partial-birth" abortion. And the conservatives struck down the District of Columbia's ban on handguns, enacted by that crime-ridden city in 1976. For the first time, the Supreme Court recognized an individual right to gun ownership, subject only to such controls as the court itself might find "reasonable." Even leading figures of the conservative legal establishment objected to the decision in *District of Columbia* v. *Heller*, comparing it to that ultimate horror, *Roe* v. *Wade*. A prominent federal appeals court judge, J. Harvie

Wilkinson III, complained that, as with *Roe*, the justices had over-
ruled "the wishes of the people's representatives" to invent a right
that had no basis in the Constitution. Another influential conservative judge, Richard Posner, condemned the use of the "freewheeling discretion" of judicial review "strongly flavored with ideology" to
tighten the court's grip on the legislative and executive branches.

For Posner, judicial review inherently involved a political judgment, and that partisanship was on display when the conservative
justices gave yet another lift to the GOP by invalidating two provisions of a major campaign law passed in 2002 over the objections
of Republican bosses—one that restricted corporate political advertising, and another, the "Millionaire's Amendment," that lifted
fund-raising limits for candidates facing wealthy opponents whose
own spending from personal funds was unrestricted. Finally, the
conservatives enabled Republicans to add several seats to their Texas
congressional delegation by rubber-stamping an egregious gerrymander cooked up by party leaders in Washington and Austin that
reapportioned districts in ways grossly favorable to GOP candidates.

Every one of these decisions was the work of a bare majority of
five justices—the phalanx plus Kennedy, who remained a swing vote,
only now swinging more right than left. Even when he swung the
other way, the phalanx stood united in dissent. Chief Justice Roberts, in his confirmation hearings, had taken pains to distinguish
his jurisprudence from the radicalism of Scalia and Thomas, yet in
2007, he voted with Scalia in almost 90 percent of nonunanimous
cases. His—and Alito's—votes in the 2006 term alone provoked Ted
Kennedy, a forty-three-year veteran of the Senate Judiciary Committee, to declare their confirmation hearings a "sham." Kennedy
wrote that their "voting record on the court reflects not the neutral,
modest judicial philosophy they promised the Judiciary Committee,
but an activist's embrace of the administration's political and ideological agenda."

In the hearings and in speeches and interviews, Roberts had promised to unify the court, promoting himself as a consensus-builder, extolling the virtue of unanimous decisions, with "one clear and focused opinion of the court." But unanimous opinions fell during his tenure, while the proportion of 5–4 votes leaped to historic highs—more than one third of all decisions in 2007. And many of these close divisions were bitter, as the court's liberals, unusually, made their anger and frustration public. Mild-mannered David Souter, dissenting when the court denied relief to the inmate who had missed the filing deadline, declared that "it is intolerable for the judicial system to treat people this way," while John Paul Stevens jabbed at the conservatives' "strained and unpersuasive reading" of the Second Amendment in the D.C. handgun case. Dissenters pointed out that the conservatives were casting away precedents on the strength of their slim majority alone—"power, not reason," as Thurgood Marshall had feared in 1991, was now the court's currency. Dismayed by the conservative assault on school integration and *Brown*, Stephen Breyer spoke emotionally for twenty minutes in open court, concluding, "It is not often in the law that so few have so quickly changed so much." Even the typically collegial Ruth Ginsburg noted that with their "partial-birth" abortion decision, the conservatives had overturned a 2000 precedent—the only distinction between the two cases, she added tartly, was that the court was "differently composed."

But for all of the precedents the phalanx erased, the chief justice also pursued a subtler strategy. He had, after all, as Ted Kennedy recalled, promised senators that he would be "a modest judge." Frequently, Roberts held back from overturning an old ruling openly. Instead he crafted an opinion that would, in Ronald Dworkin's analysis, dismiss existing law without acknowledging that it was doing so—by "subterfuge"—but "as effectively as if it had done so explicitly." Roberts would sap the precedent of its authority, leaving it an empty shell. Justice Scalia, always a maximalist where Roberts was usually a minimalist, scorned this "faux judicial restraint" as "judicial obfuscation." But such denunciations also served Roberts's purpose: they separated him from Scalia and Thomas in controversial cases, and while they filed their inflammatory concurrences, he would issue his quieter, but scarcely less far-reaching, opinions for the court.

The chief justice's "stealth" strategy and skill at playing his "moderation" against the court's extremists also enabled Roberts to pick off members of the liberal bloc, bringing them behind conservative decisions, as he did most notably in 2008, when the proportion of 5–4 decisions dropped by half from the year before. On the short end of such decisions himself all too often, dependent on the vote of the erratic Kennedy, Roberts would expand his numbers where he could, without sacrificing the results he sought. He won the support of Stevens and Breyer for a 7–2 ruling that upheld Kentucky's use of lethal injection to execute convicted criminals. They agreed in *Baze v. Rees* that the available evidence did not prove that the procedure was painful enough to constitute "cruel and unusual" punishment, although Stevens took the opportunity in a separate concurrence to explain his vote as a bow to precedent. In fact, he wrote, he favored the total abolition of the death penalty. For his part, Roberts had to leave the door open to reversing the decision if conclusive evidence appeared of the suffering caused by lethal injection, but the chief justice, a consistent defender of the death penalty, got the result he wanted.

Similarly, Stevens agreed to join the phalanx and Kennedy in a 6–3 ruling to uphold an Indiana law that, to prevent voting fraud, obliged voters to present government-issued photo identification before they were allowed to cast ballots, the toughest of a half-dozen such state laws. Liberals believed that these laws were an attempt by Republican legislators to cut Democratic turnout at the polls. Despite the fact that there had never been a documented case of voter fraud in Indiana history and despite expectations that the law might disenfranchise countless poor, disabled, elderly, and minority voters, the court's majority in *Crawford* v. *Marion County Election Board*, in an opinion written by Stevens himself, held that the measure did not put an undue burden on voting rights. Scalia and Thomas, in their concurrences, demanded a more sweeping rejection of challenges to such laws.

Stevens, who had spoken eloquently on behalf of disenfranchised voters in *Bush* v. *Gore*, may have gone along with Roberts in order to forestall such a judgment. His opinion left open the possibility that more evidence of the law's burden on voters would lead to a reversal. Shortly after the court's ruling, a dozen Indiana nuns, all in their eighties and nineties, who came to the polls in wheelchairs and on walkers, were refused ballots when they could not prove their identities. A few had expired passports; none had a driver's license. The precinct worker who had to turn them away was a nun from their convent. News reports did not indicate whether the sisters were Democrats or Republicans.

By 2008, John Paul Stevens, Chicago Republican, Ford appointee, and by his own account, "pretty darn conservative," had for almost twenty years been the leader of what remained of the judicial liberalism that once had dominated the Supreme Court. After decades of right-wing assault, the court's liberal bloc had been reduced to reliance on the wayward decision-making of Ronald Reagan's last appointee, Anthony Kennedy. "Including myself," Stevens told a journalist in 2007, "every judge who's been appointed to the court since Lewis Powell"—named by Nixon in 1971—"has been more conservative than his or her predecessor. Except maybe Justice Ginsburg. That's bound to have an effect on the court." At age eighty-eight, the survivor of countless rumors—and Republican hopes and prayers—that he would retire, Stevens was all too aware of the fragility of the constitutional principles he upheld and how close the Supreme Court was to becoming the unbreachable conservative fortress it had been through much of its history. One more Roberts or Alito, one more Scalia or Thomas, would do it.

Nothing more vividly illustrated the razor's edge on which the awesome Supreme Court perched than the cases involving presidential power in the age of Bush and Cheney. Already, the court had rejected Bush's attempt to send captives of the "war on terror" into what an official called "the legal equivalent of outer space"—a "lawless" universe beyond the reach of Constitution and courts. After the justices denied Bush his "blank check" in *Rasul* v. *Bush* and *Hamdi* v. *Rumsfeld* in 2004, the president unilaterally created military commissions to try detainees at the Guantánamo prison in Cuba. By the time a challenge to that action, brought on behalf of Salim Ahmed Hamdan, a Yemeni held since 2001, reached the court in 2006, Roberts and Alito had taken their seats on the bench. But because Roberts had already ruled on *Hamdan* v. *Rumsfeld* as an appeals court judge— upholding the administration in the decision that won Dick Cheney's heart—the new chief justice did not take part in the case. On decision day, he sat next to Stevens as the old judge read out a majority opinion that shredded Roberts's earlier work piece by piece. Stevens focused sharply on Bush's determination to consolidate all power over the detainees in the executive branch, rejecting the president's arguments that he could establish military commissions without congressional authorization and that the Supreme Court was not entitled to hear Hamdan's appeal. The 5–3 ruling was a sharp blow to Bush-Cheney unilateralism as the majority, Clarence Thomas complained in his dissent, chose to disregard the court's "well-established duty to respect the Executive's judgment in matters of military operations and foreign affairs."

The president responded quickly in the fall of 2006 by pushing the compliant Republican Congress to authorize what he had been doing all along. Despite Supreme Court rulings in the earlier cases, the new law also asserted that the court's jurisdiction did not extend to the revived military commissions. When the inevitable challenge arrived at the Supreme Court late in December 2007, Bush's solicitor general, Paul Clement, argued that the justices had no business hearing *Boumediene* v. *Bush*. "Congress here has spoken," he declared. "The political branches have spoken." As evidence grew that the military commissions were a sham—their former chief prosecutor, Colonel Morris Davis, charged that the administration planned to mount show trials, with convictions guaranteed—the Supreme Court asserted its jurisdiction over them, again holding, in a 5–4 decision, that the detainees were entitled to habeas corpus, "an indispensable mechanism for monitoring the separation of powers." As in *Hamdan*, Kennedy provided the fifth vote, and he authored the majority opinion in *Boumediene*, a harsh rebuke to both president and Congress. "To hold that the political branches may switch the Constitution on or off at will," he wrote, "would lead to a regime in which they, not this Court, say 'what the law is.'"

The conservative phalanx united in opposition, with Roberts raising the old cry of "judicial activism," accusing the majority of replacing "a review system designed by the people's representatives with a set of shapeless procedures to be defined by federal courts at some future date." Scalia went further, as he so often did, and roused a still older fear. Never mind his outrage in *Hamdi* at the administration's trade-off of liberty for security. With the country "at war with radical Islamists," Scalia now forecast chillingly, the ruling "will make the war harder on us" and "will almost certainly cause more Americans to be killed."

From the Civil War to World War II and the Cold War, that fear had inhibited the Supreme Court from defending individual rights against questionable claims of military necessity. Yet four times in four years, and with increasing severity, the court had struck down the attempts of George Bush and Dick Cheney to fashion a legal black hole in which to throw their captives, rejecting each effort the president made to meet its objections. In part, it was the formless character of the "war on terror" that emboldened the justices. That war had no fixed battlefield, no definition of victory, and no end in sight. As Souter noted in his *Boumediene* concurrence, many of the detainees, including Lakhdar Boumediene, had already been "locked up for six years" in a constitutional limbo, with the administration asserting—but refusing to prove—that they were guilty of crimes or that their imprisonment was a military necessity.

Even more, it was the extreme and persistent claims of Bush and Cheney for almost limitless and unaccountable presidential power that rankled the justices. The administration relied on a novel doctrine of "inherent executive powers that are unenumerated in the Constitution" to make "the President alone" responsible for deciding how, in all respects, to defend national security. By acting on such assertions of centralized authority, Bush and Cheney invited a rebuke, if not from Congress, controlled until 2007 by the president's own party and cowed by the administration's relentless fearmongering, then by a court that for two hundred years had reserved to itself the right and duty "to say what the law is." It was a collision waiting to happen, a great, historic clash of powers. And in the end, in the 5–4 decision of *Boumediene*, one vote, falling as it did, had greater force than the claims of the president and vice president and their armies of lawyers. One vote.

Ending Judicial Supremacy

———————

BARACK OBAMA understood the weight of that one vote. Few presidents had scrutinized the Constitution and the powers of its judicial "third branch" more closely than Obama had before entering the White House. As the first African-American president of the Harvard Law Review, he had debated the work of the Founders with his fellow editors. As a professor of constitutional law at the University of Chicago, he had delighted in opening students' eyes to a Constitution that was, as he wrote in his 2006 book, *The Audacity of Hope*, "a part not just of the past but of their present and their future."

Befitting a scholar of the ambiguities and potentialities of that charter, Obama's view of the Constitution was complex and nuanced. The Founders, he maintained in *The Audacity of Hope*, had gotten it "incredibly right" when they established a framework for "deliberative democracy." By rejecting "all forms of absolute authority," they required citizens "to engage in a process of testing their ideas against an external reality, persuading others of their point of view, and building shifting alliances of consent." But that democratic conversation broke down, he noted, "over the one subject the Founders refused to talk about"—slavery. The Constitution had provided "no protection to those outside the constitutional circle" such as black Americans like Dred Scott, "who would walk into the Supreme Court a free man and leave a slave."

If the Constitution created a structure for democratic deliberation and popular decision, the task of the Supreme Court, Obama believed, was to serve as the keeper of the rules—to preserve and extend the vibrancy of that conversation and to ensure that all Americans had an equal voice in it. The court's role, in other words, was to oversee processes, not to dictate outcomes. In *The Audacity of Hope*, Obama rejected the "originalism" of justices like Scalia and Thomas. The Founders, he wrote, told us only "*how* to think," not "*what* to think." The Constitution was "not a static but rather a living document, and must be read in the context of an ever-changing world." Its meaning was political, emerging ultimately from democratic competition in the marketplace of ideas.

By vanquishing Republican John McCain in the presidential election of 2008—and with substantial Democratic gains in Congress—Obama could claim a victory in the battle of ideas. Americans had rejected the conservative dogmas of unrestricted laissez faire and severely limited government. Instead of rampant, unregulated economic competition, Obama emphasized inclusion, equal opportunity, and collective action, values that, he promised, would be reflected in his nominations to the Supreme Court. As senator, he had opposed Bush's two court appointments because John Roberts and Samuel Alito had consistently sided with the powerful against the powerless. As a presidential candidate, Obama vowed to name justices who had real-life experience and understood "what it means to be on the outside, what it means to have the system not work for them." He wanted, he told voters, "people on the bench who have enough empathy, enough feeling, for what ordinary people are going through."

As Barack Obama took office, ordinary people were going through a wave of economic insecurity unprecedented since the Great Depression of the 1930s. Rising inequality, job losses, collapsing home values, heavy consumer indebtedness, skyrocketing health care costs, as well as the looming dangers of global climate change—all these had created a crisis of faith among Americans over the country's direction, over the government's willingness to act on behalf of ordinary Americans, and over their own future prospects. Elected on a platform of wide-ranging change, amid calls for a "new New Deal," confronted with a Republican opposition that spurned his summons to bipartisan cooperation in the crisis, President Obama faced the most daunting challenges, but also an extraordinary opportunity for transforming leadership. Would he seize it? If he did, would the Supreme Court obstruct him as it had Franklin Roosevelt seventy-five years before?

Beneath the clamor over heated social issues like abortion and homosexuality and the battles over civil rights and liberties, the Supreme Court of William Rehnquist and John Roberts had quietly been laying the groundwork for confrontation with a president and Congress elected on a platform of change. Over the previous two decades, the justices had undertaken a remarkable but little-noticed transformation in their rulings on economic issues, a slow reversal of the "constitutional revolution" of 1937, when the court had abruptly and at long last acknowledged the authority of the elected branches of government to regulate the economy. Through a widening stream of pro-business decisions in such areas as environmental regulation, equal pay and union rights, health care and retirement benefits, and a host of others, the Supreme Court stripped power from the political branches and from consumers and workers and shareholders to hold corporations and their executives to account. The court joined the elite, turn-of-century consensus that trumpeted the virtues of the free market and dog-eat-dog competition whose benefits supposedly would trickle down to hard-pressed working men and women and impoverished families. It was not only the court's powerful conservative phalanx that led the campaign to "repeal the 20th Century," as journalist Simon Lazarus put it. "Liberal" justices like Stephen Breyer and David Souter were little less hostile to restraints on business and finance. The court was in fact heavily packed with formidable free-marketeers.

A president armed with a mandate for change, committed to a new New Deal in a time of dire wants and needs, might again confront a Supreme Court that would ignore the election returns and resume the court's historic role as a choke point for progressive reforms. Once again, it would be less a battle between judges and elected officials than a conflict between *leaderships*. A Supreme Court tenacious of its supremacy built up over centuries from its roots in John Marshall's *Marbury* decision might oppose a president and Congress determined not only to protect their legislative achievements but also to settle at last the continuing constitutional struggle over leadership in American democracy.

THE SUPREME COURT's long supremacy over the Constitution has often led Americans to look to the justices for leadership in times of uncertainty and strain. It has led them to identify the court with the strength of the constitutional order and of the nation itself. And indeed, without John Marshall's determination to establish national authority against the ideologues of states' rights, and his insistence on the supremacy of constitutional law, the United States might have become far less unified. The idea of union to which Lincoln appealed in the fury and violence of civil war had its origins in the minds of George Washington and James Madison and other authors of the Constitution, but to a remarkable degree, it took shape and gathered force in the opinions of John Marshall during his three-decade domination of the Supreme Court. Because we have come to take that union for granted, the authority of the court has come to be seen as intrinsic and essential to it. Two centuries later, the Supreme Court continues to draw on the credit of John Marshall's nation-building.

Americans have also regarded the Supreme Court as the ultimate guardian of their civil rights and liberties, and the defender of individuals against government oppression, of powerless minorities against majorities. That image is a far more recent one and owes much to the leadership of another great chief justice, Earl Warren. Despite the concerted assaults of half a century, the legacy of his jurisprudence remains, as reflected in the court's bold decisions striking down George W. Bush's abuses of executive power and upholding the rights of detainees. The idea of the court as friend to the weak and powerless lingers. Yet, as we have seen, for much of its history, the Supreme Court has more often been indifferent to the wants and needs of the great majority of Americans. It has wielded its supremacy over the Constitution to deny them economic and political power. Too often, the court has been fighting history. As political scientist Philippa Strum has argued, "at every stage of the Court's existence," there have been justices "who refused to recognize that the meaning of the Constitution as written in 1787 had to change if it was to be applicable to the society of 1837, the ones who insisted that employers but not employees had legally protected economic rights when unions were already gaining political power, the ones who steadily maintained that the federal government could not enact broad social and economic statutes even as the welfare state was becoming a reality, the ones who could not understand that the urbanites, the non-whites, the women, the poor, the aged, the handicapped, the students, were all mobilizing in an unstoppable assault on the bastions of power."

Indeed, over the course of the Supreme Court's long history, the leadership of a Marshall or a Warren has been a luminous exception to the rule. In retrospect, the court has far more often been a tool for reaction, not progress. Whether in the Gilded Age of the late nineteenth century or the Gilded Age at the turn of the twenty-first, the justices have most fiercely protected the rights and liberties of the minority of the powerful and the propertied. Americans cannot look to the judicial branch for leadership. They cannot expect leadership from unelected and unaccountable politicians in robes.

If political leaders are to effectively challenge the court's supremacy and assert their own constitutional leadership, they must learn from the failures of the past. None of the many attempts to "curb the court" has succeeded, beginning with Jefferson's abortive impeachment campaign against Federalist justices. Tinkering with the numbers of justices, as politicians have attempted repeatedly, has done nothing to blunt the court's rise to constitutional supremacy. Efforts to inject accountability into judicial decision-making, by TR's idea of popular votes on the recall of decisions—or even of the justices themselves—have gotten nowhere. Initiatives to eliminate life tenure have been stillborn. Nor have proposals to temper the Supreme Court's power of judicial review had more success, whether by requiring a "supermajority" of justices for decisions to strike down federal laws, or by granting Congress, as John Marshall himself had suggested, the authority to override "opinions deem'd unsound by the legislature." Generations of reformers have urged—vehemently and in vain—the simple abolition of judicial review altogether.

Such proposals for change have never succeeded because they have never mobilized a large number of Americans behind them. Moreover, most have faced a daunting obstacle—the tortuous process of constitutional amendment.

There is another alternative, a momentous and even more daring and inspiring one. It would strike at the very roots of the Supreme Court's power while placing the burden of constitutional amendment on the *supporters* of judicial rule. It would be based on the fact that the Constitution never granted the judiciary a supremacy over the government, nor had the Framers ever conceived it. It would remind Americans that the court's vetoes of acts of Congress are founded in a ploy by John Marshall that was exploited and expanded by later conservatives until the court today stands supreme and unaccountable, effectively immune to the checks and balances that otherwise fragment and disperse power throughout the constitutional system.

Confronted by a hostile court repeatedly striking down vital progressive legislation, a president could declare that there is no place in a modern democracy for unelected judges to veto twenty-first-century laws. The president would announce flatly that he or she would not accept the Supreme Court's verdicts because the power of judicial emasculation of legislation was not—and never had been—in the Constitution. The president would invite the partisans of judicial supremacy to try to write that authority into the Constitution by proposing a constitutional amendment. Through their representatives in Congress and the state legislatures, the American people would be given the choice denied them in 1803: *to establish in the Constitution the power of judicial supremacy, or to reject that power.* Only by this route could judicial rule be legitimated, "constitutionalized." In the meantime, until the matter was settled, the president would faithfully execute the laws the Supreme Court had unconstitutionally vetoed.

It would be a risky strategy, an open defiance of constitutional customs and the myths and mysteries that have long enshrouded the court. Traditionalists would be outraged. Professors of law would express their concern in learned treatises. Powerful interests with a stake in the status quo—business groups, conservative lawyers, and their supporters in the political class—would spearhead a campaign of opposition. There might even be demands for impeachment. In the ensuing turbulence, though, the president would have an enormous strategic advantage. He would need only to sit tight. The burden would be on his adversaries to initiate the new and momentous amendment to the Constitution and to obtain a mandate for judicial rule. For once it would be the foes of reform, not the reformers, who would have to go through the constitutional hoops of amendment, with all the traps and delays.

Above all, it would be a test of leadership, of the president's ability to mobilize followers behind a transformational goal, as FDR had so markedly failed to do in 1937. He would present the idea for what it was—a revolutionary challenge to judicial business-as-usual, to minority rule by a handful of judges, a fight for the Constitution as the people's charter, not a lawyer's contract. The president would make clear—and welcome the fact—that empowering the people to rule on judicial supremacy would set off a long, boisterous, and perhaps confusing debate on its role in twenty-first-century American democracy.

If judicial rule was not ratified by the people in the amending process, the Supreme Court's exclusive grip on constitutional interpretation would be broken. Shorn of its supremacy, the court would still retain crucial tasks. It would still be called upon to interpret ambiguous statutes, adjust conflicting laws, clarify jurisdictions, and police the boundaries of federal-state power—virtually all of its present responsibilities except that of declaring federal laws unconstitutional. It would simply be brought closer to the role the Framers originally envisioned for it.

As constitutional leadership passed to the political branches, the nation's elected officials would bear the heavy and unshirkable duty to ensure that their acts were compatible with the Constitution. Without Supreme Court review or oversight, each branch would be constrained by the checks and balances already inscribed in the Constitution. But unlike the Supreme Court, whose supremacy lacks any constitutional basis, political leaders draw their authority from the charter's most fundamental principle—the sovereignty of the people. Their ultimate accountability is at the ballot box, where they face the judgment of their fellow citizens.

DOES ALL THIS seem alarming, un-American? Not if we realize that judicial rule, as it has emerged in fits and starts over two centuries to reach its modern-day pinnacle, is alien to the constitutional design. It invokes what legal scholar Edward S. Corwin, writing at the peak of FDR's battle with the Hughes Court, called a "miracle" that "supposes a kind of transubstantiation whereby the Court's opinion of the Constitution . . . becomes the very body and blood of the Constitution."

There is nothing miraculous about majority rule—it is the essence of democratic constitutionalism. It is true that Americans have long feared "naked majority rule" that would force big changes by slender majorities and threaten minority rights. The need to restrain runaway majorities has often been used to justify judicial supremacy, even though the Supreme Court has used that authority to protect entrenched interests—minorities, to be sure, but powerful ones—at the expense both of popular majorities and of powerless minorities. In fact, the constitutional structure of the Founders, from its system of checks and balances to the Bill of Rights, provides a host of protections for minorities. And, as James Madison foresaw, building a political majority in a large and diverse nation calls for endless accommodations by factions and regions, producing compromise and broad consensus. Indeed, majority rule in the United States takes a curious form—"majorities rule"—with president, Senate, and House responding to diverse national, state, and local constituencies. The abolition of judicial supremacy by the presidential challenge described above would open the way for a more potent majority rule that would reflect the needs of most of the people without destroying the rights of the minority to keep that majority under constant and critical surveillance.

Majorities, to be sure, can make dreadful mistakes, as we have seen in numerous presidencies and Congresses from John Adams to Bush II. But the Supreme Court makes bad and even dangerous decisions too, whether in ratifying the abuses of the political branches, as in *Korematsu* or the anti-Communist frenzy after World War II, or on its own initiative when it usurps political responsibility, as in *Dred Scott* and *Bush* v. *Gore*. Legislative majorities, moreover, can correct their errors in the next session or after the next election, while the court has taken decades—or nothing less than a civil war—to reverse itself. That is because presidents and legislators have to report back to the people; the justices do not.

The duty of an empowered majority is to *lead*. It is the responsibility of the minority to oppose, but not to obstruct—and much less to veto, as the Supreme Court regularly does—the acts of the majority. The British parliamentary system is the classic demonstration of this relationship. The party that wins a general election takes over the House of Commons. The defeated party might use a second chamber, the House of Lords, only to delay. In the Commons, the opposition sits on the bench across, with no power except to ask biting questions and propose alternatives, while preparing for the next election, when it might win its own majority. There is no equivalent to the American Supreme Court, no ultimate interpreter of the British constitution outside of Parliament. The British system, like other democracies, has its failings, but the power of a minority to thwart leadership by the majority is not one of them.

Still, an amorphous electoral majority is not sufficient in itself to produce broad economic and social change. Even apart from the Supreme Court's unconstitutional assertions of supremacy, the American checks-and-balances system, its separation of powers, has tended to obstruct the kind of transforming leadership that the empowerment of a majority should make possible. From the start, American politicians have sought to overcome these obstacles by converting their majority into a unified political party, as Thomas Jefferson and James Madison did with their Republicans in the 1790s. Much was made of Barack Obama's grassroots mobilization of voters in 2008 and his skill in attracting masses of disaffected voters to the polls, but as president, Obama faced the crucial test of whether he could convince his followers to give decisive backing to transformational initiatives.

Far more often, American presidents and legislators have had to act effectively as *transactional* leaders—brokers, negotiators, coalition-builders—to produce slow and incremental change. For them, as political scientist Keith Whittington has written, "constitutional disputes are more likely to be a distraction than an opportunity," a source of unnecessary conflict. They have willingly and even eagerly left such disputes to the Supreme Court. "For such beleaguered politicians, the heightened judicial authority to say what the Constitution means is a respite from the responsibility and burdens of leadership."

But leaders with transformational aspirations actively assert constitutional leadership. Empowered by new and insurgent majorities, backed by disciplined parties, thriving on conflict, presidents like Jefferson and Jackson, Lincoln and Franklin Roosevelt, have clashed with justices who refused to recognize the claims of the new majority while fiercely protecting the "minority rights" of discredited parties, interests, and ideologies. To an astonishing degree in a democracy, the Supreme Court has prevailed in these struggles for power, checkmating the popular will with its absolute veto. Against such a court armed with the dogma of its own supremacy, presidents often could win only by waiting for the next turn of the judicial roulette wheel.

. . .

THE ULTIMATE outcome of a grand national debate and decision on judicial supremacy would turn on people's capacities to relate institutions and their powers to the historic national values that are the engines of leadership and change. The essence of those values lies not in the 1787 Constitution, which mainly allots specific powers to specific institutions, but in the glowing phrases of the Declaration of Independence of 1776. In proclaiming "life, liberty and the pursuit of happiness," Jefferson and his fellow revolutionaries not only summarized in a few words what Americans were fighting for, but enunciated principles that have divided the nation since the Founding.

Leadership emerges from the conflict over core principles. The strongest appeal leaders can make to potential followers is by addressing their real wants and needs in terms of values. By mobilizing followers behind transforming goals, they generate the political force to surmount obstacles in pursuit of deep and enduring change. The presidency, Franklin Roosevelt said in 1932, was more than an administrative or engineering job. "It is preeminently a place of moral leadership," he declared, especially "at times when certain historic ideas in the life of the nation had to be clarified." Throughout our history and especially today, conservatives have defined "life" as security from internal and external threats, "liberty" as protection against intrusive and oppressive government, and "the pursuit of happiness" as the removal of impediments to individual opportunity and fulfillment. Liberals have sought to push these three values beyond such negative conceptions to a positive role for government in nurturing political, economic, and social equality—from Lincoln's Constitution, with its lost promise to secure the equal rights of freed slaves, to FDR's Four Freedoms, which included freedom from want, to Lyndon Johnson's Great Society war on economic and social inequality.

These fundamental differences over the meaning of America's

founding values have for two centuries been a driving force for the creative conflict between two major parties that vitalizes democracy. But deference to a court with extraconstitutional powers to summarily settle controversies over constitutional values has too often sapped our democracy of its vitality. It has too often muted the voice of the people in what Barack Obama termed the essential democratic conversation. It has closed off avenues to desperately needed change.

John Marshall was wrong: it is emphatically the province and duty of the American people, not of the nine justices of the United States Supreme Court, to say what the Constitution is. A national reappraisal of the all-powerful court chosen by judicial roulette is crucial if American democracy is to meet the rising challenges of the twenty-first century.

The Justices of the Supreme Court

Justice (state)	Dates of Birth and Death	Appointing President	President's Political Party	Term of Service on the Court	Reason for Leaving Seat
James Wilson (PA)	1742–1798	Washington	Federalist	1789–1798	Death
John Jay (NY) *Chief Justice*	1745–1829	Washington	Federalist	1789–1795	Resignation
William Cushing (MA)	1732–1810	Washington	Federalist	1790–1810	Death
John Blair, Jr. (VA)	1732–1800	Washington	Federalist	1790–1796	Resignation
John Rutledge (SC)	1739–1800	Washington	Federalist	1790–1791	Resignation
James Iredell (NC)	1751–1799	Washington	Federalist	1790–1799	Death
Thomas Johnson (MD)	1732–1819	Washington	Federalist	1792–1793	Resignation
William Paterson (NJ)	1745–1806	Washington	Federalist	1793–1806	Death
John Rutledge (SC) *Chief Justice*	1739–1800	Washington	Federalist	1795	Recess appointment rejected by Senate
Samuel Chase (MD)	1741–1811	Washington	Federalist	1796–1811	Death
Oliver Ellsworth (CT) *Chief Justice*	1745–1807	Washington	Federalist	1796–1800	Resignation
Bushrod Washington (VA)	1762–1829	J. Adams	Federalist	1799–1829	Death
Alfred Moore (NC)	1755–1810	J. Adams	Federalist	1800–1804	Resignation
John Marshall (VA) *Chief Justice*	1755–1835	J. Adams	Federalist	1801–1835	Death
William Johnson (SC)	1771–1834	Jefferson	Republican	1804–1834	Death
Henry Brockholst Livingston (NY)	1757–1823	Jefferson	Republican	1807–1823	Death
Thomas Todd (KY)	1765–1826	Jefferson	Republican	1807–1826	Death

continued . . .

Justice (state)	Dates of Birth and Death	Appointing President	President's Political Party	Term of Service on the Court	Reason for Leaving Seat
Gabriel Duvall (MD)	1752–1844	Madison	Republican	1811–1835	Resignation
Joseph Story (MA)	1779–1845	Madison	Republican	1812–1845	Death
Smith Thompson (NY)	1768–1843	Monroe	Republican	1823–1843	Death
Robert Trimble (KY)	1776–1828	J. Q. Adams	Republican	1826–1828	Death
John McLean (OH)	1785–1861	Jackson	Democratic	1830–1861	Death
Henry Baldwin (PA)	1780–1844	Jackson	Democratic	1830–1844	Death
James M. Wayne (GA)	1790–1867	Jackson	Democratic	1835–1867	Death
Roger B. Taney (MD) *Chief Justice*	1777–1864	Jackson	Democratic	1836–1864	Death
Philip P. Barbour (VA)	1783–1841	Jackson	Democratic	1836–1841	Death
John Catron (TN)	1786–1865	Jackson	Democratic	1837–1865	Death
John McKinley (AL)	1780–1852	Van Buren	Democratic	1838–1852	Death
Peter V. Daniel (VA)	1784–1860	Van Buren	Democratic	1842–1860	Death
Samuel Nelson (NY)	1792–1873	Tyler	Whig	1845–1872	Resignation
Levi Woodbury (NH)	1789–1851	Polk	Democratic	1845–1851	Death
Robert C. Grier (PA)	1794–1870	Polk	Democratic	1846–1870	Resignation
Benjamin R. Curtis (MA)	1809–1874	Fillmore	Whig	1851–1857	Resignation
John A. Campbell (AL)	1811–1889	Pierce	Democratic	1853–1861	Resignation
Nathan Clifford (NH)	1803–1881	Buchanan	Democratic	1858–1881	Death

Justice (state)	Dates of Birth and Death	Appointing President	President's Political Party	Term of Service on the Court	Reason for Leaving Seat
Noah H. Swayne (OH)	1804–1884	Lincoln	Republican	1862–1881	Resignation
Samuel F. Miller (IA)	1816–1890	Lincoln	Republican	1862–1890	Death
David Davis (IL)	1815–1886	Lincoln	Republican	1862–1877	Resignation
Stephen J. Field (CA)	1816–1899	Lincoln	Republican	1863–1897	Resignation
Salmon P. Chase (OH) *Chief Justice*	1808–1873	Lincoln	Republican	1864–1873	Death
William Strong (PA)	1808–1895	Grant	Republican	1870–1880	Resignation
Joseph P. Bradley (NJ)	1813–1892	Grant	Republican	1870–1892	Death
Ward Hunt (NY)	1810–1886	Grant	Republican	1873–1882	Resignation
Morrison R. Waite (OH) *Chief Justice*	1816–1888	Grant	Republican	1874–1888	Death
John Marshall Harlan (KY)	1833–1911	Hayes	Republican	1877–1911	Death
William B. Woods (GA)	1824–1887	Hayes	Republican	1881–1887	Death
T. Stanley Matthews (OH)	1824–1889	Garfield	Republican	1881–1889	Death
Horace Gray (MA)	1828–1902	Arthur	Republican	1882–1902	Resignation
Samuel Blatchford (NY)	1820–1893	Arthur	Republican	1882–1893	Death
Lucius Q. C. Lamar (MS)	1825–1893	Cleveland	Democratic	1888–1893	Death
Melville W. Fuller (IL) *Chief Justice*	1833–1910	Cleveland	Democratic	1888–1910	Death
David J. Brewer (KS)	1837–1910	B. Harrison	Republican	1890–1910	Death

continued . . .

Justice (state)	Dates of Birth and Death	Appointing President	President's Political Party	Term of Service on the Court	Reason for Leaving Seat
Henry B. Brown (MI)	1836–1913	B. Harrison	Republican	1891–1906	Resignation
George Shiras, Jr. (PA)	1832–1924	B. Harrison	Republican	1892–1903	Resignation
Howell E. Jackson (TN)	1832–1895	B. Harrison	Republican	1893–1895	Death
Edward D. White (LA)	1845–1921	Cleveland	Democratic	1894–1910	Elevated to chief justice
Rufus W. Peckham (NY)	1838–1909	Cleveland	Democratic	1896–1909	Death
Joseph McKenna (CA)	1843–1926	McKinley	Republican	1898–1925	Resignation
Oliver Wendell Holmes, Jr. (MA)	1841–1935	T. Roosevelt	Republican	1902–1932	Resignation
William R. Day (OH)	1849–1923	T. Roosevelt	Republican	1903–1922	Resignation
William H. Moody (MA)	1853–1917	T. Roosevelt	Republican	1906–1910	Resignation
Horace H. Lurton (TN)	1844–1914	Taft	Republican	1910–1914	Death
Charles Evans Hughes (NY)	1862–1948	Taft	Republican	1910–1916	Resignation
Edward D. White (LA) *Chief Justice*	1845–1921	Taft	Republican	1910–1921	Death
Willis Van Devanter (WY)	1859–1941	Taft	Republican	1911–1937	Retirement
Joseph R. Lamar (GA)	1857–1916	Taft	Republican	1911–1916	Death
Mahlon Pitney (NJ)	1858–1924	Taft	Republican	1912–1922	Resignation
James C. McReynolds (TN)	1862–1946	Wilson	Democratic	1914–1941	Retirement
Louis D. Brandeis (MA)	1856–1941	Wilson	Democratic	1916–1939	Retirement
John H. Clarke (OH)	1857–1945	Wilson	Democratic	1916–1922	Resignation

Justice (state)	Dates of Birth and Death	Appointing President	President's Political Party	Term of Service on the Court	Reason for Leaving Seat
William Howard Taft (OH) *Chief Justice*	1857–1930	Harding	Republican	1921–1930	Resignation
George Sutherland (UT)	1862–1942	Harding	Republican	1922–1938	Retirement
Pierce Butler (MN)	1866–1939	Harding	Republican	1923–1939	Death
Edward T. Sanford (TN)	1865–1930	Harding	Republican	1923–1930	Death
Harlan Fiske Stone (NY)	1872–1946	Coolidge	Republican	1925–1941	Elevated to chief justice
Charles Evans Hughes (NY) *Chief Justice*	1862–1948	Hoover	Republican	1930–1941	Retirement
Owen J. Roberts (PA)	1875–1955	Hoover	Republican	1930–1945	Resignation
Benjamin N. Cardozo (NY)	1870–1938	Hoover	Republican	1932–1938	Death
Hugo L. Black (AL)	1886–1971	F. D. Roosevelt	Democratic	1937–1971	Retirement
Stanley F. Reed (KY)	1884–1980	F. D. Roosevelt	Democratic	1938–1957	Retirement
Felix Frankfurter (MA)	1882–1965	F. D. Roosevelt	Democratic	1939–1962	Retirement
William O. Douglas (CT)	1898–1980	F. D. Roosevelt	Democratic	1939–1975	Retirement
Frank Murphy (MI)	1890–1949	F. D. Roosevelt	Democratic	1940–1949	Death
James F. Byrnes (SC)	1879–1972	F. D. Roosevelt	Democratic	1941–1942	Resignation
Harlan Fiske Stone (NY) *Chief Justice*	1872–1946	F. D. Roosevelt	Democratic	1941–1946	Death
Robert H. Jackson (NY)	1892–1954	F. D. Roosevelt	Democratic	1941–1954	Death
Wiley B. Rutledge (IA)	1894–1949	F. D. Roosevelt	Democratic	1943–1949	Death

continued . . .

Justice (state)	Dates of Birth and Death	Appointing President	President's Political Party	Term of Service on the Court	Reason for Leaving Seat
Harold H. Burton (OH)	1888–1964	Truman	Democratic	1945–1958	Retirement
Fred M. Vinson (KY) *Chief Justice*	1890–1953	Truman	Democratic	1946–1953	Death
Tom C. Clark (TX)	1899–1977	Truman	Democratic	1949–1967	Retirement
Sherman Minton (IN)	1890–1965	Truman	Democratic	1949–1956	Retirement
Earl Warren (CA) *Chief Justice*	1891–1974	Eisenhower	Republican	1953–1969	Retirement
John Marshall Harlan (NY)	1899–1971	Eisenhower	Republican	1955–1971	Retirement
William J. Brennan, Jr. (NJ)	1906–1997	Eisenhower	Republican	1956–1990	Retirement
Charles E. Whittaker (MO)	1901–1973	Eisenhower	Republican	1957–1962	Retirement
Potter Stewart (OH)	1915–1985	Eisenhower	Republican	1958–1981	Retirement
Byron R. White (CO)	1917–2002	Kennedy	Democratic	1962–1993	Retirement
Arthur J. Goldberg (IL)	1908–1990	Kennedy	Democratic	1962–1965	Resignation
Abe Fortas (TN)	1910–1982	L. B. Johnson	Democratic	1965–1969	Resignation
Thurgood Marshall (MD)	1908–1993	L. B. Johnson	Democratic	1967–1991	Retirement
Warren E. Burger (MN) *Chief Justice*	1907–1995	Nixon	Republican	1969–1986	Retirement
Harry A. Blackmun (MN)	1908–1999	Nixon	Republican	1970–1994	Retirement
Lewis F. Powell, Jr. (VA)	1907–1998	Nixon	Republican	1972–1987	Retirement
William H. Rehnquist (AZ)	1924–2005	Nixon	Republican	1972–1986	Elevated to chief justice
John Paul Stevens (IL)	1920–	Ford	Republican	1975–	

Justice (state)	Dates of Birth and Death	Appointing President	President's Political Party	Term of Service on the Court	Reason for Leaving Seat
Sandra Day O'Connor (AZ)	1930–	Reagan	Republican	1981–2006	Retirement
William H. Rehnquist (AZ) *Chief Justice*	1924–2005	Reagan	Republican	1986–2005	Death
Antonin Scalia (NY)	1936–	Reagan	Republican	1986–	
Anthony M. Kennedy (CA)	1936–	Reagan	Republican	1988–	
David H. Souter (NH)	1939–	G.H.W. Bush	Republican	1990–	
Clarence Thomas (GA)	1948–	G.H.W. Bush	Republican	1991–	
Ruth Bader Ginsburg (NY)	1933–	Clinton	Democratic	1993–	
Stephen G. Breyer (MA)	1938–	Clinton	Democratic	1994–	
John G. Roberts, Jr. (MD) *Chief Justice*	1955–	G. W. Bush	Republican	2005–	
Samuel A. Alito, Jr. (NJ)	1950–	G. W. Bush	Republican	2006–	

ACKNOWLEDGMENTS

Professor Susan Dunn offered a searching and constructive review of the manuscript of this book based on her deep immersion in American political history. Philippa Strum and Bennett Boskey gave the manuscript the benefit of their long and extensive study of the Constitution and the Supreme Court. By generously sharing their knowledge and insights, all three readers helped me to refine my ideas about the court's role in American democracy.

I am also grateful to my agent, Ike Williams, and his assistant, Hope Denekamp, for backing the work and vigorously launching it toward publication.

Laura Stickney, my editor, deserves special gratitude for her unwavering faith in the significance of this project. Her keen eye and wise suggestions improved the text in countless ways. She and her colleagues at Penguin Press were a pleasure to work with.

As she has before, Robin Keller of the Faculty Secretarial Office at Williams College helped to make communications between author and publisher smooth and easy.

The staff of Sawyer Library at Williams, and especially Alison O'Grady, the head of the Interlibrary Loan Department, offered indispensable assistance as I researched this work. The archives of the Franklin D. Roosevelt Presidential Library in Hyde Park, New York, afforded me the opportunity to dig deeply into the background of FDR's confrontation with the Supreme Court. Its director, Cynthia Koch, was most welcoming, and Robert Clark, the library's supervising archivist, generously answered detailed questions before, during, and after my visit.

Finally, this book would not have been possible without the critical and constructive participation of Milton Djuric at every stage of the work.

NOTES

CHAPTER ONE—THE FIRST COURTPACKERS

John Agresto, *The Supreme Court and Constitutional Democracy* (Cornell University Press, 1984), chs. 2–3.

Bernard Bailyn, ed., *Debate on the Constitution*, 2 vols. (Library of America, 1993).

Wilbourn E. Benton, ed., *1787: Drafting the Constitution*, 2 vols. (Texas A&M University Press, 1986).

William R. Casto, *The Supreme Court in the Early Republic: The Chief Justiceships of John Jay and Oliver Ellsworth* (University of South Carolina Press, 1995).

Susan Dunn, *Jefferson's Second Revolution: The Election of 1800 and the Triumph of Republicanism* (Houghton Mifflin, 2004).

Stanley Elkins and Eric McKitrick, *The Age of Federalism* (Oxford University Press, 1993).

Jonathan Elliot, ed., *The Debates in the Several State Conventions on the Adoption of the Federal Constitution*, 5 vols., 2nd ed. (1836; reprinted by J. B. Lippincott, 1937).

Paul Leicester Ford, ed., *Pamphlets on the Constitution of the United States* (1888; reprinted by Da Capo Press, 1968).

Landa M. Freeman, "Mr. Jay Rides Circuit," *Journal of Supreme Court History*, vol. 31, no. 1 (March 2006), pp. 18–27.

Leon Friedman and Fred L. Israel, eds., *The Justices of the United States Supreme Court, 1789–1969* (Chelsea House, 1969–78), vol. 1.

Scott Douglas Gerber, ed., *Seriatim: The Supreme Court Before John Marshall* (New York University Press, 1998).

Julius Goebel, Jr., *Antecedents and Beginnings to 1801*, vol. 1 of *History of the Supreme Court of the United States* (Macmillan, 1971).

Leslie F. Goldstein, "Popular Sovereignty, the Origins of Judicial Review, and the Revival of Unwritten Law," *Journal of Politics*, vol. 48, no. 1 (February 1986), pp. 51–71.

Charles Grove Haines, *The American Doctrine of Judicial Supremacy*, 2nd ed. (University of California Press, 1932).

Charles Grove Haines, *The Role of the Supreme Court in American Government and Politics, 1789–1835* (University of California Press, 1944).

George Lee Haskins and Herbert A. Johnson, *Foundations of Power: John Marshall, 1801–15*, vol. 2 of *History of the Supreme Court of the United States* (Macmillan, 1981).

James Haw, *John and Edward Rutledge of South Carolina* (University of Georgia Press, 1997).

James Haw et al., *Stormy Patriot: The Life of Samuel Chase* (Maryland Historical Society, 1980).

Merrill Jensen et al., eds., *The Documentary History of the Ratification of the Constitution*, 21 vols. (State Historical Society of Wisconsin, 1976–).

Larry D. Kramer, *The People Themselves: Popular Constitutionalism and Judicial Review* (Oxford University Press, 2004).

Philip B. Kurland and Ralph Lerner, eds., *The Founders' Constitution*, 5 vols. (University of Chicago Press, 1987).

Maeva Marcus and James R. Perry, eds., *The Documentary History of the Supreme Court of the United States, 1789–1800,* 9 vols. (Columbia University Press, 1985–2007).

David McCullough, *John Adams* (Simon & Schuster, 2001).

John C. Miller, *The Federalist Era, 1789–1801* (Harper & Brothers, 1960).

James R. Perry, "Supreme Court Appointments, 1789–1801: Criteria, Presidential Style, and the Press of Events," *Journal of the Early Republic,* vol. 6, no. 4 (Winter 1986), pp. 371–410.

Jack N. Rakove, "Judicial Power in the Constitutional Theory of James Madison," *William & Mary Law Review,* vol. 43, no. 4 (March 2002), pp. 1513–47.

James F. Simon, *What Kind of Nation: Thomas Jefferson, John Marshall, and the Epic Struggle to Create a United States* (Simon & Schuster, 2002).

James Morton Smith, *Freedom's Fetters: The Alien and Sedition Laws and American Civil Liberties* (Cornell University Press, 1956).

Page Smith, *James Wilson, Founding Father, 1742–1798* (University of North Carolina Press, 1956).

Kathryn Turner, "Federalist Policy and the Judiciary Act of 1801," *William and Mary Quarterly,* 3rd ser., vol. 22, no. 1 (January 1965), pp. 3–32.

Kathryn Turner, "The Midnight Judges," *University of Pennsylvania Law Review,* vol. 109, no. 4 (February 1961), pp. 494–523.

7   ["toilsome Journies"] : August 9, 1792, reprinted in Marcus and Perry, vol. 2, pp. 289–90, quoted at p. 290.

8   ["strange disorder"] : Blair to his sister, letter of July 5, 1799, in Fred L. Israel, "John Blair, Jr.," in Friedman and Israel, vol. 1, pp. 109–15, quoted at p. 115; see also letter to George Washington, October 25, 1795, in Marcus and Perry, vol. 1, part 1, p. 59.

8   ["Key-stone"] : Washington to John Jay, letter of October 5, 1789, in Marcus and Perry, vol. 1, part 1, p. 11.

8   [Supreme Court cases in first four years] : Casto, pp. 54–55.

8   ["superiority of the judicial"] : Hamilton, The Federalist No. 78, in Jacob E. Cooke, ed., *The Federalist* (Wesleyan University Press, 1961), pp. 521–30, quoted at pp. 525, 523, respectively.

9   ["various and unequal"] : Madison, The Federalist No. 10, in ibid., pp. 56–65, quoted at pp. 59, 58, 61, 64, respectively.

10   ["In framing a government"] : Madison, The Federalist No. 51, in ibid., pp. 347–53, quoted at p. 349.

11   [Convention setting] : Catherine Drinker Bowen, *Miracle at Philadelphia* (Little, Brown, 1966), pp. 23–24.

11   ["intrigue, partiality"] : June 15, 1787, in Benton, vol. 2, p. 1315.

12   ["servile dependence"] : debate in the Pennsylvania ratification convention, December 4, 1787, in Jensen et al., vol. 2, p. 495.

12   ["independent of the people"] : Brutus XV, March 20, 1788, in ibid., vol. 16, pp. 431–35, quoted at p. 432.

13   ["absolutely necessary"] : June 8, 1787, in Benton, vol. 2, p. 1459.

13   [Mason on judiciary] : Mason, "Objections to the Federal Constitution," November 11, 1787, in Jensen et al., vol. 14, pp. 149–52, quoted at p. 150.

13   ["but where the Union"] : Iredell, "Answers to Mr. Mason's Objections to the New Constitution" (1788), in Ford, *Pamphlets,* pp. 335–70, quoted at p. 343.

13   ["swallowing up"] : James Wilson, August 15, 1787, in Benton, vol. 1, p. 821.

13   ["unwise and unjust"] : James Madison, July 21, 1787, in ibid., vol. 1, p. 811.

13   ["authority to examine"] : Resolution, May 29, 1787, in ibid., vol. 1, p. 792.

13   ["improper mixture"] : John Dickinson, June 6, 1787, in ibid., vol. 1, p. 806.

13   ["In some States"] : June 4, 1787, in ibid., vol. 1, p. 793.

14   ["disapproved of the Doctrine"] : August 15, 1787, in ibid., pp. 819, 820, 821.

15   ["interpretation or construction"] : Kent, "An Introductory Lecture to a Course of Law Lectures" (1794), in Charles Hyneman and Donald S. Lutz, eds., *American Political Writing During the Founding Era, 1760–1805* (Liberty Press, 1983), vol. 2, pp. 936–49, quoted at p. 942.

15   ["rights of private property"] : Beard, *The Supreme Court and the Constitution* (1912; reprinted by Paisley Press, 1938), pp. 92, 126.

15   ["unprecedented act"] : John F. Dillon, "Address of the President" (1892), *Report of the Fifteenth Annual Meeting of the American Bar Association* (Dando Printing and Publishing, 1892), pp. 167–211, quoted at p. 203.

15   ["exalted above all"] : Brutus XV, in Jensen et al., vol. 16, p. 431.

16   ["within the limits"] : Hamilton, The Federalist No. 78, in Cooke, pp. 525, 523, respectively; see also Hamilton, The Federalist No. 81, in ibid., pp. 541–52, esp. p. 545.

16   ["dangerous encroachments"] : Madison to Thomas Jefferson, letter of October 24, 1787, in Madison, *Papers*, Robert A. Rutland et al., eds. (University Press of Virginia/University of Chicago Press, 1962–91), vol. 10, pp. 206–19, quoted at p. 211.

16   ["for the case of a disagreement"] : Madison, "Observations on Jefferson's Draft of a Constitution for Virginia," ca. October 15, 1788, in ibid., vol. 10, pp. 285–93, quoted at p. 293.

17   ["chief Pillar"] : form letter to "Associate Justices of the Supreme Court," September 30, 1789, in Washington, *Writings*, John C. Fitzpatrick, ed. (U.S. Government Printing Office, 1931–44), vol. 3, pp. 424–25, quoted at p. 425.

18   ["alternate domination"] : September 19, 1796, in Washington, *Writings*, Worthington Chauncey Ford, ed. (G. P. Putnam's, 1889–93), vol. 13, pp. 277–325, quoted at p. 303.

19   ["like a wild beast"] : Smith, *James Wilson*, p. 387.

20   ["insurrection, riot"] : reprinted in Smith, *Freedom's Fetters*, pp. 441–42 (Appendix).

20   ["constitutional difficulty"] : Ellsworth to Secretary of State Timothy Pickering, letter of December 12, 1798, quoted in Casto, p. 149.

20   ["unbounded thirst"] : quoted in Smith, *Freedom's Fetters*, p. 230.

20   ["screen from scrutiny"] : ibid., pp. 250–51.

20   ["I cannot suppress"] : quoted in Casto, p. 166.

21   ["sowing sedition"] : quoted in Smith, *Freedom's Fetters*, p. 267.

21   ["*political* sentiments"] : ibid.

21   ["There goes the President"] : ibid., p. 271.

21   ["expressly and positively"] : Madison, "Virginia Resolutions," December 21, 1798, in Madison, *Papers*, vol. 17, pp. 188–90, quoted at p. 189; for Jefferson's draft of the Kentucky resolutions, see Jefferson, *Writings*, Merrill D. Peterson, ed. (Library of America Press, 1984), pp. 449–56.

21   ["exclusively vested"] : "Resolution of the Vermont General Assembly," October 30, 1799, reprinted in Elliot, *Debates*, vol. 4, p. 539.

22   ["midnight judges"] : Haskins and Johnson, p. 126.

23   ["the judicial authority"] : Madison, "The Report of 1800," in Madison, *Papers*, vol. 17, pp. 307–50, quoted at pp. 311, 312.

23   ["in our Governments"] : Madison to Thomas Jefferson, letter of October 17, 1788, in ibid., vol. 11, pp. 295–300, quoted at p. 298.

23   ["there must be"] : Jefferson to Justice William Johnson, letter of June 12, 1823, in Jefferson, *Writings*, pp. 1469–77, quoted at p. 1476.

CHAPTER TWO—JOHN MARSHALL'S CONSTITUTION

Bruce Ackerman, *The Failure of the Founding Fathers: Jefferson, Marshall, and the Rise of Presidential Democracy* (Belknap Press, 2005).

Dean Alfange, Jr., "Marbury v Madison and Original Understandings of Judicial Review: In Defense of Traditional Wisdom," *Supreme Court Review*, vol. 1993 (1993), pp. 329–446.

Leonard Baker, *John Marshall: A Life in Law* (Macmillan, 1974).

Albert J. Beveridge, *The Life of John Marshall*, 4 vols. (Houghton Mifflin, 1916–19).

Everett S. Brown, ed., *William Plumer's Memorandum of Proceedings in the United States Senate, 1803–1807* (Macmillan, 1923).

Robert L. Clinton, Marbury v. Madison *and Judicial Review* (University Press of Kansas, 1989).

George Dangerfield, *The Era of Good Feelings* (Harcourt, Brace, 1952).

Richard E. Ellis, *The Jeffersonian Crisis: Courts and Politics in the Young Republic* (Oxford University Press, 1971).

Robert Kenneth Faulkner, *The Jurisprudence of John Marshall* (Princeton University Press, 1968).

Leon Friedman and Fred L. Israel, eds., *The Justices of the United States Supreme Court, 1789–1969* (Chelsea House, 1969–78), vol. 1.

Mark A. Graber and Michael Perhac, eds., *Marbury versus Madison* (CQ Press, 2002).

Gerald Gunther, ed., *John Marshall's Defense of* McCulloch v. Maryland (Stanford University Press, 1969).

Charles Grove Haines, *The American Doctrine of Judicial Supremacy*, 2nd ed. (University of California Press, 1932).

Charles Grove Haines, *The Role of the Supreme Court in American Government and Politics, 1789–1835* (University of California Press, 1944).

George Lee Haskins and Herbert A. Johnson, *Foundations of Power: John Marshall, 1801–1815*, vol. 2 of *History of the Supreme Court of the United States* (Macmillan, 1981).

James Haw et al., *Stormy Patriot: The Life of Samuel Chase* (Maryland Historical Society, 1980).

Charles F. Hobson, *The Great Chief Justice: John Marshall and the Rule of Law* (University Press of Kansas, 1996).

Herbert A. Johnson, *The Chief Justiceship of John Marshall, 1801–1835* (University of South Carolina Press, 1997).

Samuel J. Konefsky, *John Marshall and Alexander Hamilton: Architects of the American Constitution* (Macmillan, 1964).

Larry D. Kramer, *The People Themselves: Popular Constitutionalism and Judicial Review* (Oxford University Press, 2004).

Richard P. Longaker, "Andrew Jackson and the Judiciary," *Political Science Quarterly*, vol. 71, no. 3 (September 1956), pp. 341–64.

John Marshall, *An Autobiographical Sketch*, John Stokes Adams, ed. (University of Michigan Press, 1937).

David N. Mayer, *The Constitutional Thought of Thomas Jefferson* (University Press of Virginia, 1994), esp. ch. 9.

Donald G. Morgan, *Justice William Johnson, the First Dissenter* (University of South Carolina Press, 1954).

R. Kent Newmyer, *John Marshall and the Heroic Age of the Supreme Court* (Louisiana State University Press, 2001).

R. Kent Newmyer, *Supreme Court Justice Joseph Story: Statesman of the Old Republic* (University of North Carolina Press, 1985).

R. Kent Newmyer, "Thomas Jefferson and the Rise of the Supreme Court," *Journal of Supreme Court History*, vol. 31, no. 2 (July 2006), pp. 126–40.

Robert V. Remini, *Andrew Jackson* (Harper & Row, 1977–84), vols. 2–3.

Joel H. Silbey, *The American Political Nation, 1838–1893* (Stanford University Press, 1991).

James F. Simon, *What Kind of Nation: Thomas Jefferson, John Marshall, and the Epic Struggle to Create a United States* (Simon & Schuster, 2002).

Jean Edward Smith, *John Marshall: Definer of a Nation* (Henry Holt, 1996).

Robert Steamer, "Congress and the Supreme Court During the Marshall Era," *Review of Politics*, vol. 27, no. 3 (July 1965), pp. 364–85.

Melvin I. Urofsky, "Thomas Jefferson and John Marshall: What Kind of Constitution Shall We Have?," *Journal of Supreme Court History*, vol. 31, no. 2 (July 2006), pp. 109–25.

Sandra F. VanBurkleo, "In Defense of 'Public Reason': Supreme Court Justice William Johnson," *Journal of Supreme Court History*, vol. 32, no. 2 (August 2007), pp. 115–32.

G. Edward White, *The Marshall Court and Cultural Change, 1815–1835*, vol. 3 of *History of the Supreme Court of the United States* (Macmillan, 1988).

Christopher Wolfe, *The Rise of Modern Judicial Review: From Constitutional Interpretation to Judge-Made Law*, rev. ed. (Littlefield Adams, 1994).

25 ["all republicans"] : "First Inaugural Address," March 4, 1801, in Jefferson, *Papers*, Julian P. Boyd, ed. (Princeton University Press, 1950–), vol. 33, pp. 148–52, quoted at pp. 149, 150.

26 ["Who shall I nominate"] : Marshall, *Autobiographical Sketch*, p. 30.

26 ["pride of my life"] : Adams to Marshall, letter of August 17, 1825, in Marshall, *Papers*, Herbert A. Johnson, ed. (University of North Carolina Press, 1974–2006), vol. 10, p. 197.

27 ["rock of our political salvation"] : "To a Freeholder," *Virginia Herald* (Fredericksburg), October 2, 1798, in ibid., vol. 3, pp. 503–6, quoted at p. 504.

27 ["greatest Man"] : Marshall to James Monroe, letter of January 3, 1784, in ibid., vol. 1, pp. 113–14, quoted at p. 113.

27 ["confirmed in the habit"] : Marshall, *Autobiographical Sketch*, pp. 9–10.

27 ["no safe"] : ibid., p. 10.

28 ["well regulated Democracy"] : speech, June 10, 1788, in Marshall, *Papers*, vol. 1, pp. 256–70, quoted at p. 256.

28 ["considered by the Judges"] : speech, June 20, 1788, in ibid., vol. 1, pp. 275–86, quoted at p. 277.

28 ["good old school"] : Justice Joseph Story, *A Discourse Upon the Life, Character, and Services of the Honorable John Marshall, LL.D* (James Munroe and Co., 1835), p. 57.

28 ["stronghold"] : Jefferson to John Dickinson, letter of December 19, 1801, in Jefferson, *Works*, H. A. Washington, ed. (Townsend Mac Coun, 1884), vol. 4, pp. 424–25, quoted at p. 424.

28 ["only check"] : Giles to Jefferson, letter of March 16, 1801, in Jefferson, *Papers*, vol. 33, pp. 310–12, quoted at p. 311.

29 ["equal right"] : *Annals of Congress*, 7th Congress, 1st session, February 3, 1802, p. 179; for the omitted paragraph, see Beveridge, vol. 3, pp. 505–6 (Appendix A).

29 ["there are no words"] : 5 U.S. (1 Cranch) 299 (1803), quoted at 309.

29 ["certainly gone"] : Lee to Levin Powell, letter of July 11, 1802, quoted in Haskins and Johnson, p. 166.

31 ["appears not to be warranted"] : 5 U.S. (1 Cranch) 137 (1803), quoted at 176, 178, 177, 178, respectively.

32 ["gratuitous interference"] : Jefferson to Justice William Johnson, letter of June 12, 1823, in Jefferson, *Writings*, Merrill D. Peterson, ed. (Library of America, 1984), pp. 1469–77, quoted at p. 1474.

32   ["despotic branch"] : Jefferson to Abigail Adams, letter of September 11, 1804, in Jefferson, *Works*, vol. 4, pp. 560–62, quoted at p. 561.

32   ["travelling out"] : Jefferson to Johnson, June 12, 1823, in Jefferson, *Writings*, p. 1474.

33   ["general purgation"] : Giles to Jefferson, March 16, 1801, in Jefferson, *Papers*, vol. 33, p. 311.

33   ["fraudulent use"] : Jefferson to Dickinson, December 19, 1801, in Jefferson, *Works*, vol. 4, p. 425.

33   ["business of removing"] : entry of January 4, 1804, in Smith, *William Plumer's Memorandum*, p. 101.

33   ["the President, on application"] : entry of January 7, 1804, in ibid., p. 102.

33   [Chase's Baltimore jury charge] : quoted in Haskins and Johnson, p. 218.

34   ["mere scare-crow"] : Jefferson to Thomas Ritchie, letter of December 25, 1820, in Jefferson, *Writings*, pp. 1445–47, quoted at p. 1446.

34   ["appellate jurisdiction"] : letter of January 23, [1805], in Marshall, *Papers*, vol. 6, pp. 347–48, quoted at p. 347.

35   ["zealous democrat"] : Donald Morgan, "William Johnson," in Friedman and Israel, vol. 1, pp. 355–72, quoted at p. 358.

35   ["rest of the session"] : Johnson to Thomas Jefferson, letter of December 10, 1822, quoted in Morgan, *Justice William Johnson*, p. 182.

35   ["have a chance"] : Jefferson to Albert Gallatin, letter of September 27, 1810, in Jefferson, *Papers: Retirement Series*, J. Jefferson Looney, ed. (Princeton University Press, 2004–), vol. 3, pp. 123–25, quoted at p. 124.

36   ["pseudo-republican"] : Jefferson to Henry Dearborn, letter of July 16, 1810, in ibid., vol. 2, pp. 537–38, quoted at p. 537.

36   ["unquestionably a tory"] : Jefferson to Madison, letter of October 15, 1810, in ibid., vol. 3, pp. 165–66, quoted at p. 166.

36   ["although subscribed to"] : White, p. 192.

37   [*Fletcher*] : 10 U.S. (6 Cranch) 87 (1810), quoted at 135, 134, respectively.

38   ["sound construction"] : 14 U.S. (1 Wheaton) 304 (1816), quoted at 306.

38   ["extend to cases"] : ibid., quoted at 351, 348, respectively.

39   ["liberal latitude"] : Hamilton, "An Opinion on the Constitutionality of an Act to Establish a Bank," February 23, 1791, in Hamilton, *Papers*, Harold C. Syrett, ed. (Columbia University Press, 1961–87), vol. 8, pp. 97–134, quoted at p. 103.

39   ["emphatically and truly"] : 17 U.S. (4 Wheaton) 316 (1819), quoted at 404–5, 402, 405, respectively.

39   ["Let the end be"] : ibid., 421.

40   ["fair construction"] : ibid., 406, 407, 401, 423, respectively.

40   ["retard, impede"] : ibid., 436, 432, respectively.

40   ["judicial *coup de main*"] : Roane, first "Hampden Essay," *Richmond Enquirer*, June 11, 1819, in Gunther, pp. 106–14, quoted at pp. 110, 111; and Roane, fourth "Hampden Essay," *Richmond Enquirer*, June 22, 1819, in ibid., pp. 138–54, quoted at p. 140.

41   ["every tittle"] : Jefferson to Roane, letter of September 16, 1819, in Jefferson, *Writings*, pp. 1425–28, quoted at p. 1425.

41   ["reduce the whole instrument"] : Jefferson, "Opinion on the Constitutionality of a National Bank," February 15, 1791, in Jefferson, *Writings*, pp. 416–21, quoted at p. 418.

41   ["opinion is huddled up"] : Jefferson to Ritchie, December 25, 1820, in ibid., p. 1446.

41   ["thing of wax"] : Jefferson to Roane, September 16, 1819, in ibid., p. 1426.

41   ["Let each operate"] : *Cohens* v. *Virginia*, 19 U.S. (6 Wheaton) 264 (1821), quoted at 344.

42   ["all its departments"] : ibid., 415, 414, respectively.

43 ["perhaps two-thirds"] : diary entry, December 31, 1825, in Adams, *Memoirs*, Charles Francis Adams, ed. (J. B. Lippincott, 1874–77), vol. 7, p. 98.

43 ["Federalist heresies"] : quoted in Silbey, p. 17.

43 ["I should consider"] : see Marshall to Joseph Story, letter of May 1, 1828, in Marshall, *Papers*, vol. 11, pp. 93–94, quoted at p. 94.

44 [Georgia and the Cherokees] : *Worcester* v. *Georgia*, 31 U.S. (6 Peters) 515 (1832); see also *Cherokee Nation* v. *Georgia*, 30 U.S. (5 Peters) 1 (1831).

44 ["power to make war"] : "Special Message to the Senate," February 22, 1831, in James D. Richardson, ed., *A Compilation of the Messages and Papers of the Presidents* (Bureau of National Literature and Art, 1913), vol. 2, pp. 1099–1104, quoted at p. 1102.

44 ["made his decision"] : quoted in Longaker, p. 341.

44 ["fell still born"] : Jackson to John Coffee, letter of April 7, 1832, quoted in Remini, vol. 2, p. 276.

44 ["permitted to control"] : "Veto Message," July 10, 1832, in Richardson, vol. 2, pp. 1139–54, quoted at p. 1145.

45 ["hazard the disgrace"] : Marshall to Joseph Story, letter of October 12, 1831, in Marshall, *Papers*, vol. 12, pp. 118–20, quoted at p. 119; for Marshall's thoughts on retirement, see letter to Story, June 26, 1831, in ibid., vol. 12, pp. 93–94.

45 ["principles on the Constitution"] : Jackson to Martin Van Buren, letter of October 27, 1834, quoted in Longaker, p. 358 fn. 43.

46 [Majority rule in Marshall's court] : see *Briscoe* v. *Commonwealth Bank* and *City of New York* v. *Miln*, 33 U.S. (8 Peters) 118, Marshall's remark at 122. The two cases were eventually decided by the Taney Court; for *Briscoe*, see 36 U.S. (11 Peters) 257 (1837), and for *Miln*, 36 U.S. (11 Peters) 102 (1837).

46 ["revolutionary spirit"] : Marshall to Joseph Story, letter of May 3, 1831, in Marshall, *Papers*, vol. 12, pp. 62–63, quoted at p. 62.

46 [Marshall's dissent] : *Ogden* v. *Saunders*, 25 U.S. (12 Wheaton) 213 (1827), dissent at 332.

47 ["I yield slowly"] : letter of September 22, 1832, in Marshall, *Papers*, vol. 12, pp. 237–38, quoted at p. 238.

CHAPTER THREE—THE DRED DECISION

Henry J. Abraham, *Justices and Presidents: A Political History of Appointments to the Supreme Court*, 3rd ed. (Oxford University Press, 1992), ch. 6.

Austin Allen, *Origins of the* Dred Scott *Case: Jacksonian Jurisprudence and the Supreme Court, 1837–1857* (University of Georgia Press, 2006).

Walter Ehrlich, *They Have No Rights: Dred Scott's Struggle for Freedom* (Greenwood Press, 1979).

Nicole Etcheson, *Bleeding Kansas: Contested Liberty in the Civil War Era* (University Press of Kansas, 2004).

Don E. Fehrenbacher, *The Dred Scott Case: Its Significance in American Law and Politics* (Oxford University Press, 1978).

Paul Finkelman, *Dred Scott v. Sandford* (Bedford Books, 1997).

Leon Friedman and Fred L. Israel, eds., *The Justices of the United States Supreme Court, 1789–1969* (Chelsea House, 1969–78), vol. 2.

Mark A. Graber, "Desperately Ducking Slavery: Dred Scott and Contemporary Constitutional Theory," *Constitutional Commentary*, vol. 14, no. 2 (Summer 1997), pp. 271–318.

Charles Grove Haines, *The American Doctrine of Judicial Supremacy*, 2nd ed. (University of California Press, 1932).

Timothy S. Huebner, *The Taney Court: Justices, Rulings, and Legacy* (ABC-CLIO, 2003).

Harold M. Hyman and William M. Wiecek, *Equal Justice Under Law: Constitutional Development, 1835–1875* (Harper & Row, 1982).

William Lasser, *The Limits of Judicial Power: The Supreme Court in American Politics* (University of North Carolina Press, 1988), ch. 2.

Donald E. Lively, *Foreshadows of the Law: Supreme Court Dissents and Constitutional Development* (Praeger, 1992), ch. 2.

Earl M. Maltz, *Dred Scott and the Politics of Slavery* (University Press of Kansas, 2007).

Wallace Mendelson, "Chief Justice Taney: Jacksonian Judge," *University of Pittsburgh Law Review*, vol. 12 (Spring 1951), pp. 381–93.

Lucas E. Morel, "The *Dred Scott* Dissents: McLean, Curtis, Lincoln, and the Public Mind," *Journal of Supreme Court History*, vol. 32, no. 2 (August 2007), pp. 133–51.

David M. Potter, *The Impending Crisis, 1848–1861* (Harper & Row, 1976).

Donald L. Robinson, *Slavery in the Structure of American Politics, 1765–1820* (Harcourt Brace Jovanovich, 1971).

John R. Schmidhauser, "Judicial Behavior and the Sectional Crisis of 1837–1860," *Journal of Politics*, vol. 23, no. 4 (November 1961), pp. 615–40.

Joel H. Silbey, *The American Political Nation, 1838–1893* (Stanford University Press, 1991).

James F. Simon, *Lincoln and Chief Justice Taney: Slavery, Secession, and the President's War Powers* (Simon & Schuster, 2006).

Kenneth M. Stampp, *America in 1857: A Nation on the Brink* (Oxford University Press, 1990).

Stuart Streichler, *Justice Curtis in the Civil War Era* (University of Virginia Press, 2005).

Carl B. Swisher, *Roger B. Taney* (Macmillan, 1935).

Carl B. Swisher, *The Taney Period, 1836–64*, vol. 5 of *History of the Supreme Court of the United States* (Macmillan, 1974).

Samuel Tyler, *Memoir of Roger Brooke Taney, LL.D*, 2nd ed. (John Murphy, 1876).

Keith E. Whittington, "The Road Not Taken: Dred Scott, Judicial Authority, and Political Questions," *Journal of Politics*, vol. 63, no. 2 (May 2001), pp. 365–91.

William M. Wiecek, "Slavery and Abolition Before the United States Supreme Court, 1820–1860," *Journal of American History*, vol. 65, no. 1 (June 1978), pp. 34–59.

Xi Wang, "The *Dred Scott* Case," in Annette Gordon-Reed, ed., *Race on Trial: Law and Justice in American History* (Oxford University Press, 2002), pp. 26–47.

49   ["slavery, spittoons"] : Dickens to Charles Sumner, letter of March 13, 1842, in Dickens, *Letters*, Madeline House et al., eds. (Clarendon Press, 1965–2002), vol. 3, pp. 126–28, quoted at p. 127; Dickens, *American Notes and Pictures from Italy* (Oxford University Press, 1957), p. 120.

49   [African-American population, late 1780s] : U.S. Bureau of the Census, *Negro Population in the United States, 1790–1915* (1918; reprinted by Arno Press, 1968), p. 45 (Table 13).

51   ["consistent with the Constitution"] : quoted in Hyman and Wiecek, p. 144.

52   ["preservation of the Union"] : *Congressional Globe*, 31st Congress, 1st session, March 7, 1850, p. 476.

52   [Marshall leaving slavery to the states] : see R. Kent Newmyer, *John Marshall and the Heroic Age of the Supreme Court* (Louisiana State University Press, 2001), pp. 424–34.

53   ["debt of gratitude"] : Jackson to Taney, letter of June 25, 1834, in Tyler, pp. 222–23, quoted at p. 223.

53   [Charles River Bridge] : *Charles River Bridge* v. *Warren Bridge*, 36 U.S. 420 (1837), Taney quoted at 548; Story's dissent at 598.

54 [Taney's expansions of state powers] : see *License Cases*, 46 U.S. 504 (1847), esp. 578–80.

54 ["could not be questioned"] : 48 U.S. 1 (1849), quoted at 42.

54 ["African race"] : quoted in Simon, pp. 16, 17.

55 [Taney on interstate slave trade] : *Groves* v. *Slaughter*, 40 U.S. 449 (1841), Taney's concurrence at 508.

55 [*Strader*] : 51 U.S. 82 (1851), esp. 93–94.

55 [*Prigg*] : 41 U.S. 539 (1842).

56 ["all questions pertaining"] : quoted in Hyman and Wiecek, p. 163.

57 ["times are not now"] : quoted in Finkelman, p. 22.

58 ["dead letter"] : "Fourth Annual Message," December 2, 1856, in Richardson, vol. 4, pp. 2930–50, quoted at p. 2935.

58 ["compromise of principle"] : quoted in Fehrenbacher, p. 301.

59 [Explanations for the court's shift] : I have relied on Fehrenbacher's discussion in his ch. 13.

59 ["line of latitude"] : Grier to Buchanan, letter of February 23, 1857, quoted in ibid., p. 312.

59 [Fehrenbacher on Taney's opinion] : ibid., p. 311.

60 ["subordinate and inferior class"] : *Dred Scott* v. *Sandford*, 60 U.S. 393 (1857), quoted at 404–5, 407, 450, 426, respectively.

61 [Curtis's dissent] : ibid. at 564.

61 ["speedily and finally"] : "Inaugural Address," in Richardson, vol. 4, pp. 2961–67, quoted at p. 2962.

61 ["supreme law"] : March 15, 1857, quoted in Fehrenbacher, p. 418.

61 ["momentous and revolutionary"] : James R. Doolittle, *Congressional Globe*, 35th Congress, 2nd session, February 11, 1858, p. 665.

62 ["opposing and enduring forces"] : Seward, "The Irrepressible Conflict," speech delivered at Rochester, NY, October 25, 1858, quoted in Frederic Bancroft, *The Life of William H. Seward* (Harper & Brothers, 1900), vol. 1, p. 459.

CHAPTER FOUR—WAR POWERS: LINCOLN VS. TANEY

Arthur T. Downey, "The Conflict Between the Chief Justice and the Chief Executive: *Ex parte Merryman*," *Journal of Supreme Court History*, vol. 31, no. 3 (November 2006), pp. 262–78.

Charles Fairman, *Mr. Justice Miller and the Supreme Court, 1862–1890* (Harvard University Press, 1939).

Daniel Farber, *Lincoln's Constitution* (University of Chicago Press, 2003).

Don E. Fehrenbacher, *The Dred Scott Case: Its Significance in American Law and Politics* (Oxford University Press, 1978).

Don E. Fehrenbacher, *Lincoln in Text and Context* (Stanford University Press, 1987).

Paul Finkelman, "'Hooted Down the Page of History': Reconsidering the Greatness of Chief Justice Taney," *Journal of Supreme Court History*, vol. 1994 (1994), pp. 83–102.

George P. Fletcher, *Our Secret Constitution: How Lincoln Redefined American Democracy* (Oxford University Press, 2001).

Leon Friedman and Fred L. Israel, eds., *The Justices of the United States Supreme Court, 1789–1969* (Chelsea House, 1969–78), vol. 2.

Doris Kearns Goodwin, *Team of Rivals: The Political Genius of Abraham Lincoln* (Simon & Schuster, 2005).

Harold Holzer and Sara Vaughn Gabbard, eds., *Lincoln and Freedom: Slavery, Emancipation, and the Thirteenth Amendment* (Southern Illinois University Press, 2007).

Timothy S. Huebner, *The Taney Court: Justices, Rulings, and Legacy* (ABC-CLIO, 2003).

Harold M. Hyman, *A More Perfect Union: The Impact of the Civil War and Reconstruction on the Constitution* (Alfred A. Knopf, 1973).

Harold M. Hyman and William M. Wiecek, *Equal Justice Under Law: Constitutional Development, 1835–1875* (Harper & Row, 1982).

Gary J. Jacobsohn, "Abraham Lincoln 'On This Question of Judicial Authority': The Theory of Constitutional Aspiration," *Western Political Quarterly*, vol. 36, no. 1 (March 1983), pp. 52–70.

Willard L. King, *Lincoln's Manager, David Davis* (Harvard University Press, 1960).

Frank L. Klement, *The Limits of Dissent: Clement L. Vallandigham & the Civil War* (University Press of Kentucky, 1970).

Wallace Mendelson, "Chief Justice Taney: Jacksonian Judge," *University of Pittsburgh Law Review*, vol. 12 (Spring 1951), pp. 381–93.

Mark E. Neely, Jr., *The Fate of Liberty: Abraham Lincoln and Civil Liberties* (Oxford University Press, 1991).

Michael Stokes Paulsen, "The Merryman Power and the Dilemma of Autonomous Executive Branch Interpretation," *Cardozo Law Review*, vol. 15 (October 1993), pp. 81–111.

David M. Potter, *The Impending Crisis, 1848–1861* (Harper & Row, 1976).

David M. Silver, *Lincoln's Supreme Court* (University of Illinois Press, 1957).

James F. Simon, *Lincoln and Chief Justice Taney: Slavery, Secession, and the President's War Powers* (Simon & Schuster, 2006).

Robert M. Spector, "Lincoln and Taney: A Study in Constitutional Polarization," *American Journal of Legal History*, vol. 15, no. 3 (July 1971), pp. 199–214.

Robert L. Stern, "Chief Justice Taney and the Shadow of *Dred Scott*," *Journal of Supreme Court History*, vol. 1992 (1992), pp. 39–52.

Stuart Streichler, *Justice Curtis in the Civil War Era* (University of Virginia Press, 2005), ch. 6.

Carl B. Swisher, *Roger B. Taney* (Macmillan, 1935).

Carl B. Swisher, *The Taney Period, 1836–64*, vol. 5 of *History of the Supreme Court of the United States* (Macmillan, 1974).

The Trial of Hon. Clement Vallandigham, by a Military Commission: and the Proceedings Under His Application for a Writ of Habeas Corpus (Rickey and Carroll, 1863).

Samuel Tyler, *Memoir of Roger Brooke Taney, LL.D*, 2nd ed. (John Murphy, 1876).

63   ["I do not forget"] : "First Inaugural Address," in Lincoln, *Speeches and Writings*, Don E. Fehrenbacher, ed. (Library of America, 1989), vol. 2, pp. 215–24, quoted at pp. 220, 221, 218, respectively.

64   ["very much agitated"] : Baltimore *Daily Exchange*, March 5, 1861, quoted in Swisher, *Taney Period*, p. 741.

64   ["that bench-full"] : *Chicago Tribune*, March 4, 1861, quoted in Silver, p. 42.

64   ["Somebody has to reverse"] : speech at Chicago, July 10, 1858, quoted in Lincoln, *Speeches and Writings*, vol. 1, pp. 439–58, quoted at p. 451.

64   ["I am sensible"] : Taney to Ellis Lewis, letter of December 24, 1860, quoted in Swisher, *Taney Period*, p. 726.

65   ["arrest, or disperse"] : Lincoln to Winfield Scott, letter of April 25, 1861, in Lincoln, *Speeches and Writings*, vol. 2, pp. 236–37, quoted at p. 236.

65   ["Errors, if any"] : General George Cadwalader to Taney, letter of May 26, 1861, reprinted in Tyler, pp. 643–44 (Appendix), quoted at p. 643.

65   ["perform his constitutional duty"] : ibid., p. 645.

65   [*Merryman*] : 17 Fed.Cas. (D. Maryland 1861) 144.

66   ["vindication of the principles"] : *Baltimore Sun*, June 4, 1861, quoted in Swisher, *Taney Period*, p. 851.

66   ["aid and comfort"] : *New York Tribune*, May 30, 1861, quoted in ibid.

66   ["government of the people"] : "Message to Congress in Special Session," in Lincoln, *Speeches and Writings*, vol. 2, pp. 246–61, quoted at pp. 250, 253, 259.

68   ["one Supreme Court"] : *Congressional Globe*, 37th Congress, 2nd session, December 9, 1861, pp. 26–28, quoted at pp. 26, 27.

68   ["fully settled"] : "Speech on the Dred Scott Decision," Springfield, IL, June 26, 1857, in Lincoln, *Speeches and Writings*, vol. 1, pp. 390–403, quoted at p. 392.

68   ["run the gantlet"] : John Hay, "Life in the White House in the Time of Lincoln," *Century*, vol. 41, no. 1 (November 1890), pp. 33–37, quoted at p. 34.

70   ["without any useful purpose"] : Nelson to Justice Clifford, letter of April 19, 1861, quoted in Fairman, p. 81.

71   ["fully expressed"] : Clifford to James Buchanan, letter of July 19, 1859, quoted in Swisher, *Taney Period*, p. 733.

71   ["Constitution knows"] : quoted in Silver, p. 112.

71   ["civil war is never"] : *Prize Cases*, 67 U.S. 635 (1862), majority opinion quoted at 666, 669, 669–70; Nelson's dissent at 694.

72   ["paper trash"] : quoted in Swisher, *Taney Period*, p. 943.

72   [Legal tender case] : *Roosevelt* v. *Meyer*, 68 U.S. 512 (1863).

73   ["all persons discouraging"] : "Proclamation Suspending the Writ of Habeas Corpus," September 24, 1862, in Lincoln, *Speeches and Writings*, vol. 2, p. 371.

73   [Eighteen thousand civilian arrests] : Hyman and Wiecek, p. 233.

73   ["disregard each and every"] : quoted in Streichler, p. 157.

73   ["is authorized to suspend"] : quoted in Swisher, *Taney Period*, p. 920.

74   ["political school"] : ibid., p. 923.

74   ["wicked, cruel"] : *Trial of Vallandigham*, p. 11.

74   ["King Lincoln"] : testimony of Capt. John A. Means, in ibid., pp. 22–23.

74   ["disloyal sentiments"] : ibid., p. 11.

75   ["close confinement"] : ibid., p. 33.

75   ["when the national life"] : Judge H. H. Leavitt's Opinion of the Court, in ibid., pp. 269, 266, respectively.

75   [Lincoln and Vallandigham's arrest] : see Lincoln to General Ambrose E. Burnside, telegram of May 29, 1863, in Lincoln, *Speeches and Writings*, vol. 2, p. 451.

75   ["wily agitator"] : Lincoln to Erastus Corning and Others, letter of June 12, 1863, in ibid., vol. 2, pp. 454–63, quoted at p. 460.

76   ["to review or pronounce"] : *Ex parte Vallandigham*, 68 U.S. 243 (1863), quoted at 252.

76   ["foul and corrupt"] : quoted in Simon, p. 244.

76   ["necessary war measure"] : "Final Emancipation Proclamation," January 1, 1863, in Lincoln, *Speeches and Writings*, vol. 2, pp. 424–25, quoted at p. 424.

76   ["hot-new purpose"] : Phillips, "Speech at the Cooper Institute," December 22, 1863, in *The Liberator*, vol. 34, no. 1 (January 1, 1864), p. 2.

76   ["absolve the judicial department"] : *Baltimore Sun*, June 20, 1863, quoted in Spector, p. 207.

CHAPTER FIVE—DECONSTRUCTION: REPUBLICAN REVERSAL

Michael Les Benedict, "Preserving the Constitution: The Conservative Basis of Radical Reconstruction," *Journal of American History*, vol. 61, no. 1 (June 1974), pp. 65–90.

Michael Les Benedict, "Preserving Federalism: Reconstruction and the Waite Court," *Supreme Court Review*, vol. 1978 (1978), pp. 39–79.

Michael Les Benedict, "The Problem of Constitutionalism and Constitutional Liberty in the Reconstruction South," in Kermit L. Hall and James W. Ely, Jr., eds., *An*

Uncertain Tradition: Constitutionalism and the History of the South (University of Georgia Press, 1989), pp. 225–49.

Pamela Brandwein, "The *Civil Rights Cases* and the Lost Language of State Neglect," in Ronald Kahn and Ken I. Kersch, eds., *The Supreme Court and American Political Development* (University Press of Kansas, 2006), pp. 275–325.

Pamela Brandwein, *Reconstructing Reconstruction: The Supreme Court and the Production of Historical Truth* (Duke University Press, 1999).

Michael Kent Curtis, *No State Shall Abridge: The Fourteenth Amendment and the Bill of Rights* (Duke University Press, 1986).

Garrett Epps, "The Antebellum Background of the Fourteenth Amendment," *Law and Contemporary Problems*, vol. 67, no. 3 (Summer 2004), pp. 175–211.

Charles Fairman, *Five Justices and the Electoral Commission of 1877*, supplement to vol. 7 of *History of the Supreme Court of the United States* (Macmillan, 1988).

Charles Fairman, *Mr. Justice Miller and the Supreme Court, 1862–1890* (Harvard University Press, 1939).

Charles Fairman, *Reconstruction and Reunion, 1864–88*, vols. 6–7 of *History of the Supreme Court of the United States* (Macmillan, 1971–87).

Eric Foner, *Reconstruction: America's Unfinished Revolution, 1863–1877* (Harper & Row, 1988).

Leon Friedman and Fred L. Israel, eds., *The Justices of the United States Supreme Court, 1789–1969* (Chelsea House, 1969–78), vol. 2.

Harold Holzer and Sara Vaughn Gabbard, eds., *Lincoln and Freedom: Slavery, Emancipation, and the Thirteenth Amendment* (Southern Illinois University Press, 2007).

Harold M. Hyman, *A More Perfect Union: The Impact of the Civil War and Reconstruction on the Constitution* (Alfred A. Knopf, 1973).

Harold M. Hyman, *The Reconstruction Justice of Salmon P. Chase* (University Press of Kansas, 1997).

Harold M. Hyman and William M. Wiecek, *Equal Justice Under Law: Constitutional Development, 1835–1875* (Harper & Row, 1982).

Peter Irons, *A People's History of the Supreme Court* (Viking, 1999), chs. 16–17.

Stanley I. Kutler, *Judicial Power and Reconstruction Politics* (University of Chicago Press, 1968).

Ronald M. Labbé and Jonathan Lurie, *The Slaughterhouse Cases: Regulation, Reconstruction, and the Fourteenth Amendment* (University Press of Kansas, 2003).

Charles Lane, *The Day Freedom Died: The Colfax Massacre, the Supreme Court, and the Betrayal of Reconstruction* (Henry Holt, 2008).

William Lasser, *The Limits of Judicial Power: The Supreme Court in American Politics* (University of North Carolina Press, 1988), ch. 3.

C. Peter Magrath, *Morrison R. Waite: The Triumph of Character* (Macmillan, 1963).

Earl M. Maltz, *Civil Rights, the Constitution, and Congress, 1863–1869* (University Press of Kansas, 1990).

Roy Morris, Jr., *Fraud of the Century: Rutherford B. Hayes, Samuel Tilden, and the Stolen Election of 1876* (Simon & Schuster, 2003).

William E. Nelson, *The Fourteenth Amendment: From Political Principle to Judicial Doctrine* (Harvard University Press, 1988).

Keith Ian Polakoff, *The Politics of Inertia: The Election of 1876 and the End of Reconstruction* (Louisiana State University Press, 1973).

David A. J. Richards, *Conscience and the Constitution: History, Theory, and Law of the Reconstruction Amendments* (Princeton University Press, 1993).

Michael A. Ross, *Justice of Shattered Dreams: Samuel Freeman Miller and the Supreme Court During the Civil War Era* (Louisiana State University Press, 2003).

Frank J. Scaturro, *The Supreme Court's Retreat from Reconstruction: A Distortion of Constitutional Jurisprudence* (Greenwood Press, 2000).

Jean Edward Smith, *Grant* (Simon and Schuster, 2001).

C. Vann Woodward, *Reunion and Reaction: The Compromise of 1877 and the End of Reconstruction* (Little, Brown, 1951).

Bertram Wyatt-Brown, "The Civil Rights Act of 1875," *Western Political Quarterly*, vol. 18, no. 4 (December 1965), pp. 763–75.

79   [Population growth, postwar decades] : Susan B. Carter et al., eds., *Historical Statistics of the United States: Earliest Times to the Present* (Cambridge University Press, 2006), vol. 1, pp. 31–32 (Table Aa9).

80   ["terrible war"] : March 4, 1865, in Lincoln, *Speeches and Writings*, Don E. Fehrenbacher, ed. (Library of America, 1989), vol. 2, pp. 686–87, quoted at p. 687.

80   ["who shall have tasted"] : Lincoln to Stephen A. Hurlbut, letter of July 31, 1863, in ibid., vol. 2, pp. 485–86, quoted at p. 485.

80   ["new birth"] : November 19, 1863, in ibid., vol. 2, p. 536.

81   ["full and equal benefit"] : quoted in Hyman, *More Perfect Union*, p. 462.

82   ["injure, oppress"] : *U.S. v. Cruikshank*, 92 U.S. 542 (1875), quoted at 547.

84   ["entirely fitting"] : letter of November 8, 1873, in Grant, *Papers*, John Y. Simon, ed. (Southern Illinois University Press, 1967–), vol. 24, p. 253.

85   [Welles on Waite] : Magrath, p. 2.

85   [Waite in front rank of second-class lawyers] : Allan Nevins, *Hamilton Fish: The Inner History of the Grant Administration* (Dodd, Mead, 1937), p. 665.

85   ["fear and trembling"] : quoted in Magrath, p. 90.

86   [*Slaughterhouse*] : *Slaughter-House Cases*, 83 U.S. 36 (1873), Miller's opinion quoted at 82, 77, 75, 71, respectively.

87   ["bloodiest single act"] : Foner, p. 530.

88   ["every legal door"] : Irons, p. 205.

88   ["very highest duty"] : *Cruikshank*, quoted at 553, 556.

89   ["not exactly extinct"] : editorial, *New York Times*, June 1, 1876, p. 6.

89   ["inns, public conveyances"] : quoted in Fairman, *Reconstruction and Reunion*, vol. 7, p. 176.

89   ["I am treated"] : *Congressional Record*, 43rd Congress, 2nd session, February 3, 1875, p. 945.

89   ["depriving white people"] : quoted in Fairman, *Reconstruction and Reunion*, vol. 7, p. 564.

90   ["not to distinctions"] : 109 U.S. 3 (1883), quoted at 24, 25.

91   ["The negro will disappear"] : "The Political South Hereafter," *Nation*, vol. 24, no. 614 (April 5, 1877), pp. 202–3, quoted at p. 202.

CHAPTER SIX—A COURT FOR THE GILDED AGE

Richard L. Aynes, "Unintended Consequences of the Fourteenth Amendment," in David E. Kyvig, ed., *Unintended Consequences of Constitutional Amendment* (University of Georgia Press, 2000), pp. 110–40.

Mark Warren Bailey, *Guardians of the Moral Order: The Legal Philosophy of the Supreme Court, 1860–1910* (Northern Illinois University Press, 2004).

Michael Les Benedict, "Laissez-Faire and Liberty: A Re-Evaluation of the Meaning and Origins of Laissez-Faire Constitutionalism," *Law and History Review*, vol. 3, no. 2 (Autumn 1985), pp. 293–331.

Loren P. Beth, *The Development of the American Constitution, 1877–1917* (Harper & Row, 1971).

David J. Brewer, "The Nation's Safeguard," *Proceedings of the New York State Bar Association*, vol. 47 (1893), pp. 37–48.

David J. Brewer, "Protection to Private Property from Public Attack," *New Englander and Yale Review*, vol. 55, no. 256 (August 1891), pp. 97–110.

James MacGregor Burns, *The Workshop of Democracy* (Alfred A. Knopf, 1985), part 2.

Robert F. Durden, *The Climax of Populism: The Election of 1896* (University of Kentucky Press, 1965).

James W. Ely, Jr., *The Chief Justiceship of Melville W. Fuller, 1888–1910* (University of South Carolina Press, 1995).

James W. Ely, Jr., *The Fuller Court: Justices, Rulings, and Legacy* (ABC-CLIO, 2003).

James W. Ely, Jr., *The Guardian of Every Other Right: A Constitutional History of Property Rights*, 2nd ed. (Oxford University Press, 1998), ch. 5.

Charles Fairman, "Mr. Justice Bradley's Appointment to the Supreme Court and the Legal Tender Cases," *Harvard Law Review*, vol. 54, nos. 6 and 7 (April and May 1941), pp. 977–1034 and 1128–55.

Charles Fairman, *Mr. Justice Miller and the Supreme Court, 1862–1890* (Harvard University Press, 1939).

Charles Fairman, *Reconstruction and Reunion, 1864–88*, vols. 6–7 of *History of the Supreme Court of the United States* (Macmillan, 1971–87).

Charles Fairman, "The So-Called Granger Cases, Lord Hale, and Justice Bradley," *Stanford Law Review*, vol. 5, no. 4 (July 1953), pp. 587–679.

Charles Fairman, "What Makes a Great Justice?: Mr. Justice Bradley and the Supreme Court, 1870–1892," *Boston University Law Review*, vol. 30 (January 1950), pp. 49–102.

Harold U. Faulkner, *Politics, Reform, and Expansion, 1890–1900* (Harper & Brothers, 1959).

Harvey Fireside, *Separate and Unequal: Homer Plessy and the Supreme Court Decision That Legalized Racism* (Carroll & Graf, 2004).

Owen M. Fiss, *Troubled Beginnings of the Modern State, 1888–1910*, vol. 8 of the *History of the Supreme Court of the United States* (Macmillan, 1993).

Eric Foner, *Free Soil, Free Labor, Free Men: The Ideology of the Republican Party Before the Civil War* (Oxford University Press, 1970).

William E. Forbath, *Law and the Shaping of the American Labor Movement* (Harvard University Press, 1991).

Leon Friedman and Fred L. Israel, eds., *The Justices of the United States Supreme Court, 1789–1969* (Chelsea House, 1969–78), vols. 2–3.

Russell W. Galloway, *Justice for All?: The Rich and Poor in Supreme Court History, 1790–1990* (Carolina Academic Press, 1991), chs. 7–8.

Howard Gillman, "How Political Parties Can Use the Courts to Advance Their Agendas: Federal Courts in the United States, 1875–1891," *American Political Science Review*, vol. 96, no. 3 (September 2002), pp. 511–24.

John D. Hicks, *The Populist Revolt: A History of the Farmers' Alliance and the People's Party* (1931; reprinted by Greenwood Press, 1981).

Peter Irons, *A People's History of the Supreme Court* (Viking, 1999), chs. 16–20.

Stanley L. Jones, *The Presidential Election of 1896* (University of Wisconsin Press, 1964).

Morton Keller, *Affairs of State: Public Life in Late Nineteenth Century America* (Belknap Press, 1977).

Paul Kens, *Justice Stephen Field: Shaping Liberty from the Gold Rush to the Gilded Age* (University Press of Kansas, 1997).

Willard L. King, *Melville Weston Fuller: Chief Justice of the United States, 1888–1910* (Macmillan, 1950).

Michael J. Klarman, "The Plessy Era," *Supreme Court Review*, vol. 1998 (1998), pp. 303–414.

Gabriel Kolko, *Railroads and Regulation, 1877–1916* (Princeton University Press, 1965).

Ronald M. Labbé and Jonathan Lurie, *The Slaughterhouse Cases: Regulation, Reconstruction, and the Fourteenth Amendment* (University Press of Kansas, 2003).

Charles A. Lofgren, *The Plessy Case* (Oxford University Press, 1987).

Jonathan Lurie, "Stanley Matthews: A Case Portrait of Gilded Age High Court Jurisprudence," *Journal of Supreme Court History*, vol. 33, no. 2 (July 2008), pp. 160–69.

C. Peter Magrath, *Morrison Waite: The Triumph of Character* (Macmillan, 1963).

Robert G. McCloskey, *American Conservatism in the Age of Enterprise* (Harvard University Press, 1951), chs. 4–5.

Wayne D. Moore, "(Re)Construction of Constitutional Authority and Meaning: The Fourteenth Amendment and *Slaughter-House Cases*," in Ronald Kahn and Ken I. Kersch, eds., *The Supreme Court and American Political Development* (University Press of Kansas, 2006), pp. 229–74.

James O'Hara, "The Gilded Age and the Supreme Court," *Journal of Supreme Court History*, vol. 33, no. 2 (July 2008), pp. 123–33.

Arnold M. Paul, *Conservative Crisis and the Rule of Law: Attitudes of Bar and Bench, 1887–1895* (Cornell University Press, 1960).

Norman Pollack, *The Populist Response to Industrial America: Midwestern Populist Thought* (Harvard University Press, 1962).

Linda Przybyszewski, "The Dissents of John Marshall Harlan I," *Journal of Supreme Court History*, vol. 32, no. 2 (August 2007), pp. 152–61.

Sidney Ratner, "Was the Supreme Court Packed by President Grant?," *Political Science Quarterly*, vol. 50, no. 3 (September 1935), pp. 343–58.

John P. Roche, "Civil Liberty in the Age of Enterprise," *University of Chicago Law Review*, vol. 31, no. 1 (Autumn 1963), pp. 103–35.

Michael A. Ross, *Justice of Shattered Dreams: Samuel Freeman Miller and the Supreme Court During the Civil War Era* (Louisiana State University Press, 2003).

William G. Ross, *A Muted Fury: Populists, Progressives, and Labor Unions Confront the Courts, 1890–1937* (Princeton University Press, 1994).

Joel H. Silbey, *The American Political Nation, 1838–1893* (Stanford University Press, 1991).

Robert Stanley, *Dimensions of Law in the Service of Order: Origins of the Federal Income Tax, 1861–1913* (Oxford University Press, 1993).

William F. Swindler, *Court and Constitution in the Twentieth Century: The Old Legality, 1889–1932* (Bobbs-Merrill, 1969), chs. 1–4.

James B. Weaver, *A Call to Action* (Iowa Printing Co., 1892).

Alan F. Westin, "The Supreme Court, the Populist Movement and the Campaign of 1896," *Journal of Politics*, vol. 15, no. 1 (February 1953), pp. 3–41.

William M. Wiecek, "Justice David J. Brewer and 'the Constitution in Exile,'" *Journal of Supreme Court History*, vol. 33, no. 2 (July 2008), pp. 170–85.

Tinsley E. Yarbrough, *Judicial Enigma: The First Justice Harlan* (Oxford University Press, 1995).

94 [*Hepburn*] : 75 U.S. 603 (1870).

94 ["curious spectacle"] : "The Legal Tender Cases of 1871," *American Law Review*, vol. 7 (1872), pp. 146–47, quoted at p. 146. Holmes was editor of the review and presumed author of this "book notice."

95 ["Chief Justice has resorted"] : letter of April 21, 1870, quoted in Fairman, *Mr. Justice Miller*, pp. 170, 171.

95 [*Legal Tender Cases*] : 79 U.S. 457 (1871).

95 ["base compliance"] : quoted in Ratner, p. 348.

95 ["although he required"] : entry of October 28, 1876, quoted in Allan Nevins, *Hamilton Fish: The Inner History of the Grant Administration* (Dodd, Mead, 1937), pp. 306–7.

96 ["profoundly wrong"] : Fairman, "Mr. Justice Bradley's Appointment," p. 1133.

96   [Railroad worker casualties, 1889] : Irons, p. 192.

98   ["distinguishing privilege"] : *Slaughter-House Cases*, 83 U.S. 36 (1873), quoted at
      110, 101, 110, respectively.

99   [Hopkins] : Frederick Rudolph, *Mark Hopkins and the Log: Williams College, 1836–
      1872* (Yale University Press, 1956), esp. ch. 2.

100   [*Munn*] : 94 U.S. 113 (1877), Waite's opinion quoted at 131, 130, respectively; Field's
      dissent at 148, 140, respectively.

101   ["labor is prior to"] : "Address Before the Wisconsin State Agricultural Society,"
      Milwaukee, September 30, 1859, in Lincoln, *Collected Works*, Roy P. Basler, ed.
      (Rutgers University Press, 1953–55), vol. 3, pp. 471–82, quoted at p. 478.

101   ["Unrestricted monopolies"] : Bradley, "Outline of my views on the subject of the
      Granger Cases," reprinted as an appendix to Fairman, "The So-Called Granger
      Cases," quoted at p. 670.

103   ["oppressive and tyrannical"] : quoted in Hicks, p. 147.

103   ["power of government"] : "People's Platform," July 4, 1892, reprinted in Arthur
      M. Schlesinger, Jr., ed., *History of American Presidential Elections* (Chelsea House,
      1971), vol. 2, pp. 1741–44, quoted at p. 1742.

103   ["Imperial Supreme Court"] : Weaver, pp. 133, 132, 134, 135, respectively.

104   ["marched to the polls"] : Alex Arnett, *The Populist Movement in Georgia*
      (Longmans, Green, 1922), p. 154.

104   ["best and most beneficial"] : Miller to David Davis, letter of September 7, 1873,
      quoted in Labbé and Lurie, p. 14.

104   ["It is vain"] : quoted in Swindler, p. 10.

105   ["duty of the people"] : Fuller, "Address in Commemoration of the Inauguration of
      George Washington," December 11, 1889, 132 U.S. 707 (1889), quoted at 732.

105   [Harlan on Lincoln's "perversion" of Union cause] : Yarbrough, p. 57.

106   [Harlan's dissent in seamen case] : *Robertson* v. *Baldwin*, 165 U.S. 275 (1897), dissent
      at 288.

107   [*Santa Clara Co.*] : 118 U.S. 394 (1886).

107   [*Wabash*] : 118 U.S. 557 (1886).

107   [*Chicago, Milwaukee*] : 134 U.S. 418 (1890), majority opinion by Blatchford quoted
      at 458; Bradley's dissent at 462. See also Fiss, pp. 203–4.

108   ["love of acquirement"] : Brewer, "Protection to Private Property," p. 99.

108   [*Reagan*] : 154 U.S. 362 (1894), quoted at 412, 399, respectively.

109   [*Pollock*] : 158 U.S. 601 (1895), Jackson's dissent quoted at 706; Fuller's majority
      opinion at 634.

109   ["unvarying law"] : Brewer, "Nation's Safeguard," p. 39.

109   [*Knight*] : 156 U.S. 1 (1895).

110   ["third House"] : "Triumph of the Sugar Trust over the People of the United
      States," *American Law Review*, vol. 29 (March–April 1895), pp. 293–306, quoted at
      p. 306.

110   ["chief end"] : Brewer, "Nation's Safeguard," p. 39.

110   ["special exigency"] : 158 U.S. 564 (1895), Brewer's opinion quoted at 592, 593.

110   ["greed over need"] : May 21, 1895, quoted in Swindler, p. 3.

111   ["government by injunction"] : "Democratic Platform" (1896), in Schlesinger, vol. 2,
      pp. 1827–31, quoted at p. 1830.

111   ["government by the mob"] : ex-President Benjamin Harrison, quoted in Westin,
      p. 34.

112   [*Plessy*] : 163 U.S. 537 (1896), majority opinion quoted at 544, 551, 552; Harlan's
      dissent at 559, 557, 559, respectively.

113   ["black flag"] : Brewer, "Nation's Safeguard," p. 47.

113   ["do all that it can"] : quoted in Fiss, p. 73.

CHAPTER SEVEN—THE TRIUMPHANT MR. TAFT

Henry J. Abraham, *Justices and Presidents: A Political History of Appointments to the Supreme Court*, 3rd ed. (Oxford University Press, 1992), ch. 8.

Leonard Baker, *Brandeis and Frankfurter* (Harper & Row, 1984).

Loren P. Beth, *The Development of the American Constitution, 1877–1917* (Harper & Row, 1971).

James E. Bond, *I Dissent: The Legacy of Chief Justice James Clark McReynolds* (George Mason University Press, 1992).

L. B. Boudin, "Government by Judiciary," *Political Science Quarterly*, vol. 26, no. 2 (June 1911), pp. 238–70.

David H. Burton, *Taft, Holmes, and the 1920s Court* (Fairleigh Dickinson University Press, 1998).

David P. Currie, "The Constitution in the Supreme Court, 1910–1921," *Duke Law Journal*, vol. 1985, no. 6 (December 1985), pp. 1111–62.

David J. Danelski, *A Supreme Court Justice Is Appointed* (Random House, 1964).

W. F. Dodd, "Social Legislation and the Courts," *Political Science Quarterly*, vol. 28, no. 1 (March 1913), pp. 1–17.

James W. Ely, Jr., *The Chief Justiceship of Melville W. Fuller, 1888–1910* (University of South Carolina Press, 1995).

James W. Ely, Jr., *The Fuller Court: Justices, Rulings, and Legacy* (ABC-CLIO, 2003).

Peter G. Fish, "William Howard Taft and Charles Evans Hughes: Conservative Politicians as Chief Judicial Reformers," *Supreme Court Review*, vol. 1975 (1975), pp. 123–45.

Owen M. Fiss, *Troubled Beginnings of the Modern State, 1888–1910*, vol. 8 of *History of the Supreme Court of the United States* (Macmillan, 1993).

Leon Friedman and Fred L. Israel, eds., *The Justices of the United States Supreme Court, 1789–1969* (Chelsea House, 1969–78), vol. 3.

John A. Garraty, "Holmes's Appointment to the U.S. Supreme Court," *New England Quarterly*, vol. 22, no. 3 (September 1949), pp. 291–303.

Howard Gillman, *The Constitution Besieged: The Rise and Decline of Lochner Era Police Powers Jurisprudence* (Duke University Press, 1993).

M. Paul Holsinger, "The Appointment of Supreme Court Justice Van Devanter: A Study of Political Preferment," *American Journal of Legal History*, vol. 12, no. 4 (October 1968), pp. 324–35.

Herbert Hovenkamp, *Enterprise and American Law, 1836–1937* (Harvard University Press, 1991).

Charles Evans Hughes, *Autobiographical Notes*, David J. Danelski and Joseph S. Tulchin, eds. (Harvard University Press, 1973).

Peter Irons, *A People's History of the Supreme Court* (Viking, 1999), chs. 20–22.

Paul Kens, *Judicial Power and Reform Politics: The Anatomy of* Lochner v. New York (University Press of Kansas, 1990).

Jonathan Lurie, "Chief Justice Taft and Dissents: Down with the Brandeis Briefs!," *Journal of Supreme Court History*, vol. 32, no. 2 (August 2007), pp. 178–89.

Alpheus T. Mason, *Brandeis: A Free Man's Life* (Viking, 1946).

Alpheus T. Mason, "The Conservative World of Mr. Justice Sutherland, 1883–1910," *American Political Science Review*, vol. 32, no. 3 (June 1938), pp. 443–77.

Alpheus T. Mason, *Harlan Fiske Stone: Pillar of the Law* (Viking, 1956).

Alpheus T. Mason, *The Supreme Court from Taft to Warren* (Louisiana State University Press, 1958).

Alpheus T. Mason, *William Howard Taft: Chief Justice* (Simon and Schuster, 1965).

Daniel S. McHargue, "President Taft's Appointments to the Supreme Court," *Journal of Politics*, vol. 12, no. 3 (August 1950), pp. 478–510.

George E. Mowry, *Theodore Roosevelt and the Progressive Movement* (University of Wisconsin Press, 1946).

Paul L. Murphy, *The Constitution in Crisis Times, 1918–1969* (Harper & Row, 1972), chs. 1–4.

Lewis J. Paper, *Brandeis* (Prentice-Hall, 1983).

Joel Francis Paschal, *Mr. Justice Sutherland: A Man Against the State* (Princeton University Press, 1951).

Richard Polenberg, *Fighting Faiths: The Abrams Case, the Supreme Court, and Free Speech* (Viking, 1987).

Walter F. Pratt, Jr., *The Supreme Court Under Edward Douglass White*, 1910-1921 (University of South Carolina Press, 1999).

Henry F. Pringle, *The Life and Times of William Howard Taft*, 2 vols. (Farrar & Rinehart, 1939).

Merlo J. Pusey, *Charles Evans Hughes*, 2 vols. (Macmillan, 1951).

William L. Ransom, *Majority Rule and the Judiciary* (Charles Scribner's Sons, 1912).

Peter G. Renstrom, *The Taft Court: Justices, Rulings, and Legacy* (ABC-CLIO, 2003).

Theodore Roosevelt, *An Autobiography* (Macmillan, 1913).

William G. Ross, *A Muted Fury: Populists, Progressives, and Labor Unions Confront the Courts, 1890–1937* (Princeton University Press, 1994).

Stephen Stagner, "The Recall of Judicial Decisions and the Due Process Debate," *American Journal of Legal History*, vol. 24, no. 3 (July 1980), pp. 257–72.

Philippa Strum, *Louis D. Brandeis: Justice for the People* (Harvard University Press, 1984).

William F. Swindler, *Court and Constitution in the Twentieth Century: The Old Legality, 1889–1932* (Bobbs-Merrill, 1969).

David M. Tucker, "Justice Horace Harmon Lurton: The Shaping of a National Progressive," *American Journal of Legal History*, vol. 13, no. 3 (July 1969), pp. 223–32.

G. Edward White, *Justice Oliver Wendell Holmes: Law and the Inner Self* (Oxford University Press, 1993).

115 ["strong and efficient"] : Roosevelt, *Autobiography*, p. 462.

116 ["malefactors of great wealth"] : e.g., Roosevelt, "The Thraldom of Names," *Outlook*, vol. 92 (June 19, 1909), pp. 391–95, quoted at p. 395.

116 ["chief lawmakers"] : "Eighth Annual Message to Congress," December 8, 1908, in Roosevelt, *Works*, Hermann Hagedorn, ed. (Charles Scribner's Sons, 1926), vol. 15, pp. 489–545, quoted at p. 511.

116 ["constructive statesmen"] : "Speech of the President of the United States at the Dinner to Mr. Justice Harlan" on the 25th anniversary of his service on the Supreme Court, December 9, 1902, *American Law Review*, vol. 37 (January–February 1903), pp. 93–95, quoted at p. 93.

116 ["negative action"] : Roosevelt, *Autobiography*, p. 463.

117 ["life of the law"] : Holmes, *The Common Law* (Little, Brown, 1881), p. 1.

117 ["ordinary and low sense"] : letter of July 10, 1902, in Roosevelt, *Letters*, Elting E. Morison, ed. (Harvard University Press, 1951–54), vol. 3, pp. 288–90, quoted at p. 289.

118 [TR on Moody] : Roosevelt to William Allen White, letter of November 30, 1908, in ibid., vol. 6, pp. 1392–93, quoted at p. 1393.

118 [*Northern Securities*] : *Northern Securities* v. *U.S.*, 193 U.S. 197 (1904), Brewer quoted at 363; Holmes's dissent at 401.

119 ["went wild"] : Adams to Elizabeth Cameron, letter of March 20–21, 1904, in Adams, *Letters*, J. C. Levenson et al., eds. (Belknap Press, 1982–88), vol. 5, pp. 563–65, quoted at p. 564.

119 ["long outgrown philosophy"] : "Eighth Annual Message," p. 511.

119 ["all-pervading power"] : *Lochner* v. *New York*, 198 U.S. 45 (1905), quoted at 59, 57, 64, respectively.

119 ["treasured freedom"] : brief for Joseph Lochner, quoted in Irons, p. 255.

119 ["this case is decided"] : *Lochner*, quoted at 75.

120 ["choice between"] : Freund, "Limitations of Hours of Labor and the Federal Supreme Court," *Green Bag*, vol. 17 (July 1905), pp. 411–17, quoted at p. 416.

120 [*Adair*] : 208 U.S. 161 (1908).

120 [*Loewe*]: 208 U.S. 274 (1908).

120 [Brandeis's brief in *Muller*] : see Mason, *Brandeis*, pp. 248–52.

120 [*Muller*] : 208 U.S. 412 (1908), quoted at 423, 422, respectively.

120 ["very slovenly"] : "Eighth Annual Message," p. 515. The decision TR referred to was *Employers' Liability Cases*, 207 U.S. 463 (1908).

121 ["you beloved individual"] : letter of August 2, 1906, in Roosevelt, *Letters*, vol. 5, pp. 341–43, quoted at p. 341.

122 ["menace to the welfare"] : Roosevelt to Henry Stimson, letter of February 5, 1912, in ibid., vol. 7, pp. 494–95, quoted p. 495.

122 ["people themselves"] : "Roosevelt's Own Creed Set Forth," *New York Times*, August 7, 1912, pp. 8–9, quoted at p. 8.

122 ["suspension of the Constitution"] : "Taft Shows Peril in Roosevelt's Policy," ibid., March 9, 1912, pp. 1, 10, quoted at p. 10.

122 ["wild scheme"] : "Progressing Backward" (editorial), ibid., February 27, 1912, p. 8.

122 ["cause of all the trouble"] : "Reversing John Marshall" (editorial), ibid., February 25, 1912, p. 10.

122 ["serious question"] : "Mr. Roosevelt's Startling New Issue," *Current Literature*, vol. 52 (April 1912), pp. 371–74, quoted at p. 372.

123 ["effectively control"] : quoted in "Roosevelt Pleads for Removal of Special Interest Control," *Wall Street Journal*, September 1, 1910, p. 6.

123 ["ultimate sovereign power"] : Roosevelt to Joseph P. Cotton, Jr., letter of April 30, 1912, quoted in Ross, p. 140.

123 ["it is the people"] : Roosevelt, "Introduction," in Ransom, pp. 3–24, quoted at p. 6.

124 ["fundamental law"] : Lurton, "A Government of Laws or a Government of Men?," *North American Review*, vol. 193 (January 1911), pp. 9–25, quoted at pp. 24, 20, respectively.

125 [Van Devanter as commander-in-chief] : Harlan Fiske Stone, in Mason, *Stone*, p. 590 fn.

125 ["modify itself"] : Holmes, "The Gas-Stokers' Strike," *American Law Review*, vol. 7 (1873), reprinted in "The Early Writings of O. W. Holmes, Jr.," Felix Frankfurter, ed., *Harvard Law Review*, vol. 44, no. 5 (March 1931), pp. 795–96, quoted at p. 796.

125 ["felt necessities"] : Holmes, *The Common Law*, p. 1.

125 ["Considerable latitude"] : *Otis* v. *Parker*, 187 U.S. 606 (1903), quoted at 608–9.

126 ["determinations of what the law is"] : Isaac F. Marcosson, "Woodrow Wilson, Presidential Possibility" (interview), October 1911, in Wilson, *Papers*, Arthur S. Link, ed. (Princeton University Press, 1966–94), vol. 23, pp. 366–72, quoted at p. 370.

126 ["way to purify"] : "An Address to the General Assembly of Maryland," March 7, 1912, in ibid., vol. 24, pp. 227–36, quoted at p. 236.

126 ["I see the female"] : quoted in Polenberg, p. 204.

126 [McReynolds on "evil" Democratic platform] : David Burner, "James C. McReynolds," in Friedman and Israel, vol. 3, pp. 2023–33, quoted at p. 2025.

127 [Mason on Brandeis's "laboratory"] : Mason, "Louis D. Brandeis," in ibid., vol. 3, pp. 2043–59, quoted at p. 2044.

127 ["not a fit person"] : quoted in Mason, *Brandeis*, p. 489.

127 ["judicial temperament"] : quoted in Paper, p. 217.

127 ["dominant reasons"] : quoted in Mason, *Brandeis*, p. 491.

128   ["into the wilderness"] : Henry Morgenthau, Sr., quoted in ibid., p. 503.

128   ["Men are not necessarily made"] : ibid., p. 554.

128   ["presumption of constitutionality"] : see *O'Gorman & Young* v. *Hartford Fire Insurance,* 282 U.S. 251 (1931), esp. 257–58.

129   [*Schenck*] : 249 U.S. 47 (1919), quoted at 52.

129   ["You must also remember"] : quoted in Baker, p. 247. Felix Frankfurter was the friend.

129   ["poor and puny"] : 250 U.S. 616 (1919), quoted at 629, 630.

130   ["best qualified man"] : Executive Committee of the American Bar Association, quoted in Mason, *Taft,* p. 69.

130   ["White will not end"] : Taft to Gus V. Karger, letter of January 3, 1916, quoted in Pringle, vol. 2, p. 952.

131   ["Four years president"] : Taft to Karger, letter of May 19, 1921, quoted in ibid., vol. 2, p. 958.

131   ["noisy dissenter"] : quoted in Mason, *Taft,* p. 161.

131   ["Taft's *modus operandi*"] : Abraham, p. 186.

132   ["The good sought"] : *Bailey* v. *Drexel Furniture Co.,* 259 U.S. 20 (1922), Taft's opinion for the court quoted at 37.

132   ["any law"] : Taft, "The Attacks on the Courts and Legal Procedure," *Kentucky Law Journal,* vol. 5, no. 2 (October 1916), pp. 3–24, quoted at p. 8.

132   ["overwhelming mass"] : Taft, *The Presidency: Its Duties, Its Powers, Its Opportunities, and Its Limitations* (Charles Scribner's Sons, 1916), p. 9.

133   [Fuller and Taft vetoes of legislation] : Swindler, pp. 344–45 (Appendix D).

133   ["hasty action"] : Taft, "Veto Message," August 22, 1911, in Taft, *Collected Works,* David H. Burton et al., eds. (Ohio University Press, 2001–2004), vol. 4, pp. 149–58, quoted at p. 152.

133   ["high duty"] : *Bailey,* quoted at 37.

133   ["truculent labor leaders"] : quoted in "Taft Denounces the Clayton Act," *New York Times,* May 27, 1915, p. 12; see also Taft, *Justice and Freedom for Industry* (National Association of Manufacturers, 1915).

133   ["business of the butcher"] : *Wolff Packing* v. *Court of Industrial Relations,* 262 U.S. 522 (1923), Taft's opinion for the court quoted at 537.

134   ["no evidence"] : *Gitlow* v. *New York,* 268 U.S. 652 (1925), quoted at 656, 668, 669.

134   [*Whitney*] : 274 U.S. 357 (1927), Sanford's majority opinion quoted at 371; Brandeis's dissent at 377.

135   [Taft's dissents] : The count was made by Taft's successor, Chief Justice Hughes. See 285 U.S. (1931), at xxxiv.

135   ["attitude of protest"] : Taft to Stone, letter of January 26, 1927, quoted in Mason, *Stone,* p. 257.

136   [Brandeis's advice to judges] : ibid., p. 118.

136   ["colors the rest of the day"] : Taft to Helen Taft Manning, letter of January 8, 1928, quoted in Mason, *Taft,* p. 295.

136   ["if a number of us die"] : Taft to Horace Taft, letter of December 8, 1929, quoted in Mason, *Stone,* p. 276.

136   ["leviathan"] : Taft, *The Anti-trust Act and the Supreme Court* (1914), in Taft, *Collected Works,* vol. 5, p. 189.

136   ["form of government"] : Taft, *Popular Government* (1913), in ibid., vol. 5, quoted at p. 116.

136   ["prevent the Bolsheviki"] : Taft to Horace Taft, letter of December 1, 1929, quoted in Pringle, vol. 2, p. 967.

137   ["era of regulation"] : Hughes, *The Supreme Court of the United States: Its Foundation, Methods, and Achievements* (Columbia University Press, 1928), p. 96.

CHAPTER EIGHT—FDR'S BOLDEST GAMBLE

Bruce Ackerman, *We the People: Transformations* (Belknap Press, 1998).

Joseph Alsop and Turner Catledge, *The 168 Days* (Doubleday, Doran, 1938).

Stephen R. Alton, "Loyal Lieutenant, Able Advocate: The Role of Robert H. Jackson in Franklin D. Roosevelt's Battle with the Supreme Court," *William & Mary Bill of Rights Journal*, vol. 5 (Summer 1997), pp. 527–618.

Leonard Baker, *Back to Back: The Duel Between FDR and the Supreme Court* (Macmillan, 1967).

James E. Bond, *I Dissent: The Legacy of Chief Justice James Clark McReynolds* (George Mason University Press, 1992).

Irving Brant, *Storm over the Constitution* (Bobbs-Merrill, 1936).

James MacGregor Burns, *Roosevelt: The Lion and the Fox, 1882–1940* (Harcourt, Brace, 1956).

Gregory A. Caldeira, "Public Opinion and the U.S. Supreme Court: FDR's Court-Packing Plan," *American Political Science Review*, vol. 81, no. 4 (December 1987), pp. 1139–53.

Frank V. Cantwell, "Public Opinion and the Legislative Process," *American Political Science Review*, vol. 40, no. 5 (October 1946), pp. 924–35.

John W. Chambers, "The Big Switch: Justice Roberts and the Minimum-Wage Cases," *Labor History*, vol. 10, no. 1 (Winter 1969), pp. 44–73.

Edward S. Corwin, *Court over Constitution: A Study of Judicial Review as an Instrument of Popular Government* (Princeton University Press, 1938).

Barry Cushman, "The Secret Lives of the Four Horsemen," *Virginia Law Review*, vol. 83, no. 3 (April 1997), pp. 559–645.

Katherine B. Fite and Louis B. Rubinstein, "Curbing the Supreme Court: State Experiences and Federal Proposals," *Michigan Law Review*, vol. 35, no. 5 (March 1937), pp. 762–87.

Osmond K. Fraenkel, "What Can Be Done About the Constitution and the Supreme Court?," *Columbia Law Review*, vol. 37, no. 2 (February 1937), pp. 212–26.

Paul A. Freund, "Charles Evans Hughes as Chief Justice," *Harvard Law Review*, vol. 81, no. 1 (November 1967), pp. 4–43.

Richard D. Friedman, "Switching Time and Other Thought Experiments: The Hughes Court and Constitutional Transformation," *University of Pennsylvania Law Review*, vol. 142, no. 6 (June 1994), pp. 1891–1984.

Samuel Hendel, *Charles Evans Hughes and the Supreme Court* (Russell & Russell, 1968).

M. Paul Holsinger, "Mr. Justice Van Devanter and the New Deal," *Historian*, vol. 31, no. 1 (November 1968), pp. 57–63.

Ronald F. Howell, "The Judicial Conservatives Three Decades Ago: Aristocratic Guardians of the Prerogatives of Property and the Judiciary," *Virginia Law Review*, vol. 49, no. 8 (December 1963), pp. 1447–82.

Charles Evans Hughes, *Autobiographical Notes*, David J. Danelski and Joseph S. Tulchin, eds. (Harvard University Press, 1973), esp. ch. 18.

Dennis J. Hutchinson and David J. Garrow, *The Forgotten Memoir of John Knox: A Year in the Life of a Supreme Court Clerk in FDR's Washington* (University of Chicago Press, 2002).

Harold L. Ickes, *The Secret Diary* (Simon and Schuster, 1953–54), vols. 1–2.

Peter Irons, *The New Deal Lawyers* (Princeton University Press, 1982).

Peter Irons, *A People's History of the Supreme Court* (Viking, 1999), chs. 23–25.

Robert H. Jackson, *The Struggle for Judicial Supremacy: A Study of a Crisis in American Power Politics* (Alfred A. Knopf, 1941).

David E. Kyvig, "The Road Not Taken: FDR, the Supreme Court, and Constitutional Amendment," *Political Science Quarterly*, vol. 104, no. 3 (Autumn 1989), pp. 463–81.

Joseph P. Lash, *Dreamers and Dealers* (Doubleday, 1988), ch. 21.

Charles A. Leonard, *A Search for a Judicial Philosophy: Mr. Justice Roberts and the Constitutional Revolution of 1937* (Kennikat Press, 1971).

Max Lerner, "The Great Constitutional War," *Virginia Quarterly Review*, vol. 18, no. 4 (Autumn 1942), pp. 530–45.

William E. Leuchtenburg, *The Supreme Court Reborn: The Constitutional Revolution in the Age of Roosevelt* (Oxford University Press, 1995).

William E. Leuchtenburg, "When the People Spoke, What Did They Say?: The Election of 1936 and the Ackerman Thesis," *Yale Law Journal*, vol. 108, no. 8 (June 1999), pp. 2077–2114.

Joseph L. Lewinson, *Limiting Judicial Review* (Parker, Stone & Baird, 1937).

Richard A. Maidment, *The Judicial Response to the New Deal: The US Supreme Court and Economic Regulation, 1934–1936* (Manchester University Press, 1991).

Alpheus T. Mason, *Harlan Fiske Stone: Pillar of the Law* (Viking, 1956).

Alpheus T. Mason, "Politics and the Supreme Court: President Roosevelt's Proposal," *University of Pennsylvania Law Review and American Law Register*, vol. 85, no. 7 (May 1937), pp. 659–77.

Alpheus T. Mason, *The Supreme Court: Vehicle of Revealed Truth or Power Group, 1930-1937* (Boston University Press, 1953).

Marian C. McKenna, *Franklin Roosevelt and the Great Constitutional War: The Court-Packing Crisis of 1937* (Fordham University Press, 2002).

Michael Nelson, "The President and the Court: Reinterpreting the Court-Packing Episode of 1937," *Political Science Quarterly*, vol. 103, no. 2 (Summer 1988), pp. 267–93.

Michael E. Parrish, "The Hughes Court, the Great Depression, and the Historians," *Historian*, vol. 40, no. 2 (February 1978), pp. 286–308.

Michael E. Parrish, *The Hughes Court: Justices, Rulings, and Legacy* (ABC-CLIO, 2002).

Joel Francis Paschal, *Mr. Justice Sutherland: A Man Against the State* (Princeton University Press, 1951).

James T. Patterson, *Congressional Conservatism and the New Deal: The Growth of the Conservative Coalition in Congress, 1933–1939* (University of Kentucky Press, 1967), esp. ch. 3.

Drew Pearson and Robert S. Allen, *The Nine Old Men* (Doubleday, Doran, 1937).

Barbara A. Perry, *The Priestly Tribe: The Supreme Court's Image in the American Mind* (Praeger, 1999), esp. ch. 1.

Merlo J. Pusey, *Charles Evans Hughes* (Macmillan, 1951), esp. vol. 2, chs. 69–71.

Merlo J. Pusey, *The Supreme Court Crisis* (Macmillan, 1937).

Arthur M. Schlesinger, Jr., *The Politics of Upheaval, 1935–1936* (Houghton Mifflin, 1960), esp. part 3.

Torbjorn Sirevag, "Rooseveltian Ideas and the 1937 Court Fight: A Neglected Factor," *Historian*, vol. 33, no. 4 (August 1971), pp. 578–95.

William F. Swindler, *Court and Constitution in the Twentieth Century: The New Legality, 1932-1968* (Bobbs-Merrill, 1970), ch. 1.

139   ["action, and action now"] : "Inaugural Address," March 4, 1933, in Roosevelt, *Public Papers and Addresses*, Samuel I. Rosenman, comp. (Random House, 1938–50), vol. 2, pp. 11–16, quoted at p. 12.

139   ["bold, persistent"] : "Address at Oglethorpe University," May 22, 1932, in ibid., vol. 1, pp. 639–47, quoted at p. 646.

140   ["great cooperative movement"] : "Recommendation to the Congress to Enact the National Industrial Recovery Act to Put People to Work," May 17, 1933, in ibid., vol. 2, pp. 202–4, quoted at p. 202.

141   ["encroachments upon the sanctity"] : *Home Building & Loan Association* v. *Blaisdell*, 290 U.S. 398 (1934), Sutherland's dissent quoted at 448, 451, 453.

141 [Black Monday cases] : *Louisville Joint Stock Land Bank* v. *Radford*, 295 U.S. 555 (1935) (farm bankruptcy bill); *Humphrey's Executor* v. *U.S.*, 295 U.S. 602 (1935) (FTC); *Schechter*, 295 U.S. 495 (1935), quoted at 542, 528, respectively.

142 ["pathetic appeals"] : press conference, May 31, 1935, in Roosevelt, *Public Papers*, vol. 4, pp. 200–222, quoted at pp. 201, 212, 221, 222.

142 [*Butler*] : 297 U.S. 1 (1936), quoted at 61.

142 [*Carter*] : 298 U.S. 238 (1936), quoted at 291, 304, 308.

143 ["just as much a local activity"] : Charles I. Dawson, quoted in Schlesinger, p. 476.

143 ["'no-man's-land'"] : press conference, June 2, 1936, in Roosevelt, *Public Papers*, vol. 5, pp. 191–92, quoted at p. 192.

143 ["Clearly, it is running"] : entry of December 27, 1935, in Ickes, vol. 1, p. 495.

144 ["intervene reasonably"] : "Memorandum for AAA File," January 24, 1936, in Elliott Roosevelt, ed., *F.D.R.: His Personal Letters* (Duell, Sloane, and Pearce, 1947–50), vol. 3, pp. 548–49, quoted at p. 548.

144 ["continuous constitutional convention"] : *Congressional Record*, 74th Congress, 2nd session, vol. 80, part 2, February 12, 1936, p. 1883.

144 ["It takes twelve men"] : quoted in "House Bloc Weighs High Court Check," *New York Times*, January 12, 1936, p. 23.

144 ["something should be done"] : "Hoover Advocates Women's Wage Law," ibid., June 7, 1936, p. 1. The New York minimum wage law case was *Morehead* v. *New York ex rel. Tipaldo*, 298 U.S. 587 (1936).

144 ["lift the Dead Hand"] : quoted in George Creel, *Rebel at Large* (G. P. Putnam's Sons, 1947), p. 291.

144 ["no two people agree"] : Roosevelt to Charles C. Burlingham, letter of February 23, 1937, in Roosevelt, *F.D.R.: His Personal Letters*, vol. 3, pp. 661–62, quoted at p. 661.

145 ["The real difficulty"] : letter of January 29, 1936, in Cummings, *Selected Papers*, Carl B. Swisher, ed. (Charles Scribner's Sons, 1939), pp. 148–49, quoted at p. 148.

145 ["private, social philosophy"] : "Memorandum for AAA file," pp. 548–49.

145 [Metropolitan Life study] : Schlesinger, p. 493.

145 ["number of Justices"] : "A 'Fireside Chat' Discussing the Plan for Reorganization of the Judiciary," March 9, 1937, in Roosevelt, *Public Papers*, vol. 6, pp. 122–35, quoted at p. 129.

145 [FDR's court-packing plan] : see ibid., vol. 6, pp. 51–66.

145 ["enemies of peace"] : "Campaign Address at Madison Square Garden," New York City, October 31, 1936, in ibid., vol. 5, pp. 566–73, quoted at p. 568.

146 ["means must be found"] : January 6, 1937, in ibid., vol. 5, pp. 634–42, quoted at pp. 639–40.

146 ["where I cash in"] : quoted in Burns, p. 294.

147 ["fully abreast"] : quoted in Mason, *Stone*, p. 451.

147 ["more judges to hear"] : quoted in Baker, p. 158.

147 ["until I read about it"] : Stone to Irving Brant, letter of April 20, 1937, quoted in Mason, *Stone*, p. 453.

147 ["shrewdly, Hughes chose"] : entry of March 26, 1937, in Ickes, vol. 2, p. 104.

148 ["We have begun"] : March 4, 1937, in Roosevelt, *Public Papers*, vol. 6, pp. 113–21, quoted at p. 114.

148 ["three horse team"] : "Fireside Chat," March 9, 1937, in ibid., vol. 6, quoted at pp. 123, 126.

148 ["slightest degree"] : Hughes, p. 311.

149 ["fully conscious"] : quoted in Mason, *Stone*, p. 456fn.

149 [Hughes's *West Coast Hotel* opinion] : 300 U.S. 379 (1937), quoted at 391, 399.

149 [Farm bankruptcy law decision] : *Wright* v. *Vinton Branch*, 300 U.S. 440 (1937).
149 [Railroad labor law decision] : *Virginian Railway* v. *System Federation*, 300 U.S. 515 (1937).
149 [Firearms tax decision] : *Sonzinsky* v. *U.S.*, 300 U.S. 506 (1937).
150 ["fundamental right"] : 301 U.S. 1 (1937), quoted at 33, 37, 41.
150 ["poking his pencil"] : quoted in Irons, *People's History*, p. 322.
150 ["private owner is deprived"] : *Jones & Laughlin*, quoted at 103.
150 ["chortling all morning"] : press conference, April 13, 1937, in Roosevelt, *Public Papers*, vol. 6, pp. 153–56, quoted at pp. 153, 154.
151 ["weaken the prestige"] : entry of March 30, 1937, in Ickes, vol. 2, p. 107.
151 [Polls after White Monday] : see Cantwell, p. 92.
151 ["decision of crucial constitutional issues"] : quoted in McKenna, p. 423.
151 ["make this Government"] : quoted in Baker, p. 230.
152 ["nomadic existence"] : Perry, pp. 8, 10.
154 ["violated an express provision"] : "Fireside Chat," March 9, 1937, in Roosevelt, *Public Papers,* vol. 6, quoted at p. 125.
155 ["layman's document"] : "Address on Constitution Day," September 17, 1937, in Roosevelt, *Public Papers*, vol. 6, pp. 359–67, quoted at pp. 362, 363, 365, 364, respectively.

CHAPTER NINE—"WILD HORSES": THE ROOSEVELT COURT

Henry J. Abraham, *Justices and Presidents: A Political History of Appointments to the Supreme Court,* 3rd ed. (Oxford University Press, 1992), ch. 9.
Francis A. Allen, "Chief Justice Vinson and the Theory of Constitutional Government," *Northwestern University Law Review*, vol. 49, no. 3 (March–April 1954), pp. 3–25.
David N. Atkinson, "From New Deal Liberal to Supreme Court Conservative: The Metamorphosis of Justice Sherman Minton," *Washington University Law Quarterly*, vol. 1975 (1975), pp. 361–94.
Leonard Baker, *Brandeis and Frankfurter* (Harper & Row, 1984).
Howard Ball and Philip J. Cooper, "Fighting Justices: Hugo L. Black and William O. Douglas and Supreme Court Conflict," *American Journal of Legal History*, vol. 38, no. 1 (January 1994), pp. 1–37.
Howard Ball and Philip J. Cooper, *Of Power and Right: Hugo Black, William O. Douglas, and America's Constitutional Revolution* (Oxford University Press, 1992).
Michal R. Belknap, *Cold War Political Justice: The Smith Act, the Communist Party, and American Civil Liberties* (Greenwood Press, 1977).
Herman Belz, "Changing Conceptions of Constitutionalism in the Era of World War II and the Cold War," *Journal of American History*, vol. 59, no. 3 (December 1972), pp. 640–69.
Mary Frances Berry, *Stability, Security, and Continuity: Mr. Justice Burton and Decision-Making in the Supreme Court, 1945–1958* (Greenwood Press, 1978).
George D. Braden, "Mr. Justice Minton and the Truman Bloc," *Indiana Law Journal*, vol. 26, no. 2 (Winter 1951), pp. 153–68.
James F. Byrnes, *All in One Lifetime* (Harper & Brothers, 1958), part 3.
Marquis W. Childs, "The Supreme Court To-Day," *Harper's*, vol. 176 (May 1938), pp. 581–88.
Tom Clark, "Reminiscences of an Attorney General Turned Associate Justice," *Houston Law Review*, vol. 6, no. 4 (March 1969), pp. 623–29.
Richard C. Cortner, *The Supreme Court and the Second Bill of Rights: The Fourteenth Amendment and the Nationalization of Civil Liberties* (University of Wisconsin Press, 1981).

William Domnarski, *The Great Justices, 1941–54: Black, Douglas, Frankfurter & Jackson in Chambers* (University of Michigan Press, 2006).

William O. Douglas, *The Court Years, 1939–1975* (Random House, 1980).

William O. Douglas, "Diary," Philip E. Urofsky, ed., *Journal of Supreme Court History*, vol. 1995 (1995), pp. 80–112.

William O. Douglas, *Go East, Young Man: The Early Years* (Random House, 1974).

Gerald T. Dunne, *Hugo Black and the Judicial Revolution* (Simon and Schuster, 1977).

John D. Fassett, *New Deal Justice: The Life of Stanley Reed of Kentucky* (Vantage Press, 1994).

John M. Ferren, *Salt of the Earth, Conscience of the Court: The Story of Justice Wiley Rutledge* (University of North Carolina Press, 2004).

John P. Frank, "Fred Vinson and the Chief Justiceship," *University of Chicago Law Review*, vol. 21, no. 2 (Winter 1954), pp. 212–46.

Max Freedman, ed., *Roosevelt and Frankfurter: Their Correspondence, 1928–1945* (Little, Brown, 1967).

Leon Friedman and Fred L. Israel, eds., *The Justices of the United States Supreme Court, 1789–1969* (Chelsea House, 1969–78), vols. 3–4.

Eugene C. Gerhart, *America's Advocate: Robert H. Jackson* (Bobbs-Merrill, 1958).

Linda C. Gugin and James E. St. Clair, *Sherman Minton: New Deal Senator, Cold War Justice* (Indiana Historical Society, 1997).

Walton Hamilton, "Preview of a Justice" (Felix Frankfurter), *Yale Law Journal*, vol. 48, no. 5 (March 1939), pp. 819–38.

Fowler V. Harper, *Justice Rutledge and the Bright Constellation* (Bobbs-Merrill, 1965).

Robert Harrison, "The Breakup of the Roosevelt Supreme Court: The Contribution of History and Biography," *Law and History Review*, vol. 2, no. 2 (Autumn 1984), pp. 165–221.

Jeffrey D. Hockett, *New Deal Justice: The Constitutional Jurisprudence of Hugo L. Black, Felix Frankfurter, and Robert H. Jackson* (Rowman & Littlefield, 1996).

J. Woodford Howard, Jr., *Mr. Justice Murphy* (Princeton University Press, 1968).

Dennis J. Hutchinson, "'The Achilles Heel' of the Constitution: Justice Jackson and the Japanese Exclusion Cases," *Supreme Court Review*, vol. 2002 (2002), pp. 455–94.

Dennis J. Hutchinson, "The Black-Jackson Feud," *Supreme Court Review*, vol. 1988 (1988), pp. 203–43.

Peter Irons, *Justice at War* (Oxford University Press, 1983).

Peter Irons, *A People's History of the Supreme Court* (Viking, 1999), chs. 25–28.

Joseph P. Lash, ed., *From the Diaries of Felix Frankfurter* (W. W. Norton, 1975).

William E. Leuchtenburg, *The Supreme Court Reborn: The Constitutional Revolution in the Age of Roosevelt* (Oxford University Press, 1995).

Stefanie A. Lindquist et al., "The Impact of Presidential Appointments to the U.S. Supreme Court: Cohesive and Divisive Voting Within Presidential Blocs," *Political Research Quarterly*, vol. 53, no. 4 (December 2000), pp. 795–814.

Constance L. Martin, "The Life and Career of Justice Robert H. Jackson," *Journal of Supreme Court History*, vol. 33, no. 1 (March 2008), pp. 42–67.

Alpheus T. Mason, *Harlan Fiske Stone: Pillar of the Law* (Viking, 1956).

Alpheus T. Mason, *The Supreme Court from Taft to Warren* (Louisiana State University Press, 1958), esp. ch. 4.

Robert G. McCloskey, *The Modern Supreme Court* (Harvard University Press, 1972).

Wesley McCune, *The Nine Young Men* (Harper & Brothers, 1947).

Wallace Mendelson, "Mr. Justice Frankfurter and the Process of Judicial Review," *University of Pennsylvania Law Review*, vol. 103, no. 3 (December 1954), pp. 295–320.

Bruce Allen Murphy, *Wild Bill: The Legend and Life of William O. Douglas* (Random House, 2003).

Paul L. Murphy, *The Constitution in Crisis Times, 1918–1969* (Harper & Row, 1972), chs. 5–9.

Roger K. Newman, *Hugo Black* (Pantheon, 1994).

David M. O'Brien, "Packing the Supreme Court," *Virginia Quarterly Review*, vol. 62, no. 2 (Spring 1986), pp. 189–212.

Richard L. Pacelle, Jr., *The Transformation of the Supreme Court's Agenda: From the New Deal to the Reagan Administration* (Westview Press, 1991).

Michael E. Parrish, "Cold War Justice: The Supreme Court and the Rosenbergs," *American Historical Review*, vol. 82, no. 4 (October 1977), pp. 805–42.

Michael E. Parrish, *The Hughes Court: Justices, Rulings, and Legacy* (ABC-CLIO, 2002).

William Petit, "Justice Byrnes and the United States Supreme Court," *South Carolina Law Quarterly*, vol. 6 (1954), pp. 423–28.

C. Herman Pritchett, *Civil Liberties and the Vinson Court* (University of Chicago Press, 1954).

C. Herman Pritchett, "The President and the Supreme Court," *Journal of Politics*, vol. 11, no. 1 (February 1949), pp. 80–92.

C. Herman Pritchett, *The Roosevelt Court: A Study in Judicial Politics and Values, 1937–1947* (Macmillan, 1948).

Peter G. Renstrom, *The Stone Court: Justices, Rulings, and Legacy* (ABC-CLIO, 2001).

Frances Howell Rudko, *Truman's Court: A Study in Judicial Restraint* (Greenwood Press, 1988).

James E. St. Clair and Linda C. Gugin, *Chief Justice Fred M. Vinson of Kentucky* (University Press of Kentucky, 2002).

Bernard Schwartz, *The Supreme Court: Constitutional Revolution in Retrospect* (Ronald Press, 1957).

John F. Simon, *The Antagonists: Hugo Black, Felix Frankfurter, and Civil Liberties in Modern America* (Simon and Schuster, 1989).

Robert J. Steamer, *Chief Justice: Leadership and the Supreme Court* (University of South Carolina Press, 1986).

Steve Suitts, *Hugo Black of Alabama* (NewSouth Books, 2005).

William F. Swindler, *Court and Constitution in the Twentieth Century: The New Legality, 1932–1968* (Bobbs-Merrill, 1970).

Jacobus tenBroek et al., *Prejudice, War, and the Constitution* (University of California Press, 1954).

Melvin I. Urofsky, "Conflict Among the Brethren," *Duke Law Journal*, vol. 1988, no. 1 (February 1988), pp. 71–113.

Melvin I. Urofsky, *Division and Discord: The Supreme Court Under Stone and Vinson, 1941–1953* (University of South Carolina Press, 1997).

Melvin I. Urofsky, "The Roosevelt Court," in William H. Chafe, ed., *The Achievement of American Liberalism: The New Deal and Its Legacies* (Columbia University Press, 2003), pp. 63–98.

G. Edward White, *The Constitution and the New Deal* (Harvard University Press, 2000).

William M. Wiecek, *The Birth of the Modern Constitution: The United States Supreme Court, 1941–1953*, vol. 12 of *History of the Supreme Court of the United States* (Cambridge University Press, 2006).

David A. Yalof, *Pursuit of Justices: Presidential Politics and the Selection of Supreme Court Nominees* (University of Chicago Press, 1999), ch. 2.

Tinsley E. Yarbrough, *Mr. Justice Black and His Critics* (Duke University Press, 1988).

157 [Roberts's dissents, 1945] : Wiecek, p. 71.
158 ["absolute anomaly"] : Joseph Alsop and Turner Catledge, *The 168 Days* (Doubleday, Doran, 1938), p. 300.

158   ["have to take him"] : James A. Farley, *Jim Farley's Story* (McGraw-Hill, 1948),
      p. 98.
158   ["worst insult"] : Edward E. Cox, quoted in "Selection of Black Splits Congress,"
      New York Times, August 13, 1937, pp. 1, 4, at p. 4.
158   ["did the trick"] : quoted in Farley, p. 100.
159   ["presidential boner"] : *Kiplinger Washington Letter*, September 18, 1937, quoted in
      Leuchtenburg, p. 195.
159   ["Well, Stanley"] : quoted in Fassett, p. 198.
159   ["half brother"] : quoted in Wiecek, p. 85.
160   ["give the Jew baiters"] : White to Paul Kellogg, letter of September 16, 1938,
      in White, *Selected Letters, 1899–1943*, Walter Johnson, ed. (Henry Holt, 1947),
      pp. 389–90, quoted at p. 390.
160   ["identified the Constitution"] : memorandum for FDR, February 18, 1937, in
      Freedman, pp. 384–87, quoted at p. 386.
160   ["You know"] : Frankfurter, *Felix Frankfurter Reminisces* (Reynal, 1960), p. 283.
161   ["new job for you"] : quoted in Douglas, *Go East*, p. 463.
161   ["Catholic piety"] : Wiecek, p. 100.
161   ["broader view"] : quoted in Howard, p. 232.
162   ["losing the smoothest"] : McCune, p. 244.
163   ["don't think I can stand"] : quoted in Urofsky, *Division and Discord*, p. 28.
163   ["assistant President"] : Walter F. Murphy, "James F. Byrnes," in Friedman and
      Israel, vol. 4, pp. 2517–33, quoted at p. 2530.
164   ["not a radical"] : Fred L. Israel, "Wiley Rutledge," in ibid., vol. 4, pp. 2593–2601,
      quoted at p. 2593.
164   [Hughes on chief justice] : Hughes, *The Supreme Court of the United States:
      Its Foundation, Methods, and Achievements* (Columbia University Press, 1928),
      p. 58.
164   [Frankfurter on Hughes] : Frankfurter, "Chief Justices I Have Known," *Virginia
      Law Review*, vol. 39, no. 7 (November 1953), pp. 883–905, quoted at p. 901.
164   ["don't work for Hughes"] : quoted in Douglas, *The Court Years*, p. 219.
164   ["not a philosopher"] : Steamer, p. 74.
165   ["With Sutherland off"] : Stone to his sons, letter of February 10, 1938, quoted in
      Mason, *Stone*, p. 488.
165   ["fatal way"] : quoted in ibid., p. 487.
166   [*Carolene*] : 304 U.S. 144 (1938), quoted at 152–53.
167   [*Edwards*] : 314 U.S. 160 (1941).
167   [Stone on "the job"] : Stone to Sterling Carr, letter of November 25, 1941, quoted in
      Mason, *Stone*, p. 580.
167   [*Journal* on justices] : Eugene S. Duffield, "Yesterday Was the First 'Decision
      Day' This Term Without Noisy Dissent," *Wall Street Journal*, November 25,
      1941, p. 3.
167   [Nonunanimous opinions] : Urofsky, *Division and Discord*, p. 40.
167   ["Collection of fleas"] : Stone to Sterling Carr, letter of June 13, 1943, quoted in
      ibid., p. 40.
168   ["mischievous phrase"] : *Kovacs* v. *Cooper*, 336 U.S. 77 (1949), Frankfurter's
      concurrence quoted at 91, 92.
169   ["national unity"] : *Gobitis*, 310 U.S. 586 (1940), quoted at 595.
169   ["too tight a rein"] : Frankfurter to Stone, note of May 27, 1940, quoted in Mason,
      Stone, p. 527.
169   ["vulgar intrusion"] : Stone to Frankfurter, undated note, quoted in ibid., p. 527.
169   ["searching judicial inquiry"] : *Gobitis*, quoted at 606.
169   ["between legislatively allowable"] : note of May 27, 1940, quoted in Wiecek,
      p. 222.

169   [*Opelika*] : 316 U.S. 584 (1942), Black, Douglas, and Murphy quoted at 624; Stone at 608.
170   [*Barnette*] : 319 U.S. 624 (1943), Jackson quoted at 642; Frankfurter at 649, 648, 666, respectively.
170   [*Murdock*] : 319 U.S. 105 (1943), quoted at 115.
171   ["holy cause"] : Frankfurter conference notes, December 5, 1942, quoted in Urofsky, *Division and Discord*, p. 53.
171   ["Criticism of"] : *Schneiderman*, 320 U.S. 118 (1943), quoted at 138.
171   ["appeal to reason"] : *Milk Wagon Drivers Union* v. *Meadowmoor Dairies*, 312 U.S. 287 (1941), quoted at 293.
172   ["to hell with *habeas corpus*"] : quoted in tenBroek et al., p. 86.
172   ["nobody's constitutional rights"] : Lippmann, "The Fifth Column on the Coast," *Washington Post*, February 12, 1942, p. 9.
172   [*Hirabayashi*] : 320 U.S. 81 (1943), quoted at 93.
173   [*Korematsu*] : 323 U.S. 214 (1944), Black's opinion quoted at 219, 218, respectively; see also Mason, *Stone*, pp. 677–78.
173   ["always regretted"] : Douglas, *Court Years*, p. 280.
173   [*Endo*] : 323 U.S. 283 (1944).
173   ["once loyalty is shown"] : Douglas's conference notes, October 16, 1944, quoted in Ball and Cooper, p. 115.
173   ["legalization of racism"] : *Korematsu*, quoted at 242.
174   ["Olympian infallibility"] : quoted in Mason, *Stone*, p. 798.
174   ["smooth over the discords"] : Felix Belair, Jr., "Vinson Named Chief Justice," *New York Times*, June 7, 1946, pp. 1, 4, quoted at p. 1.
175   ["secret, conspiratorial"] : quoted in Wiecek, pp. 543, 544.
175   ["Congress was not forbidden"] : *Dennis* v. *U.S.*, 341 U.S. 494 (1951), quoted at 552.
176   ["diabolical conspiracy"] : U.S. district judge Irving Kaufman, quoted in Parrish, p. 811.
176   ["before we allow"] : the text of Douglas's stay is reprinted as an appendix to his dissent in *Rosenberg* v. *U.S.*, 346 U.S. 273 (1953), quoted at 321.
176   ["race for death"] : quoted in Wiecek, p. 616.
176   ["loyalty-security mania"] : Alexander M. Bickel, *The Supreme Court and the Idea of Progress* (Harper & Row, 1970), p. 5.
176   ["History teaches"] : *Dennis*, 525.

CHAPTER TEN—LEADERSHIP: THE WARREN COURT

Henry J. Abraham, *Justices and Presidents: A Political History of Appointments to the Supreme Court*, 3rd ed. (Oxford University Press, 1992), ch. 10.
Howard Ball and Phillip J. Cooper, "Fighting Justices: Hugo L. Black and William O. Douglas and Supreme Court Conflict," *American Journal of Legal History*, vol. 38, no. 1 (January 1994), pp. 1–37.
William M. Beaney, "The Warren Court and the Political Process," *Michigan Law Review*, vol. 67, no. 2 (December 1968), pp. 343–52.
Michal R. Belknap, "The Warren Court and Equality," in Sandra F. VanBurkleo et al., eds., *Constitutionalism and American Culture* (University Press of Kansas, 2002), pp. 211–39.
Alexander M. Bickel, *The Supreme Court and the Idea of Progress* (Harper & Row, 1970).
Herbert Brownell, *Advising Ike* (University Press of Kansas, 1993).
Joseph A. Califano, Jr., *The Triumph & Tragedy of Lyndon Johnson: The White House Years* (Simon and Schuster, 1991).
James E. Clayton, *The Making of Justice: The Supreme Court in Action* (E. P. Dutton, 1964).

Richard C. Cortner, *The Supreme Court and the Second Bill of Rights: The Fourteenth Amendment and the Nationalization of Civil Liberties* (University of Wisconsin Press, 1981).

Archibald Cox, *The Warren Court: Constitutional Decision as an Instrument of Reform* (Harvard University Press, 1968).

Michael D. Davis and Hunter R. Clark, *Thurgood Marshall: Warrior at the Bar, Rebel on the Bench* (Birch Lane Press, 1992).

William O. Douglas, *The Court Years, 1939–1975* (Random House, 1980).

Kim Isaac Eisler, *A Justice for All: William J. Brennan, Jr., and the Decisions That Transformed America* (Simon and Schuster, 1993).

Leon Friedman and Fred L. Israel, eds., *The Justices of the United States Supreme Court, 1789–1969* (Chelsea House, 1969–78), vol. 4.

Fred P. Graham, *The Self-Inflicted Wound* (Macmillan, 1970).

Morton J. Horwitz, *The Warren Court and the Pursuit of Justice* (Hill and Wang, 1998).

Dennis J. Hutchinson, "'The Ideal New Frontier Judge'" (Byron White), *Supreme Court Review*, vol. 1997 (1997), pp. 373–402.

Dennis J. Hutchinson, *The Man Who Once Was Whizzer White* (Free Press, 1998).

Dennis J. Hutchinson, "The Man Who Once Was Whizzer White," *Yale Law Journal*, vol. 103, no. 1 (October 1993), pp. 43–56.

Peter Irons, *A People's History of the Supreme Court* (Viking, 1999), chs. 29–31.

Ronald Kahn, *The Supreme Court and Constitutional Theory, 1953–1993* (University Press of Kansas, 1994), chs. 2–3.

Thomas M. Keck, *The Most Activist Supreme Court in History: The Road to Modern Judicial Conservatism* (University of Chicago Press, 2004), esp. chs. 2–3.

Michael J. Klarman, *From Jim Crow to Civil Rights: The Supreme Court and the Struggle for Racial Equality* (Oxford University Press, 2004).

Richard Kluger, *Simple Justice: The History of* Brown v. Board of Education *and Black America's Struggle for Equality* (Alfred A. Knopf, 1976).

Philip B. Kurland, "Earl Warren, the 'Warren Court,' and the Warren Myths," *Michigan Law Review*, vol. 67, no. 2 (December 1968), pp. 353–58.

Philip B. Kurland, *Politics, the Constitution, and the Warren Court* (University of Chicago Press, 1970).

Clifford M. Lytle, *The Warren Court & Its Critics* (University of Arizona Press, 1968).

David E. Marion, *The Jurisprudence of Justice William J. Brennan, Jr.* (Rowman & Littlefield, 1997).

Alpheus T. Mason, "Judicial Activism: Old and New," *Virginia Law Review*, vol. 55, no. 3 (April 1969), pp. 385–426.

Alpheus T. Mason, "Understanding the Warren Court: Judicial Self-Restraint and Judicial Duty," *Political Science Quarterly*, vol. 81, no. 4 (December 1966), pp. 523–63.

John Massaro, "LBJ and the Fortas Nomination for Chief Justice," *Political Science Quarterly*, vol. 97, no. 4 (Winter 1982–83), pp. 603–21.

Michael S. Mayer, "With Much Deliberation and Some Speed: Eisenhower and the Brown Decision," *Journal of Southern History*, vol. 52, no. 1 (February 1986), pp. 43–76.

Bruce Allen Murphy, *Fortas: The Rise and Ruin of a Supreme Court Justice* (William Morrow, 1988).

Paul L. Murphy, *The Constitution in Crisis Times, 1918–1969* (Harper & Row, 1972), chs. 10–13.

Jim Newton, *Justice for All: Earl Warren and the Nation He Made* (Riverhead, 2006).

David M. O'Brien, "LBJ and Supreme Court Politics in the Light of History," in Bernard J. Firestone and Robert C. Vogt, eds., *Lyndon Baines Johnson and the Uses of Power* (Greenwood Press, 1988), pp. 149–60.

James T. Patterson, *Brown v. Board of Education: A Civil Rights Milestone and Its Troubled Legacy* (Oxford University Press, 2001).

Jack Harrison Pollack, *Earl Warren: The Judge Who Changed America* (Prentice-Hall, 1979).

Lucas A. Powe, Jr., *The Warren Court and American Politics* (Belknap Press, 2000).

C. Herman Pritchett, *Congress Versus the Supreme Court, 1957–1960* (University of Minnesota Press, 1961).

Bernard Schwartz, *Decision: How the Supreme Court Decides Cases* (Oxford University Press, 1996).

Bernard Schwartz, "Felix Frankfurter and Earl Warren: A Study of a Deteriorating Relationship," *Supreme Court Review*, vol. 1980 (1980), pp. 115–42.

Bernard Schwartz, *Super Chief: Earl Warren and His Supreme Court* (New York University Press, 1983).

Bernard Schwartz, ed., *The Warren Court: A Retrospective* (Oxford University Press, 1996).

Martin Shapiro, *Law and Politics in the Supreme Court* (Free Press of Glencoe, 1964).

Kate Stith, "Byron R. White: The Last of the New Deal Liberals," *Yale Law Journal*, vol. 103, no. 1 (October 1993), pp. 19–35.

William F. Swindler, *Court and Constitution in the Twentieth Century: The New Legality, 1932–1968* (Bobbs-Merrill, 1970).

Dennis L. Thompson, "The Kennedy Court: Left and Right of Center," *Western Political Quarterly*, vol. 26, no. 2 (June 1973), pp. 263–79.

Mark Tushnet, ed., *The Warren Court in Historical and Political Perspective* (University Press of Virginia, 1993).

Melvin I. Urofsky, *The Warren Court: Justices, Rulings, and Legacy* (ABC-CLIO, 2001).

Earl Warren, *Memoirs* (Doubleday, 1977).

Herbert Wechsler, "The Courts and the Constitution," *Columbia Law Review*, vol. 65, no. 6 (June 1965), pp. 1001–14.

Stephen J. Wermiel, "The Nomination of Justice Brennan: Eisenhower's Mistake?," *Constitutional Commentary*, vol. 11, no. 3 (Winter 1994), pp. 515–37.

Alan F. Westin, "Liberals and the Supreme Court: Making Peace with the 'Nine Old Men,'" *Commentary*, vol. 22, no. 1 (July 1956), pp. 20–26.

William M. Wiecek, *The Birth of the Modern Constitution: The United States Supreme Court, 1941–1953*, vol. 12 of *History of the Supreme Court of the United States* (Cambridge University Press, 2006).

David A. Yalof, *Pursuit of Justices: Presidential Politics and the Selection of Supreme Court Nominees* (University of Chicago Press, 1999), chs. 3–4.

Tinsley E. Yarbrough, *John Marshall Harlan: Great Dissenter of the Warren Court* (Oxford University Press, 1992).

180   ["repetition of Pearl Harbor"] : quoted in Lawrence E. Davies, "Coast Axis Aliens Face Business Ban," *New York Times*, January 31, 1942, p. 8.

180   ["personal promise"] : quoted in Yalof, p. 46.

181   ["Earl Warren's a Democrat"] : quoted in Pollack, p. 97.

181   ["breaking his word"] : quoted in Yalof, p. 49.

181   ["truth was"] : Eisenhower, *Mandate for Change, 1953–1956* (Doubleday, 1963), p. 228.

181   ["high ideals"] : quoted in Swindler, p. 220.

182   ["helpful as direction"] : quoted in Schwartz, *Super Chief*, p. 149.

182   ["Be a judge"] : ibid., p. 261.

182   ["worst Chief Justice"] : quoted in Pollack, p. 197.

182   ["just uncongenial"] : ibid., p. 257.

183   [1948 restrictive covenants decision] : *Shelley* v. *Kraemer*, 334 U.S. 1 (1948).

183   [Three 1950 segregation cases] : *McLaurin* v. *Oklahoma State Regents*, 339 U.S. 637 (1950); *Sweatt* v. *Painter*, 339 U.S. 629 (1950) (Texas law school); *Henderson* v. *U.S.*, 339 U.S. 816 (1950) (railway dining cars).

183   ["South's Magna Carta"] : Powe, p. 21.
183   ["enforced separation"] : 163 U.S. 537 (1896), quoted at 551.
183   ["not go out"] : quoted in Wiecek, p. 691.
183   ["long continued interpretations"] : Clark conference notes, December 12, 1952, quoted in ibid., p. 697.
184   ["inherent inferiority"] : quoted in Schwartz, *Super Chief*, p. 86.
184   ["minimum of emotion"] : ibid., p. 88.
184   ["different handling"] : ibid., p. 91.
184   [*Brown* opinion] : 347 U.S. 483 (1954), quoted at 495, 494, 495, respectively.
185   ["end of the world"] : quoted in Kluger, p. 711.
185   ["familiar prophecy"] : Krock, "A Milestone in More Ways Than One," *New York Times*, May 18, 1954, p. 28.
185   [Eastland on *Brown* and court] : *Congressional Record*, 83rd Congress, 2nd session, vol. 100, part 6, May 27, 1954, p. 7254.
185   ["as the Supreme Court interprets it"] : "The President's News Conference," September 5, 1956, in Eisenhower, *Public Papers* (U.S. Government Printing Office, 1958–61), vol. 1956, pp. 732–45, quoted at pp. 737, 736, respectively.
185   ["sweet little girls"] : quoted in Warren, *Memoirs*, p. 291.
186   ["most principled"] : Irons, p. 430.
186   ["outstanding"] : quoted in Wermiel, p. 525.
187   ["always wanted"] : Stephen J. Friedman, "William J. Brennan," in Friedman and Israel, vol. 4, pp. 2849–65, quoted at p. 2851.
188   ["believes that the Constitution"] : quoted in Swindler, p. 233.
188   ["closely akin"] : *Barenblatt* v. *U.S.*, 360 U.S. 109 (1959), quoted at 143.
188   [Red Monday decisions] : *Watkins* v. *U.S.*, 354 U.S. 178 (1957) (HUAC); *Sweezy* v. *New Hampshire*, 354 U.S. 234 (1957) (state attorney general); *Yates* v. *U.S.*, 354 U.S. 298 (1957) (Smith Act); *Service* v. *Dulles*, 354 U.S. 363 (1957) (State Department).
189   ["spectacle of a Court"] : *Congressional Record*, 85th Congress, 1st session, vol. 103, part 10, July 26, 1957, pp. 12806, 12807.
189   [*Gitlow* and incorporation] : see *Gitlow* v. *New York*, 268 U.S. 652 (1925), at 666.
190   [Black's argument for total incorporation] : see *Adamson* v. *California*, 332 U.S. 46 (1947), Black's dissent at 68–123.
190   [*Colegrove*] : 328 U.S. 549 (1946), quoted at 552, 556. The Taney opinion was *Luther* v. *Borden*, 48 U.S. 1 (1849).
191   [Warren on his most important decision] : Warren, *Memoirs*, p. 306.
191   ["political vicissitudes"] : Harlan to Whittaker and Stewart, letter of October 11, 1961, quoted in Newton, p. 390.
191   ["made change hopeless"] : Warren, *Memoirs*, p. 307.
191   ["citizen's right"] : *Baker* v. *Carr*, 369 U.S. 186 (1962), quoted at 208, 231.
191   ["one person, one vote"] : 372 U.S. 368 (1963), quoted at 368.
191   ["great day"] : quoted in Schwartz, *Super Chief*, p. 424.
191   ["massive repudiation"] : *Baker*, quoted at 267.
192   ["I never know"] : *Denver Post*, April 1, 1962, quoted in Hutchinson, "The Ideal New Frontier Judge," p. 394.
192   ["You didn't think"] : quoted in Clayton, p. 52.
193   ["With five votes"] : quoted in Irons, p. 416.
193   [Warren Court's use of judicial review] : Keck, pp. 40–41 (Tables 2.1 and 2.2).
193   ["new law"] : *Miranda* v. *Arizona*, 384 U.S. 436 (1966), White's dissent quoted at 531.
194   [Precedents overturned by Warren Court] : see Powe, p. 405.
195   ["durable principles"] : Bickel, p. 99.
195   ["First Amendment allows"] : *Ginzburg* v. *U.S.*, 383 U.S. 463 (1966), Douglas's dissent quoted at 491.
195   [*Griswold*] : 381 U.S. 479 (1965), Douglas quoted at 484; Black at 510, 511, 522.

196   ["powerful weapon"] : Irons, p. 416.
196   [*Mapp*] : 367 U.S. 643 (1961).
196   [*Gideon*] : 372 U.S. 335 (1963).
197   [*Escobedo*] : 378 U.S. 478 (1964).
197   [*Miranda*] : 384 U.S. 436 (1966).
197   ["wear him down"] : quoted in Murphy, *Fortas*, p. 176.
199   ["effective at your pleasure"] : quoted in Newton, p. 491.
200   ["with deep regret"] : "Statement by the President Upon Withdrawing the Nomination of Justice Abe Fortas," October 2, 1968, in Johnson, *Public Papers* (U.S. Government Printing Office, 1965–70), vol. 1968–69, part 2, p. 1000.
200   ["indicated his willingness"] : "Statement by the President Upon Declining to Submit an Additional Nomination," October 10, 1968, in ibid., vol. 1968–69, part 2, p. 1024.

CHAPTER ELEVEN—REPUBLICANS AS ACTIVISTS

Henry J. Abraham, *Justices, Presidents, and Senators: A History of the U.S. Supreme Court Appointments from Washington to Clinton*, 4th ed. (Rowman & Littlefield, 1999), chs. 2, 11–12.
Stephen E. Ambrose, *Nixon*, 2 vols. (Simon and Schuster, 1987–89).
R. W. Apple, Jr., "Sununu Tells How and Why He Pushed Souter for Court," *New York Times*, July 25, 1990, p. A12.
Jack M. Balkin and Sanford Levinson, "Understanding the Constitutional Revolution," *Virginia Law Review*, vol. 87, no. 6 (October 2001), pp. 1045–1109.
Paul Barrett et al., *A Year in the Life of the Supreme Court*, Rodney A. Smolia, ed. (Duke University Press, 1995).
Martin H. Belsky, ed., *The Rehnquist Court* (Oxford University Press, 2002).
Joan Biskupic, *Sandra Day O'Connor* (Ecco, 2005).
Janet L. Blasecki, "Justice Lewis F. Powell: Swing Voter or Staunch Conservative?," *Journal of Politics*, vol. 52, no. 2 (May 1990), pp. 530–47.
Donald E. Boles, *Mr. Justice Rehnquist, Judicial Activist: The Early Years* (Iowa State University Press, 1987).
Lincoln Caplan, *The Tenth Justice: The Solicitor General and the Rule of Law* (Alfred A. Knopf, 1987).
Stephen Carter, "The Confirmation Mess," *Harvard Law Review*, vol. 101, no. 6 (April 1988), pp. 1185–1201.
"The Changing Social Vision of Justice Blackmun," *Harvard Law Review*, vol. 96, no. 3 (January 1983), pp. 717–36.
Hunter R. Clark, *Justice Brennan: The Great Conciliator* (Birch Lane Press, 1995).
Michael Comiskey, "The Rehnquist Court and American Values," *Judicature*, vol. 77, no. 5 (March–April 1994), pp. 261–67.
Michael Comiskey, *Seeking Justices: The Judging of Supreme Court Nominees* (University Press of Kansas, 2004).
John W. Dean, *The Rehnquist Choice* (Free Press, 2001).
Neal Devins, "The Countermajoritarian Paradox" (review of Garrow, *Liberty and Sexuality*), *Michigan Law Review*, vol. 93, no. 6 (May 1995), pp. 1433–59.
Elizabeth Drew, *On the Edge: The Clinton Presidency* (Simon and Schuster, 1994), ch. 15.
John Ehrlichman, *Witness to Power: The Nixon Years* (Simon and Schuster, 1982).
John P. Frank, *Clement Haynsworth, the Senate, and the Supreme Court* (University Press of Virginia, 1991).
Leon Friedman and Fred L. Israel, eds., *The Justices of the United States Supreme Court, 1789–1969* (Chelsea House, 1969–78), vols. 4–5.
Richard Y. Funston, *Constitutional Counterrevolution? The Warren Court and the Burger Court: Judicial Policy-Making in Modern America* (Schenkman, 1977).

Martin Garbus, *Courting Disaster: The Supreme Court and the Unmaking of American Law* (Times Books, 2002).

David J. Garrow, "Justice Souter Emerges," *New York Times Magazine*, September 25, 1994, pp. 36–43, 52–55, 64, 67.

David J. Garrow, *Liberty and Sexuality: The Right to Privacy and the Making of* Roe *v.* Wade (Lisa Drew, 1994).

David J. Garrow, "The Rehnquist Reins," *New York Times Magazine*, October 6, 1996, pp. 65–71, 82, 85.

David J. Garrow, "The Unlikely Center" (review of Biskupic, *O'Connor*, and Yarbrough, *Souter*), *New Republic*, vol. 234, no. 8 (March 6, 2006), pp. 33–37.

Elizabeth E. Gillman and Joseph M. Micheletti, "Justice Ruth Bader Ginsburg," *Seton Hall Constitutional Law Journal*, vol. 3 (Fall 1993), pp. 657–63.

Jan Crawford Greenburg, *Supreme Conflict: The Inside Story of the Struggle for Control of the United States Supreme Court* (Penguin, 2007).

Linda Greenhouse, *Becoming Justice Blackmun* (Times Books, 2005).

Thomas R. Hensley, *The Rehnquist Court: Justices, Rulings, and Legacy* (ABC-CLIO, 2006).

Richard Hodder-Williams, "Ronald Reagan and the Supreme Court," in Joseph Hogan, ed., *The Reagan Years* (Manchester University Press, 1990), pp. 143–63.

Richard Hodder-Williams, "The Strange Story of Judge Robert Bork and a Vacancy on the United States Supreme Court," *Political Studies*, vol. 36 (1988), pp. 613–37.

A. E. Dick Howard, "Mr. Justice Powell and the Emerging Nixon Majority," *Michigan Law Review*, vol. 70, no. 3 (January 1972), pp. 445–68.

Peter Irons, *Brennan vs. Rehnquist: The Battle for the Constitution* (Alfred A. Knopf, 1994).

Peter Irons, *A People's History of the Supreme Court* (Viking, 1999), chs. 32–35.

John C. Jeffries, Jr., *Justice Lewis F. Powell, Jr.* (Charles Scribner's Sons, 1994).

John A. Jenkins, "The Partisan" (William Rehnquist), *New York Times Magazine*, March 3, 1985, pp. 28–35, 88, 100–101.

Ronald Kahn, *The Supreme Court and Constitutional Theory, 1953–1993* (University Press of Kansas, 1994), part 2.

Bruce H. Kalk, "The Carswell Affair: The Politics of a Supreme Court Nomination in the Nixon Administration," *American Journal of Legal History*, vol. 42, no. 3 (July 1998), pp. 261–87.

Thomas M. Keck, *The Most Activist Supreme Court in History: The Road to Modern Judicial Conservatism* (University of Chicago Press, 2004).

Charles M. Lamb and Stephen C. Halpern, eds., *The Burger Court: Political and Judicial Profiles* (University of Illinois Press, 1991).

Frederick P. Lewis, *The Context of Judicial Activism: The Endurance of the Warren Court Legacy in a Conservative Age* (Rowman & Littlefield, 1999).

Clifford M. Lytle, *The Warren Court & Its Critics* (University of Arizona Press, 1968).

Earl M. Maltz, *The Chief Justiceship of Warren Burger, 1969–1986* (University of South Carolina Press, 2000).

John Massaro, *Supremely Political: The Role of Ideology and Presidential Management in Unsuccessful Supreme Court Nominations* (State University of New York Press, 1990).

Ann Carey McFeatters, *Sandra Day O'Connor: Justice in the Balance* (University of New Mexico Press, 2005).

Kevin Merida and Michael A. Fletcher, *Supreme Discomfort: The Divided Soul of Clarence Thomas* (Doubleday, 2007).

David M. O'Brien, *Judicial Roulette* (Priority Press, 1988).

David M. O'Brien, "The Politics of Professionalism: President Gerald R. Ford's Appointment of Justice John Paul Stevens," in Bernard J. Firestone and Alexej

Ugrinsky, eds., *Gerald R. Ford and the Politics of Post-Watergate America* (Greenwood Press, 1993), vol. 1, pp. 111–36.

Barbara A. Perry, *The Priestly Tribe: The Supreme Court's Image in the American Mind* (Praeger, 1999).

Barbara A. Perry and Henry J. Abraham, "A 'Representative' Supreme Court?," *Judicature*, vol. 81, no. 4 (January–February 1998), pp. 158–65.

L. A. Powe, Jr., "The Politics of American Judicial Review: Reflections on the Marshall, Warren, and Rehnquist Courts," *Wake Forest Law Review*, vol. 38, no. 2 (Summer 2003), pp. 697–732.

Jeremy Rabkin, "A Supreme Court in the Culture Wars," *Public Interest*, no. 125 (Fall 1996), pp. 3–26.

Jamin B. Raskin, *Overruling Democracy: The Supreme Court vs. The American People* (Routledge, 2003).

Jeffrey Rosen, "The Agonizer" (Anthony Kennedy), *New Yorker*, vol. 72, no. 34 (November 11, 1996), pp. 82–90.

Jeffrey Rosen, "A Majority of One" (Sandra Day O'Connor), *New York Times Magazine*, June 23, 2001, pp. 32–37, 64–79.

Jeffrey Rosen, "The New Look of Liberalism on the Court" (Ruth Bader Ginsburg), *New York Times Magazine*, October 5, 1997, pp. 60–65, 86, 90, 96–97.

William Saletan, *Bearing Right: How Conservatives Won the Abortion War* (University of California Press, 2003).

David G. Savage, *Turning Right: The Making of the Rehnquist Court* (John Wiley & Sons, 1992).

Bernard Schwartz, ed., *The Burger Court: Counter-Revolution or Confirmation?* (Oxford University Press, 1998).

Bernard Schwartz, *Decision: How the Supreme Court Decides Cases* (Oxford University Press, 1996).

Bernard Schwartz, *The New Right and the Constitution: Turning Back the Legal Clock* (Northeastern University Press, 1990).

Herman Schwartz, ed., *The Burger Years: Rights and Wrongs in the Supreme Court, 1969–1986* (Viking, 1987).

Herman Schwartz, *Packing the Courts: The Conservative Campaign to Rewrite the Constitution* (Charles Scribner's Sons, 1988).

Herman Schwartz, ed., *The Rehnquist Court: Judicial Activism on the Right* (Hill and Wang, 2002).

Herman Schwartz, "The Supreme Court's Federalism: Fig Leaf for Conservatives," *Annals of the American Academy of Political and Social Science*, vol. 574 (March 2001), pp. 119–31.

Mark Silverstein, "Bill Clinton's Excellent Adventure: Political Development and the Modern Confirmation Process," in Howard Gillman and Cornell Clayton, eds., *The Supreme Court in American Politics* (University Press of Kansas, 1999), pp. 133–47.

Mark Silverstein, *Judicious Choices: The New Politics of Supreme Court Confirmations* (W. W. Norton, 1994).

James F. Simon, *The Center Holds: The Power Struggle Inside the Rehnquist Court* (Simon and Schuster, 1995).

James F. Simon, *In His Own Image: The Supreme Court in Richard Nixon's America* (David McKay, 1973).

Christopher E. Smith, *Justice Antonin Scalia and the Supreme Court's Conservative Moment* (Praeger, 1993).

Christopher E. Smith, "The Supreme Court in Transition: Assessing the Legitimacy of the Leading Legal Institution," *Kentucky Law Journal*, vol. 79 (1991), pp. 317–46.

Christopher E. Smith and Thomas R. Hensley, "Unfulfilled Aspirations: The Court-Packing

Efforts of Presidents Reagan and Bush," *Albany Law Review*, vol. 57 (Fall 1994), pp. 1111–31.

Kate Stith, "Byron R. White: The Last of the New Deal Liberals," *Yale Law Journal*, vol. 103, no. 1 (October 1993), pp. 19–35.

Margaret Talbot, "Supreme Confidence: The Jurisprudence of Justice Antonin Scalia," *New Yorker*, vol. 81, no. 6 (March 28, 2005), pp. 40–55.

Jeffrey Toobin, *The Nine: Inside the Secret World of the Supreme Court* (Doubleday, 2007).

Mark Tushnet, *A Court Divided: The Rehnquist Court and the Future of Constitutional Law* (W. W. Norton, 2005).

Norman Vieira and Leonard Gross, *Supreme Court Appointments: Judge Bork and the Politicization of Senate Confirmations* (Southern Illinois University Press, 1998).

J. Harvie Wilkinson III, "The Rehnquist Court at Twilight: The Lures and Perils of Split-the-Difference Jurisprudence," *Stanford Law Review*, vol. 58, no. 6 (April 2006), pp. 1969–96.

Bob Woodward and Scott Armstrong, *The Brethren: Inside the Supreme Court* (Simon and Schuster, 1979).

David A. Yalof, *Pursuit of Justices: Presidential Politics and the Selection of Supreme Court Nominees* (University of Chicago Press, 1999), chs. 5–6.

Tinsley E. Yarbrough, *The Burger Court: Justices, Rulings, and Legacy* (ABC-CLIO, 2000).

Tinsley E. Yarbrough, *David Hackett Souter: Traditional Republican on the Rehnquist Court* (Oxford University Press, 2005).

Tinsley E. Yarbrough, *The Rehnquist Court and the Constitution* (Oxford University Press, 2000).

Robert Zelnick, "Whizzer White and the Fearsome Foursome," *Washington Monthly*, vol. 4, no. 10 (December 1972), pp. 46–54.

201 ["above politics"] : "Conversation with Newsmen," May 22, 1969, in Nixon, *Public Papers* (U.S. Government Printing Office, 1971–75), vol. 1969, pp. 389–99, quoted at pp. 391, 392.

202 ["gone too far"] : Robert B. Semple, Jr., "Nixon Decries 'Lawless Society' and Urges Limited Wiretapping," *New York Times*, May 9, 1968, pp. 1, 32, quoted at p. 1; see also, e.g., "Nixon Denounces Humphrey Views," ibid., September 7, 1968, pp. 1, 20.

203 ["all deliberate speed"] : *Brown* v. *Board of Education of Topeka* (II), 349 U.S. 294 (1955), quoted at 301.

203 ["Our personal opinions"] : "Radio and Television Address to the American People on the Situation in Little Rock," September 24, 1957, in Eisenhower, *Public Papers* (U.S. Government Printing Office, 1958–61), vol. 1957, pp. 689–94, quoted at p. 690.

203 ["busing the child"] : quoted in Ambrose, vol. 2, p. 169.

203 ["Court will not be used"] : "Conversation with Newsmen," May 22, 1969, p. 391.

204 ["come out ahead"] : entry of November 21, 1969, in H. R. Haldeman, *Diaries: Inside the Nixon White House* (G. P. Putnam's Sons, 1994), p. 110.

204 ["play it very tough"] : ibid.

204 ["real Southern judge"] : quoted in Simon, *In His Own Image*, p. 116.

204 ["absurd constructionist"] : quoted in ibid., p. 122.

204 ["Even if he were mediocre"] : Spencer Rich, "Hruska Calls Foes of Carswell Unfair," *Washington Post*, March 17, 1970, p. A2.

204 ["I have reluctantly"] : "Remarks to Reporters About Nominations to the Supreme Court," April 9, 1970, in Nixon, *Public Papers*, vol. 1970, p. 345.

206 ["right of society"] : quoted in Dean, p. 269.

206   [Nixon on Rehnquist] : ibid., p. 86; and transcript of recorded conversation between Nixon and John Ehrlichman, July 24, 1971, in Abraham, p. 268.
206   ["salt away"] : Ehrlichman, quoted in Dean, p. 139.
207   ["was right"] : quoted in ibid., p. 275.
207   ["be as mean"] : quoted in Tushnet, p. 31.
207   ["4 more years"] : "Remarks at Ontario, California," November 4, 1972, in Nixon, *Public Papers*, vol. 1972, pp. 1129–34, quoted at p. 1133.
208   ["would have to stand"] : Burger to Douglas, note of December 18, 1971, quoted in Garrow, *Liberty and Sexuality*, p. 534.
208   ["sweeping consequences"] : *Roe v. Wade*, 410 U.S. 113 (1973), quoted at 208.
208   ["sensitive and emotional"] : ibid., quoted at 116.
209   ["raw judicial power"] : ibid., quoted at 222.
210   [*Nixon*] : 418 U.S. 683 (1974), quoted at 703.
210   ["last hound dog"] : Douglas, *The Court Years, 1939–1975* (Random House, 1980), p. 377.
211   ["most qualified woman"] : "Transcript of Ronald Reagan's Remarks at News Conference in Los Angeles," *New York Times*, October 15, 1980, p. A24.
212   ["interpret the law"] : memo on judicial selection criteria, June 18, 1981, quoted in Yalof, p. 138.
212   ["personally repugnant"] : quoted in McFeatters, p. 4.
212   ["most conservative woman"] : quoted in Savage, p. 114.
212   [*Akron*] : 462 U.S. 416 (1983), quoted at 463.
213   ["refusal to create"]: quoted in Yalof, pp. 143, 144.
213   ["Original Intention"] : Meese, "The Attorney General's View of the Supreme Court: Toward a Jurisprudence of Original Intention," *Public Administration Review*, vol. 45 (November 1985), pp. 701–4.
213   ["arrogance cloaked"] : quoted in Clark, p. 270.
213   [Rehnquist on interpreting the First Amendment] : Savage, p. 150.
213   ["paradigmatic example"] : quoted in Greenburg, p. 41.
213   ["generally rudderless"] : "Report on Justice William Rehnquist," quoted in Yalof, p. 150.
214   ["commitment to principles"] : quoted in Greenburg, p. 44.
214   ["archconservative Catholic"] : William Stern, quoted in Irvin Molotsky, "Judge with Tenacity and Charm," *New York Times*, June 18, 1986, p. A31.
214   [Scalia as "perfect"] : quoted in Greenburg, p. 42.
215   ["determined moderate"] : Stuart Taylor, Jr., "Opening for Reagan," *New York Times*, June 27, 1987, pp. 1, 32, quoted at p. 1.
215   ["evenhanded"] : "Remarks Announcing the Nomination of Robert H. Bork," July 1, 1987, in Reagan, *Public Papers* (U.S. Government Printing Office, 1982–91), vol. 1987, p. 736.
215   ["Robert Bork's America"] : *Congressional Record*, 100th Congress, 1st session, vol. 133, no. 110, July 1, 1987, p. S9188.
215   ["they'll object to"] : "Remarks to New Jersey Republican State Committee," October 13, 1987, in Reagan, *Public Papers*, vol. 1987, pp. 1172–75, quoted at p. 1175.
216   ["disturbing aspects"] : quoted in Greenburg, p. 55.
216   [Conservative bloc voting, 1988, 1989] : Hensley, p. 15.
216   [*Croson*] : 488 U.S. 469 (1989).
216   [Decisions on searches and religious liberty] : *Skinner v. Railway Labor Executives' Association*, 489 U.S. 602 (1989) and *National Treasury Employees Union v. Von Raab*, 489 U.S. 656 (1989); *Employment Division, Oregon Department of Human Resources v. Smith*, 494 U.S. 872 (1990).

216   [*Webster*] : 492 U.S. 490 (1989), O'Connor's concurrence quoted at 526; Blackmun's dissent at 538.

217   ["home run"] : Philip Shenon, "Conservative Says Sununu Assured Him on Souter," *New York Times*, August 24, 1990, p. A15.

218   ["high-tech lynching"] : "Excerpts from Senate's Hearings on the Thomas Nomination," *New York Times*, October 12, 1991, p. 14.

219   [*Payne*] : 501 U.S. 808 (1991), Rehnquist's opinion for the court quoted at 827, 828; Marshall's dissent at 845, 844, respectively.

219   [Hensley on court's decisions] : Hensley, p. 20. For this discussion of the conservative bloc's dissolution, I have relied on Hensley, pp. 18–22.

220   ["Court was mistaken"] : 505 U.S. 833 (1992), Rehnquist's opinion—joined by White, Scalia, and Thomas—quoted at 953.

220   ["decision to overrule"] : ibid., 869, 846, respectively.

220   ["unquestionably qualified"] : Ruth Marcus and Joan Biskupic, "Justice White to Retire After 31 Years," *Washington Post*, March 20, 1993, pp. A1, A12, quoted at p. A12.

221   ["emotional connection"] : Ann Devroy and Ruth Marcus, "After 87 Days, Tortuous Selection Process Came Down to Karma," ibid., June 15, 1993, p. A11.

221   ["mother to boot"] : quoted in Gillman and Micheletti, p. 658.

221   ["decide the case"] : Neil A. Lewis, "Ginsburg Promises Judicial Restraint If She Joins Court," *New York Times*, July 21, 1993, pp. A1, A13, quoted at p. A13.

222   ["principled moderate"] : quoted in "Senate Panel Gives Breyer Its Approval," ibid., July 20, 1994, p. A10.

223   [Court's record in striking down federal statutes] : Keck, p. 40 (Table 2.1).

223   ["most activist"] : ibid., passim.

223   ["courts retain the power"] : *City of Boerne* v. *Flores*, 521 U.S. 507 (1997), quoted at 536.

CHAPTER TWELVE—HARD RIGHT: THE CHENEY-BUSH COURT

Bruce Ackerman, ed., *Bush v. Gore: The Question of Legitimacy* (Yale University Press, 2002).

Perry Bacon, Jr., and Mike Allen, "The Cool Fervor of Judge Alito," *Time*, vol. 167, no. 3 (January 16, 2006), pp. 40–44.

Thomas E. Baker and John F. Stack, Jr., eds., *At War with Civil Rights and Civil Liberties* (Rowman & Littlefield, 2006).

Jack M. Balkin, "Bush v. Gore and the Boundary Between Law and Politics," *Yale Law Journal*, vol. 110, no. 8 (June 2001), pp. 1407–58.

Rachel E. Barkow, "More Supreme than Court? The Fall of the Political Question Doctrine and the Rise of Judicial Supremacy," *Columbia Law Review*, vol. 102, no. 2 (March 2002), pp. 237–336.

Jo Becker and Dale Russakoff, "Proving His Mettle in the Reagan Justice Dept." (Alito), *Washington Post*, January 9, 2006, pp. A1, A8–9.

E. J. Dionne, Jr., and William Kristol, eds., *Bush v. Gore* (Brookings Institution Press, 2001).

Ronald Dworkin, ed., *A Badly Flawed Election: Debating* Bush v. Gore, *the Supreme Court, and American Democracy* (New Press, 2002).

Ronald Dworkin, "The Supreme Court Phalanx," *New York Review of Books*, vol. 54, no. 14 (September 27, 2007), pp. 92–101.

James L. Gibson et al., "The Supreme Court and the US Presidential Election of 2000: Wounds, Self-Inflicted or Otherwise?," *British Journal of Political Science*, vol. 33, no. 4 (October 2003), pp. 535–56.

Howard Gillman, *The Votes That Counted: How the Court Decided the 2000 Presidential Election* (University of Chicago Press, 2001).

Jan Crawford Greenburg, *Supreme Conflict: The Inside Story of the Struggle for Control of the United States Supreme Court* (Penguin, 2007).

Thomas R. Hensley, *The Rehnquist Court: Justices, Rulings, and Legacy* (ABC-CLIO, 2006).

Samuel Issacharoff, "Political Judgments," *University of Chicago Law Review*, vol. 68, no. 3 (Summer 2001), pp. 637–56.

Thomas M. Keck, *The Most Activist Supreme Court in History: The Road to Modern Judicial Conservatism* (University of Chicago Press, 2004).

Jerry Landay, "The Conservative Cabal That's Transforming American Law," *Washington Monthly*, vol. 32, no. 3 (March 2000), pp. 19–23.

Simon Lazarus, "More Polarizing than Rehnquist," *American Prospect*, vol. 18, no. 5 (May 2007), pp. 23–27.

Eric Lichtblau, *Bush's Law: The Remaking of American Justice* (Pantheon, 2008).

Dahlia Lithwick, "Realignment?," *Washington Post National Weekly Edition*, June 23–July 6, 2008, p. 25.

Jonathan Mahler, *The Challenge:* Hamdan v. Rumsfeld *and the Fight over Presidential Power* (Farrar, Straus and Giroux, 2008).

Janet Malcolm, "The Art of Testifying," *New Yorker*, vol. 82, no. 4 (March 13, 2006), pp. 70–79.

Joseph Margulies, *Guantánamo and the Abuse of Presidential Power* (Simon and Schuster, 2006).

Thomas R. Marshall, *Public Opinion and the Rehnquist Court* (State University of New York Press, 2008).

Lois Romano and Juliet Eilperin, "Republicans Were Masters in the Race to Paint Alito," *Washington Post*, February 2, 2006, pp. A1, A10.

Jeffrey Rosen, "The Dissenter" (John Paul Stevens), *New York Times Magazine*, September 23, 2007, pp. 50–57, 72, 76–79, 81.

Jeffrey Rosen, "Narrow Minded: John Roberts Does Obama a Favor," *New Republic*, vol. 238, no. 12 (July 9, 2008), pp. 8–11.

Jeffrey Rosen, "Rehnquist the Great?," *Atlantic*, vol. 295, no. 3 (April 2005), pp. 79–90.

Jeffrey Rosen, "Supreme Leader: The Arrogance of Justice Anthony Kennedy," *New Republic*, vol. 236, no. 18 (June 18, 2007), pp. 16–22.

Charlie Savage, *Takeover: The Return of the Imperial Presidency and the Subversion of American Democracy* (Little, Brown, 2007).

Louis Seidman, "Romer's Radicalism: The Unexpected Revival of Warren Court Activism," *Supreme Court Review*, vol. 1996 (1996), pp. 67–121.

Cass R. Sunstein and Richard A. Epstein, eds., *The Vote: Bush, Gore, and the Supreme Court* (University of Chicago Press, 2001).

Jeffrey Toobin, *The Nine: Inside the Secret World of the Supreme Court* (Doubleday, 2007).

Mark Tushnet, ed., *The Constitution in Wartime: Beyond Alarmism and Complacency* (Duke University Press, 2005).

Mark Tushnet, *A Court Divided: The Rehnquist Court and the Future of Constitutional Law* (W. W. Norton, 2005).

David Von Drehle, "Inside the Incredibly Shrinking Role of the Supreme Court," *Time*, vol. 170, no. 17 (October 22, 2007), pp. 40–49.

225 ["unsought responsibility"] : *Bush* v. *Gore*, 531 U.S. 98 (2000), majority opinion quoted at 111.

226 ["respect for federalism"] : ibid., Rehnquist's concurrence quoted at 112.

226 ["fundamental right"] : ibid., majority opinion quoted at 105, 109.

227 ["threaten irreparable harm"] : Supreme Court's grant of certiorari, 531 U.S. 1046 (2000), quoted at 1047.

227   ["if not disposed of"] : *Bush* v. *Gore*, quoted at 133.

227   ["Congress, being a political body"] : ibid., quoted at 155.

227   ["wholly without merit"] : ibid., quoted at 128, 127, 128–29, respectively.

228   [Gore's concession] : transcript in *New York Times*, December 14, 2000, p. A26.

228   ["Desirable result"] : DiIulio, "Equal Protection Run Amok," *Weekly Standard*, December 25, 2000, reprinted in Dionne and Kristol, pp. 321–23, quoted at p. 323.

228   ["legitimizing symbols"] : Gibson et al., p. 553.

228   [2001 term cases] : *Whitman* v. *American Trucking Associations*, 531 U.S. 457 (2001) (environmental law); *Board of Trustees of the University of Alabama* v. *Garrett*, 531 U.S. 356 (2001) (disability discrimination suits); *Atwater* v. *City of Lago Vista*, 532 U.S. 318 (2001) (full arrests for misdemeanors); *FEC* v. *Colorado Republican Federal Campaign Committee*, 533 U.S. 431 (2001) (campaign finance law); see also Linda Greenhouse, "The High Court and the Triumph of Discord," *New York Times*, July 15, 2001, sect. 4, pp. 1, 4; Charles Lane, "Laying Down the Law, Justices Ruled with Confidence," *Washington Post*, July 1, 2001, p. A6.

230   ["strictly interpret"] : "Transcript of Debate Between Vice President Gore and Governor Bush," *New York Times*, October 4, 2000, pp. A30–33, quoted at p. A31.

230   [Bush's favorite justices] : Robert S. Greenberger and Jackie Calmes, "Next President Likely to Tip Balance of Supreme Court," *Wall Street Journal*, October 2, 2000, p. A36.

230   ["forum for ideas"] : executive director Eugene Meyer, quoted in Landay, p. 23.

231   [Michelman-Bopp exchange] : Robin Toner and Neil A. Lewis, "Lobbying Starts as Groups Foresee Vacancy on Court," *New York Times*, June 8, 2003, pp. 1, 36, quoted at p. 36.

231   ["prayer offensive"] : "Evangelist Calls for New Court," *New York Times*, July 16, 2003, p. A12.

232   [*Romer*] : 517 U.S. 620 (1996), quoted at 633.

232   [*Boerne*] : 521 U.S. 507 (1997).

232   [*Lawrence*] : 539 U.S. 558 (2003), Kennedy quoted at 579; Scalia's dissent at 602. The precedent overturned was *Bowers* v. *Hardwick*, 478 U.S. 186 (1986).

232   ["most dangerous man"] : quoted in Jason DeParle, "In Battle to Pick Next Justice, Right Says Avoid a Kennedy," *New York Times*, June 27, 2005, pp. A1, A12, quoted at p. A12.

233   [Cheney's vetting of potential nominees] : see Jo Becker and Barton Gellman, "Taking on the Supreme Court Case," *Washington Post*, June 26, 2007, p. A10.

233   [*Rasul*] : 542 U.S. 466 (2004).

233   [*Hamdi*] : 542 U.S. 507 (2004), O'Connor's opinion quoted at 536; Scalia's at 578.

234   ["don't think we need"] : quoted in Greenburg, pp. 19, 20.

235   ["comprehensive philosophy"] : ibid., p. 191.

235   ["Geneva Convention cannot"] : *Hamdan* v. *Rumsfeld*, 415 F.3d 33 (D.C. Circuit 2005), quoted at 39.

235   ["good colleague"] : quoted in Greenburg, p. 205.

236   ["settled law"] : "I Believe No One Is Above the Law Under Our System," excerpts from Roberts's Senate confirmation hearings, *New York Times*, September 14, 2005, quoted at p. A26.

236   ["They make sure"] : "I Come Before the Committee with No Agenda. I Have No Platform," transcript of Roberts's opening statement to Senate Judiciary Committee, *New York Times*, September 13, 2005, p. A28.

236   ["narrow and cramped"] : Sheryl Gay Stolberg and Adam Liptak, "Roberts Fields Questions on Privacy and Precedents," *New York Times*, September 14, 2005, pp. A1, A25, quoted at p. A25.

236 ["invincible pleasantness"] : Malcolm, p. 72.
237 ["servant's mentality"] : Ron Key, quoted in Richard A. Serrano et al., "Few Clues to Miers' Convictions," *Los Angeles Times*, October 6, 2005, pp. A1, A16–17, quoted at p. A16.
237 ["I know her heart"] : "President Nominates Harriet Miers as Supreme Court Justice," October 3, 2005, http://georgewbush-whitehouse.archives.gov/news/releases/2005/10/20051003.html
237 ["president's secretary"] : see Greenburg, p. 269.
238 ["deep interest"] : David D. Kirkpatrick, "1985 Document Opens a Window to Alito's Views," *New York Times*, November 15, 2005, pp. A1, A21, quoted at p. A21.
238 ["one of the most outstanding"] : quoted in Becker and Russakoff, p. A1.
238 ["He was on the bench"] : quoted in Toobin, p. 300.
238 ["repugnant"] : *Planned Parenthood of Southeastern Pennsylvania v. Casey*, 505 U.S. 833 (1992), quoted at 898; see also Toobin, pp. 299–300.
238 ["radical right"] : Ralph G. Neas, president of People for the American Way, quoted in Romano and Eilperin, p. A10.
239 [Dworkin on conservative "phalanx"] : Dworkin, "Supreme Court Phalanx," p. 92.
239 [School integration case] : *Parents Involved in Community Schools v. Seattle School District No. 1*, No. 05-908, slip opinion (U.S. June 28, 2007).
239 [Exclusionary rule case] : *Hudson v. Michigan*, 547 U.S. 586 (2006).
239 [Filing deadline case] : *Bowles v. Russell*, No. 06-5306, slip opinion (U.S. June 14, 2007).
239 [Free speech cases] : *Garcetti v. Ceballos*, 547 U.S. 410 (2006); and *Morse v. Frederick*, No. 06-278, slip opinion (U.S. June 25, 2007).
239 ["Faith-based" funding case] : *Hein v. Freedom From Religion Foundation*, No. 06-157, slip opinion (U.S. June 25, 2007).
239 ["Partial-birth" abortion case] : *Gonzales v. Carhart*, No. 05-380, slip opinion (U.S. April 18, 2007).
239 [*Heller*] : No. 07-290, slip opinion (U.S. June 26, 2008).
240 ["wishes of the people's representatives"] : Adam Liptak, "Ruling on Guns Elicits Rebuke from the Right," *New York Times*, October 21, 2008, pp. A1, A15, quoted at p. A15.
240 ["freewheeling discretion"] : Posner, "In Defense of Looseness," *New Republic*, vol. 239, no. 3 (August 27, 2008), pp. 32–35, quoted at p. 32.
240 [Corporate political advertising case] : *FEC v. Wisconsin Right to Life*, No. 06-969, slip opinion (U.S. June 25, 2007).
240 ["Millionaire's Amendment" case] : *Davis v. FEC*, No. 07-320, slip opinion (U.S. June 26, 2008).
240 [Texas gerrymander case] : *League of United Latin American Citizens v. Perry*, 548 U.S. 399 (2006).
240 [Roberts-Scalia voting, 2007] : Linda Greenhouse, "In Steps Big and Small, Supreme Court Moved Right," *New York Times*, July 1, 2007, pp. 1, 18, figure at p. 18.
240 [Kennedy on hearings "sham"] : Kennedy, "Roberts and Alito Misled Us," *Washington Post*, July 30, 2006, pp. B1, B4, quoted at p. B4.
241 ["one clear and focused"] : quoted in Reynolds Holding, "In Defense of Dissents," *Time*, vol. 169, no. 9 (February 26, 2007), p. 44.
241 ["it is intolerable"] : *Bowles v. Russell*, Souter dissent, slip opinion quoted at 1.
241 ["strained and unpersuasive"] : *District of Columbia v. Heller*, Stevens dissent, slip opinion quoted at 3–4.
241 ["power, not reason"] : *Payne v. Tennessee*, 501 U.S. 808 (1991), Marshall's dissent quoted at 844.

241 ["It is not often"] : Linda Greenhouse, "Justices Limit the Use of Race in School Plans for Integration," *New York Times*, June 29, 2007, pp. A1, A24 , quoted at p. A24.

241 ["differently composed"] : *Gonzales* v. *Carhart*, Ginsburg dissent, slip opinion quoted at 24. The 2000 precedent was *Stenberg* v. *Carhart*, 530 U.S. 914 (2000).

241 ["modest judge"] : quoted in Lazarus, p. 24.

241 [Dworkin on Roberts's "subterfuge"] : Dworkin, "Supreme Court Phalanx," p. 98.

242 ["faux judicial restraint"] : *FEC* v. *Wisconsin Right to Life*, Scalia concurrence, slip opinion quoted at 17 fn. 7.

242 [5–4 decisions, 2008] : Linda Greenhouse, "On Court That Defied Labeling, Kennedy Made the Boldest Mark," *New York Times*, June 29, 2008, pp. 1, 18, figure at p. 1.

242 [*Baze*] : No. 07-5439, slip opinion (U.S. April 16, 2008).

243 [*Crawford*] : No. 07-21, slip opinion (U.S. April 28, 2008).

243 [Indiana nuns] : Deborah Hastings, "Indiana Nuns Lacking ID Denied at Poll by Fellow Sister," May 6, 2008, Associated Press article posted on Breitbart.com, http://www.breitbart.com/article.php?id=D90GBCNO0&show_article=1.

243 ["pretty darn conservative"] : quoted in Rosen, "The Dissenter," p. 52.

243 ["Including myself"] : ibid., pp. 52–53.

244 ["legal equivalent"] : State Department lawyer David Bowker quoting the words of a colleague, in Michael Isikoff and Stuart Taylor, Jr., "The Gitmo Fallout," *Newsweek*, vol. 148, no. 3 (July 17, 2006), pp. 22–25, quoted at p. 23.

244 [*Hamdan*] : No. 05-184, slip opinion (U.S. June 26, 2006), Thomas dissent quoted at 1.

245 ["Congress here has spoken"] : quoted in Linda Greenhouse, "Justices Ready to Answer Detainee Rights Questions," *New York Times*, December 6, 2007, p. A32.

245 [Davis on show trials] : Ross Tuttle, "Rigged Trials at Gitmo," *Nation*, vol. 286, no. 9 (March 10, 2008), pp. 4–6.

245 [*Boumediene*] : No. 06-1195, slip opinion (U.S. June 12, 2008), opinion of the court quoted at 5.

245 ["judicial activism"] : ibid., Roberts dissent, slip opinion quoted at 6, 1, respectively.

245 ["at war"] : ibid., Scalia dissent, slip opinion quoted at 2.

246 ["locked up"] : ibid., Souter concurrence, slip opinion quoted at 2.

246 ["inherent executive powers"] : John Yoo, Deputy Assistant Attorney General, "The President's Constitutional Authority to Conduct Military Operations Against Terrorists and Nations Supporting Them," Memorandum Opinion for the Deputy Counsel to the President, September 25, 2001. http://www.usdoj.gov/olc/warpowers925.htm.

EPILOGUE—ENDING JUDICIAL SUPREMACY

David Adamany, "Legitimacy, Realigning Elections, and the Supreme Court," *Wisconsin Law Review*, vol. 3 (1978), pp. 790–846.

James MacGregor Burns, *Leadership* (Harper & Row, 1978).

James MacGregor Burns, *Transforming Leadership: The New Pursuit of Happiness* (Grove/Atlantic, 2003).

Edward S. Corwin, *Court over Constitution: A Study of Judicial Review as an Instrument of Popular Government* (Princeton University Press, 1938).

Robert A. Dahl, "Decision-Making in a Democracy: The Supreme Court as a National Policy-Maker," *Journal of Public Law*, vol. 6 (1957), pp. 279–95.

Neal Devins and Keith E. Whittington, eds., *Congress and the Constitution* (Duke University Press, 2005).

Louis Fisher, *Constitutional Dialogues: Interpretation as Political Process* (Princeton University Press, 1988).

Daniel Hamilton, ed., "A Symposium on *The People Themselves* (Kramer)," *Chicago-Kent Law Review*, vol. 81, no. 3 (2006).

Ronald Kahn and Ken I. Kersch, eds., *The Supreme Court and American Political Development* (University Press of Kansas, 2006).

Larry D. Kramer, *The People Themselves: Popular Constitutionalism and Judicial Review* (Oxford University Press, 2004).

Robert Kuttner, *Obama's Challenge: America's Economic Crisis and the Power of a Transformative Presidency* (Chelsea Green, 2008).

Simon Lazarus, "Repealing the 20th Century," *American Prospect*, vol. 18, no. 12 (December 2007), pp. 19–22.

Sanford Levinson, ed., *Responding to Imperfection: The Theory and Practice of Constitutional Amendment* (Princeton University Press, 1995).

Gary L. McDowell, *Curbing the Courts: The Constitution and the Limits of Judicial Power* (Louisiana State University Press, 1988).

Barack Obama, *The Audacity of Hope: Thoughts on Reclaiming the American Dream* (Crown, 2006).

J. Mitchell Pickerell, *Constitutional Deliberation in Congress: The Impact of Judicial Review in a Separated System* (Duke University Press, 2004).

Jamin B. Raskin, *Overruling Democracy: The Supreme Court vs. The American People* (Routledge, 2003).

Jeffrey Rosen, "Supreme Court Inc.," *New York Times Magazine*, March 16, 2008, pp. 38–45, 66–71.

Mark Tushnet, "Democracy Versus Judicial Review," *Dissent*, vol. 52, no. 2 (Spring 2005), pp. 59–63.

Mark Tushnet, *The New Constitutional Order* (Princeton University Press, 2003).

Mark Tushnet, *Taking the Constitution Away from the Courts* (Princeton University Press, 1999).

John R. Vile, *The Constitutional Amending Process in American Political Thought* (Praeger, 1992).

John R. Vile, *Contemporary Questions Surrounding the Constitutional Amending Process* (Praeger, 1993).

G. Edward White, "The Constitutional Journey of 'Marbury v. Madison,'" *Virginia Law Review*, vol. 89, no. 6 (October 2003), pp. 1463–1573.

Keith E. Whittington, *Political Foundations of Judicial Supremacy: The Presidency, the Supreme Court, and Constitutional Leadership in U.S. History* (Princeton University Press, 2007).

Norman R. Williams, "The People's Constitution" (review of Kramer), *Stanford Law Review*, vol. 57, no. 1 (October 2004), pp. 257–90.

247   ["not just of the past"] : Obama, p. 85.

247   ["incredibly right"] : ibid., pp. 90, 92, 93, 92, 95, respectively.

248   ["*how* to think"] : ibid., pp. 89, 90.

248   ["what it means"] : quoted in Stephanie Mencimer, "The Stakes 2008: The Courts," *Washington Monthly*, vol. 40, no. 9 (August–September–October 2008), pp. 20–22, quoted at p. 21.

249   ["people on the bench"] : quoted in David G. Savage, "Two Visions of the Supreme Court," *Los Angeles Times*, May 19, 2008, p. A8.

250   ["repeal the 20th Century"] : Lazarus.

251   ["at every stage"] : Strum, "Leadership and Equality: A Social Scientist at Work," in Michael R. Beschloss and Thomas E. Cronin, eds., *Essays in Honor of James MacGregor Burns* (Prentice-Hall, 1989), pp. 181–205, quoted at p. 183.

252   ["opinions deem'd unsound"] : Marshall to Justice Samuel Chase, letter of January

23, [1805], in Marshall, *Papers,* Herbert A. Johnson, ed. (University of North Carolina Press, 1974–2006), vol. 6, pp. 347–48, quoted at p. 347.

255 ["kind of transubstantiation"] : Corwin, p. 68.

257 ["constitutional disputes"] : Whittington, p. 287.

258 ["preeminently a place"] : Anne O'Hare McCormick, "Roosevelt's View of the Big Job," *New York Times Magazine,* September 11, 1932, pp. 1–2, 16, quoted at p. 2.

INDEX

on judicial salaries, 76
licensing, and free speech, 169
regulatory, 149
by states, 39–41
Taxpayers Associations, 103
Tennessee, 190
Payne v. *Tennessee*, 219, 220
terror, war on, 233–34, 244–46
Texas, 51, 240
City of Boerne, 232
Lawrence, 232
Roe, 207–9
Thomas, Clarence, 230, 244, 248
appointed to Supreme Court, 218
Bush v. *Gore* and, 225–27
as conservative activist, 219, 222, 235, 240,
242, 243
as member of conservative "phalanx,"
239–41, 242
presidential power and, 233, 244
Thompson, Smith, 44
Thornberry, Homer, 199
Thurmond, Strom, 188
Tilden, Samuel, 90–91, 97
Todd, Thomas, 35
Truman, Harry, 180, 181
Supreme Court appointments by,
174–75, 188
trust-busting, *see* antitrust actions
Tyler, John, 58

unions, 110, 120, 128, 133, 143, 149–50, 171, 249,
251; *see also* labor and workers' rights
U.S. v. *Butler*, 142, 143
U.S. v. *Carolene Products*, 166, 168, 169
U.S. v. *Cruikshank*, 88–89
U.S. v. *E. C. Knight Co.*, 109–10
U.S. v. *Nixon*, 209–10

Vallandigham, Clement, 74–76
Van Buren, Martin, 52
Van Devanter, Willis, 124–25, 140, 147
retirement of, 151, 157, 158
Vermont, 21
Vietnam War, 194, 202, 206, 230
Vinson, Fred, 180, 184
appointed chief justice, 174
Brown and, 183–84
domestic communism and, 174–76, 188
judicial restraint and, 174–75
Virginia, 21, 27–28, 38, 40–41, 52, 65
City of Richmond v. *Croson*, 216
Cohens, 41–42
Martin, 38, 41
voting rights:
Bush v. *Gore* and, 225–27
denial of, to African Americans, 82, 83,
87–89, 90, 198

Fifteenth Amendment and, 82, 89
malapportionment and, 190–91, 197
voting fraud law and, 242–43

Wabash, St. Louis & Pacific R.R. v. *Illinois*, 107
Wagner Act (1935), 149–50
Waite, Morrison R., 96, 105
African-American rights and, 88–89
appointed chief justice, 85
state regulatory powers and, 100, 101
states' rights and, 88, 100
Wall Street Journal, 167
War of 1812, 39, 43, 152
Warren, Earl, 179–200, 251–52
appointed chief justice, 179–81
Brown and, 184–85
civil liberties and, 188–90, 193–97, 251
criminal justice and, 196–97
leadership of court by, 180, 184–185, 188,
191, 201, 223
liberal judicial activism of, 180, 181–82, 192,
193–97, 223, 226
opposition to, 185–86, 188–89, 193–95, 196,
199, 202–3, 205, 206, 207, 210, 238
relations with colleagues, 182, 187
resignation of, 199, 200, 207
voting rights and, 190–91
Washington, Bushrod, 34, 154
appointed to Supreme Court, 19
as Marshall ally, 19, 36, 45
Washington, D.C., 3, 22, 30, 152, 239–40
Washington, George, 11, 121, 250
court-packing by, 7–8, 17, 20, 26 ,34, 35, 157
Federalism of, 17–18, 23, 39
Marshall and, 27
on Supreme Court's role, 8, 17, 18–19, 22–23
Watergate, 209–10, 230
Wayne, James, 58, 67, 71
Wealth of Nations (Smith), 98
Weaver, James B., 103
Webster, Daniel, 52
Webster v. *Reproductive Health Services*,
216–17, 220
Welles, Gideon, 85
West Coast Hotel v. *Parrish*, 148–49
West Virginia, 143, 169, 170
West Virginia Board of Education v. *Barnette*,
170
Wheeler, Burton, 147
Whig party, 51, 53, 54, 56, 58, 59, 73, 85, 105
Whiskey Rebellion, 20
White, Byron "Whizzer," 195, 221
appointed to Supreme Court, 192
as judicial conservative, 192–93, 216, 218,
219, 222
Roe and, 209
White, Edward D., 124, 130, 131
White, G. Edward, 36